Praise for "Nanny to the Rescue!"

Lots of good parenting ideas from someone who has been there. Easy to understand and user friendly
  Thomas W. Phelan, PhD
  Author of *1-2-3 Magic: Effective Discipline for Children 2-12*

Nanny to the Rescue! is the most practical guide I have read on the topic of pre-school parenting. Michelle LaRowe covers all the major decisions and dilemmas parents will face while raising their preschoolers. As a parent and a family advocate, I appreciate her insight and realistic solutions to common every day occurrences. I encourage all caregivers to read this book.
  Joseph A. Sapienza
  Senior Pastor, Celebration International Church
  Founder, Bread of Compassion

Michelle LaRowe has put the "parent" back in parenting with her no-non-sense approach to the world's greatest profession. Our family loved her con-fident "that's just the way we do it" approach so much that now even our girls say it to one another.
  Lynne Kenney Markan, PsyD
  CEO, Real Time Moms

Michelle LaRowe knows her stuff! As a former nanny to the stars and now a parent myself, I can assure you her talk is straight and her tips are excel-lent. Her suggestions are so helpful and easy to put into action that even Mary Poppins would have carried this little treasure in her magic bag.
  Suzanne Hansen
  Author of *You'll Never Nanny In This Town Again, The True Adventures of a Hollywood Nanny*

D1312428

MICHELLE R. LaROWE
nanny to the rescue!

STRAIGHT TALK & SUPER TIPS FOR PARENTING IN THE EARLY YEARS

W PUBLISHING GROUP
A Division of Thomas Nelson Publishers
Since 1798

www.wpublishinggroup.com

Published by W Publishing Group, a Division of Thomas Nelson, Inc., P.O. Box 141000, Nashville, TN 37214.

The author is represented by the literary agency of WordServe Literary Group, 10152 S. Knoll Circle, Highlands Ranch, CO 80130.

All Scripture quotations, unless otherwise indicated, are taken from The Holy Bible, New International Version®. Copyright © 1973, 1978, 1984 by International Bible Society. Used by permission of Zondervan Bible Publishers. All rights reserved. Scriptures marked NLT are taken from The Holy Bible, New Living Translation®. Copyright © 1996. Used by permission of Tyndale House Publishers, Inc., Wheaton, Illinois 60189. All rights reserved. Scriptures marked NCV are taken from the New Century Version®. Copyright © 1987, 1988, 1991 by Thomas Nelson, Inc. All rights reserved. Scriptures marked NKJV are taken from the New King James Version (NKJV®), copyright 1979, 1980, 1982, Thomas Nelson, Inc., Publishers.

Library of Congress Cataloging-in-Publication Data

LaRowe, Michelle R.
    Nanny to the rescue! : straight talk & super tips for parenting in the early years / Michelle R. LaRowe.
        p. cm.
    Includes bibliographical references.
    ISBN: 978-0-8499-1232-0
    1. Child rearing. 2. Parenting. 3. Parent and child. 4. Toddlers.
5. Preschool children. 6. Parenting—Religious aspects—Christianity.
I. Title.
HQ769.L2494 2005
649'.123—dc22   2005024088

Printed in the United States of America
06 07 08 09 10 VG 9 8 7 6 5 4 3 2 1

contents

Section Three   Embracing the Joys of Parenting

To the Kuntz family,
whom I have served
for more than six years

ACKNOWLEDGMENTS

Whew! If I didn't cry out and praise God for this one, the rocks certainly would. This project was a God thing from the get-go. Thank You, Lord. I give You all the glory.

I am also deeply grateful to the following people:

Karen and Rick Kuntz—You gave me the privilege of loving your children unconditionally, and you allow me to do my job to the best of my ability. You welcomed me into your family, home, and hearts, and I treasure the bond that we have built. It's been amazing to see your family grow. I've been blessed by you.

Austin—Your spirit makes my heart smile. I love *you* more than the biggest ice-cream sundae. That day you stretched your arms out and told me, "Shell, I love you this much," I knew I had done my job well and had conveyed to you the unconditional love that I have for you—the same love that God has for each one of us. Near or far, that love will remain strong and last forever.

Fraser—You're right: we will be "old friends." At the young age of four, when you first shared this with me, I bet you didn't know the depth of those words or what they would mean in times to come. Over the years, those words have brought me great comfort. I love you with as much love as I know how to give.

Boys, remember what I have taught you. I certainly remember all the things you have taught me. Love and respect your parents, always.

Mom—You gave me two amazing gifts that helped me get where I am today. You taught me the meaning of unconditional love, and you assured me that I could achieve anything I put my mind to. You gave me a strong foundation in a Christian home. You've been my best friend, my encourager, and my supporter, and you taught me more about parenting than we ever knew! I love you. You've done your job well.

Greg Johnson—I'll never forget answering my phone and hearing a voice on the other end ask, "Are you a woman of faith?" That was the question that got us where we are today. Thank you for taking a chance on me and bringing this project, and others to come, into being. Your love, guidance, patience, and commitment to me and to our projects have made the magic happen.

Becky Johnson—Go ahead and confess it: you are an angel. You literally taught me how to write and how to find my voice. Your loving, kind way of teaching and encouraging me made me press on and never give up. Thanks for investing in me.

Debbie Wickwire and the W Publishing Group team—As you said, I think we broke some records! Overnight, we brought a dream into reality. You made the unlikely, likely. Thanks for your passion and dedication to our project.

Jeanie Flynn—The risk you took paid off! Thanks for putting the PR time in on this kid, long before we knew what was to come.

P. K. Walsh, Hair Solutions for Women—Here, hair!

Members of the International Nanny Association, Christian Nannies, National Association of Nannies, Boston Area Nannies, and all the local Boston agencies that have unwaveringly supported me over the years—Thank you. I hope you are as proud of me as I am of you in the amazing strides we have made in the nanny industry.

Barbara Chandra, Sylvia Greenbaum, and the Boston Nanny Centre team—The day you told my employers you found "their perfect nanny," you were right! Thank you.

Katherine Leary Robinson of Beacon Hill Nannies—You are a great mentor. Thanks for your guidance and support over the years.

The members of Celebration International Church—Your prayers and encouragement have been felt. I'm glad we are family.

Kim and all the young adults at CIC—I love you! Press on in unity.

My friends who support me always, through the good, the bad, and the ugly—Thank you, thank you, thank you.

INTRODUCTION

Ever had a crying child who wouldn't eat her dinner? Or a screaming toddler who wouldn't give up until he got his way?

Bedtime troubles? Overly rough playing with friends? Snacks and sugar battles?

Fights over TV? Naptime? Getting dressed?

Welcome to the wonderful world of parenting.

Perhaps the following is a typical scene from your life: It's Monday, and you've just picked up your child from preschool. Deciding to make a quick stop at the grocery store to get supplies for dinner, you unbuckle your child, carry him into the store, and load him into the shopping cart.

Maneuvering as quickly as possible through the produce and meat departments, it happens . . . again. You've carefully avoided the snack and candy aisle, next to the milk you so desperately need, but it's too late. Your preschooler catches a glimpse of the sparkly box that holds his favorite treat: "Bob the Builder" fruit snacks. You slyly move your cart in the opposite direction, but his protest is already in full swing.

"I want fruit snacks!"

"Not now, honey," you answer calmly but firmly. "We're only here for things on the dinner list."

He ignores you, his demand increasing. Same song, second verse—a little bit louder and a little bit worse.

The negotiator in you kicks in: "If you stop crying and let Mommy finish shopping, I will make a cake for us to eat after we have our dinner."

Nothing doing. Delayed gratification is not what he has in mind. He wants what he wants when he wants it . . . and he lets the whole world know.

Everyone, it seems, is now watching your little drama. One woman, feeling benevolent, approaches you and says, "Oh, we all have these days, honey. Don't let it get to you." You try to finish your shopping, pretending that the trauma in aisle six is not happening, but you and your screaming child have become the focus of every disapproving eye in the store.

Embarrassed, you reluctantly abandon your half-full grocery cart in the middle of the store and head back to the car, sans dinner. As you drive away, the crying ceases. Your little angel has fallen fast asleep, his face peaceful and serene. You, in contrast, have knots in your stomach and a pounding headache, and you drive through for fast food on the way home.

Does this story sound familiar? All parents of preschoolers have experienced it at least once, but more likely multiple times.

Did you realize there are five good parenting rules that were broken in the grocery store illustration? Here are the five mistakes the fictional mom made:

1. She didn't keep to a schedule.
2. She didn't set clear expectations for her child.
3. She didn't realize you cannot negotiate with a preschooler.
4. She chose the temporary, easy solution.
5. She took a tired child (and mommy) on errands.

Don't worry if you didn't get all the answers right at first; we'll be sure to cover these and other important topics in the pages ahead.

Never fear—here comes *Nanny to the Rescue!*

Much the way Mary Poppins pulled magic out of her flowered carpetbag, in this book, I will share every nanny secret in my toolbox for preschool children. If you are consistent with my tried-and-true Nanny Tips and parenting ideas, not only will your children enjoy their days more fully, but so will you. By the last page of this book, you'll have all the best ideas of the nanny trade tucked in your own parenting pockets. Then I'll pop open my umbrella and catch the next good, strong wind out of here, satisfied that I've done my job, knowing your children are in *excellent* hands.

In this book, you will be given the tools to handle even the most trying situations with assured authority, and you'll be empowered to implement these tools.

(After all, you are the parent in charge of your preschooler at large!) God created you to be a loving, nurturing parent who raises happy, secure, and well-balanced children. Yet, as you have no doubt discovered, good parenting isn't an easy task.

In times past, new parents lived near their parents, grandparents, and other relatives, so they had mentors to guide them through the disorienting world of raising young kids. Not only are today's parents often living across the country from the help of Grandma and Grandpa, but they are often both working outside the home. No wonder parents are stressed!

Enter an innovative, if old-fashioned-sounding, solution—nannies.

What Can I Learn from a Nanny?

This book is all about *you*, the parent. But before we get started, you need to know a few things about me . . . and why a professional nanny like me has anything to say to you, the real parents in the trenches, about raising your little bundles of joy.

In today's world of dual-income families, many parents have turned to professional nannies to help care for their children. In fact, one million of them have. Yes, nannies can be more expensive than day care or a baby-sitter, so our services aren't for everyone. And you as a parent aren't looking for anyone to have more influence on your child than you do. But the truth is, nanny care serves as a wonderful solution to the childcare dilemma for many families. Having a nanny allows children to receive personal care in their own home and enables parents to play an active role in their children's day-to-day care. The nanny solution also allows parents to decide exactly who will be caring for and influencing their children on a consistent and long-term basis.

Through the popular TV reality shows *Nanny 911* and *Supernanny*, America is learning about *what* a nanny does, but we haven't learned *why* or *how*. Parents have been able to catch a few good ideas, but they have not been given the reasoning behind these ideas or the confidence to implement them. My aim in this book is to give you all three: the logic behind effective parenting methods, the confidence to use these methods in your family, and practical Nanny Tips for dealing with everyday problems!

Unlike yesterday's baby-sitter, today's American nanny is often an educated professional who has a working knowledge of and genuine love for children. Many nannies have college degrees, often specializing in early childhood education. Some have even taken additional parenting and professional development courses. Like other professionals, nannies often hold membership in professional organizations and take part in industry-related conferences and events. We keep current in industry trends and work hard to advance our field.

Nannies also often have more experience in dealing with children than parents, especially first-time parents. Nannies know from experience which childrearing techniques are most effective. A nanny can separate herself emotionally from the children because, although she loves the children, they are not hers; thus, she does not have a strong, maternal response to their crying. She can endure the embarrassment of a tantrum at the mall, because she knows that the tantrum is only momentary but the lesson will last a lifetime. A nanny is not preoccupied with asking herself, "Am I being a bad mommy?" or dealing with hurt feelings when a child says, "I hate you." A nanny does not underestimate the value of teaching a child the meaning of no . . . even if everyone at the mall is staring as the child threatens to hold his breath until he passes out.

I'm not attempting to sell you on the idea of hiring a nanny; that's a decision you must make for your own family. But I am here with several years of intense experience, my sleeves rolled up, ready to offer aid and comfort to moms and dads like you. My desire in this book is to empower, encourage, and share some tricks of the childrearing trade that may be lifesavers for parents who feel adrift in conflicting advice.

I grew up working with children, teaching Sunday school, and volunteering in the church nursery. This evolved into baby-sitting and, later, to becoming a professional nanny. I met my current charges—twin boys—when they were just ten days old. When I held them for the first time, I fell in love and knew in my heart that I would be their nanny. It's amazing to see them today, in grade school, knowing that I was there almost from the start of their precious lives. Because I have a chemistry degree but have chosen to work with children, the boys' parents were assured that I was a nanny by choice—not because I was unqualified for anything else.

Over the years, the family and I have built a special relationship. The parents respect me, and I respect them. They value my input and advice because they know, without a doubt, that any decision I make or action I take is in the best interest of their children. They know that my advice and input are objective.

Although I love their children deeply, I raise them in a way that will both teach them well and serve their family well. The children love me as much as I love them, and they respect me as a third authority figure. When children know that you love them and feel secure in that love, they heed your discipline quickly.

My charges are well-behaved children because from the beginning I (and their parents) did things right. Sometimes we did things wrong, but we were *consistently* wrong (which may sound odd—more on that later). The boys have had the same rules since they could walk, and they know what to expect day to day. I have never done for them what they could do for themselves. As a result, they are confident kids. Sure, there were times when it would have been much quicker if I had gotten them dressed or made their beds for them, but the rewards of letting them do it themselves were worth being late.

I have learned that I must be constantly aware that I'm a role model for the children in my care. I must be mindful of teaching them right from wrong, not only in word but in deed. I must be consistent at all times, which sometimes means saying no when it would be easier to say yes. I must live my life in a way that makes me proud of my choices and makes the children proud of me. I share in the successes of my charges as they share in mine.

I have been entrusted with a great responsibility, and I love the joy of pleasing God through my work—whether it is as mundane as changing a diaper or as meaningful as reminding a child of how loved and special he is to his Creator.

I hope this book, written from my heart, provides you with a window to see more objectively how to maximize the joy of raising babies and young children. You may never have a need to hire a nanny, but all parents need a healthy dose of encouragement now and then. Most are eager for tips, tricks, and secrets to make their family life flow more smoothly.

So think of me as your personal nanny in book form. Perhaps you can take a few afternoons away while the kids are asleep and read the book straight through (before you fall asleep too!). Or put this book on your nightstand and open up the pages when you need a boost or a tip or a friend who understands your unique challenges. Or open to the chapter that addresses your highest felt need right now. Whatever works for you, I'm here to help!

SECTION
ONE

THE BASICS
OF GREAT PARENTING

CHAPTER ONE

WHO'S THE BOSS?

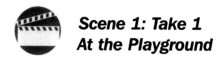 **Scene 1: Take 1**
At the Playground

MOM. Allie, it's time to go.

ALLIE, *pouting*. But, Mommy, I don't wanna go!

MOM. We need to leave in five minutes.

(Five minutes pass.)

MOM. OK, sugar, time's up. Let's go.

ALLIE. No! I don't wanna go home!

MOM. OK, five more minutes. That's it.

(Five minutes pass.)

MOM. Allie, time's up. No more minutes left.

ALLIE. I'm not done playing!

MOM, *taking a deep, aggravated breath*. Fine. You tell me when you're done.

(Ten minutes pass.)

MOM. I've waited long enough. I'm going to leave you here if you don't come
     with me right now.

ALLIE, *stamping feet*. I'm not going!

MOM, *walking away*. Fine. Stay here, then. Bye!

ALLIE, *screaming*. Mommy! Mommy!

MOM, *walking back, irritated*. If you would listen to me the first time,
     we wouldn't have to keep going through this frustration!

(She picks up Allie and carries her to the car.)

Why does it seem that parents today are afraid to be *parents*? When did it become more acceptable to be a child's best friend instead of her mom or dad? In our society, many parents have lost touch with the simple, profound commission of leading their children and confidently rising to the role of being in charge. In fact, some children have taken advantage of their parents' fear of authority and turned into pint-size dictators, having trained their parents to obey their every immature whim.

The Bible tells us that God only gives us what we can handle, and He will equip us to handle what He gives (1 Corinthians 10:13). So even though you may feel inadequate for this task, be assured that God has given you all you need to parent the children He has given you. You may need to learn some healthy parenting techniques and perhaps even overcome your own dysfunctional rearing, but within you is the miraculous making of the mom or dad who perfectly fits what your children need.

Build Trust with Your Baby

When blessed with a new child, most parents know the basics: you must feed, change, respond to, and give love to your new bundle of joy. Most new moms and dads grasp the basic fundamentals of infant care fairly quickly, but they often do not realize how important these fundamentals are for the future of their precious child.

When you meet all the needs of a new baby—feeding her, changing her, responding to her cries, and giving her lots of expressions of love—you are building trust with your child. Your new baby quickly learns that you are there to meet her every real need and that she is solely dependent on you. She begins to trust you from day one, and this trust gives her a sense of security. As King David, the world's most beloved psalmist, wrote, "You made me trust you while I was just a baby" (Psalm 22:9 NCV). When you show your baby that she can trust you to care for her basic needs, not only are you establishing your authority as a parent, but you are, at an even deeper level, preparing your child to someday trust in a good and faithful God.

Besides caring for your baby's basic needs, you can also give your newborn a sense of trust and security in the world through your body language and sound. I have learned over the years that the old saying is true: "It's not what you say, but how you say it." When you approach a baby with confidence, he will respond with confidence because he feels safe—and when a child feels safe, he also feels secure.

If you have ever witnessed someone holding a new baby for the first time, you may have sensed the adult's insecurity and nervousness. Now imagine being held in those same arms! How would you respond? Babies can sense nervousness and tension, and they respond to it accordingly. If someone was holding you and didn't seem to know what he was doing, how long would you want to stay in his arms?

So one way to build confidence in your infant is to learn to hold your baby in a way that helps him relax. He will soon trust that you are in charge and that you know what you're doing. Infants love to be held closely, often close enough to feel your familiar heartbeat. Sometimes all it takes to soothe your baby's crying is swaddling him in a soft blanket and cradling him in your arms, head near your heart.

Sometimes infants are over-stimulated, and their crying means, "Take me away from all this chaos!" You will learn to decipher your baby's different cries. At times like this, turning the lights low, cradling your baby, and slowly rocking back and forth will do the trick. You can also gently rock him up and down while holding him. Babies usually respond to consistent, rhythmic movement. They also respond to consistent rhythmic sounds, such as "Ahh, ahh, baby," repeated over and over in a soft, reassuring voice.

Nanny Tip

When holding a baby who is unfamiliar with you, don't look him in the eyes at first: it's too overwhelming for the baby. If the baby is old enough to have some head control (about one month), hold him face out, against your tummy, one arm under his arms, one arm under his bottom. This way, he feels secure because he can connect to his familiar environment and explore his world. (It also helps that he isn't confused by the unfamiliar smell of your perfume, which he recognizes quickly as not belonging to Mommy.)

Soothing your baby when she's upset is another good way to build trust. A gassy baby is usually soothed when you rub her belly in a circular motion while she is lying on her back. Moving her legs as if she is riding a bicycle often helps too. Don't be too quick to label your baby "colicky." I am sure that some babies genuinely have symptoms that at the time seem inconsolable, but *colic* has become a generic term for infant crying—ranging from tiredness and general fussiness to real tummy aches. I believe almost any baby can be soothed, and holding babies in the way that they feel most safe and secure usually does the trick (eventually).

Talking lovingly and softly to your baby and holding her in a way that comforts her provide safety and security that lays the foundation for your future interaction with her. If a child feels safe and secure in the arms of her parent, why would she waver from what the parent teaches? If she knows that her parents have met all her needs, why would she begin to doubt that they will now? (Well, there is the normal toddler testing period—often called the "first adolescence"—when your child will pull at the reins. The point is, your kids may throw a fit, but ultimately, they will know from their earliest memories that you love them, and if you set limits or have to say no, you are only doing so to protect them.)

The family system has been orchestrated with great wisdom. Each stage of your child's development is like a building block. As babies move through infancy with a sense of trust and toddlers arrive at preschool secure in their parents' care, they will continue this process to adulthood and hopefully extend that sense of trust to include a solid faith in a good and loving heavenly Father.

Create a Routine That Works for You

As all parents know, having a new baby in the house quickly turns life upside down! Suddenly you are completely responsible for someone who is utterly helpless, while being more sleep deprived than you could ever imagine. Your former life as you knew it no longer exists. Your well-planned schedule is now thrown into what seems to be unpredictable chaos. And it may soon get worse.

So what type of parent will you be? Will you parent the way *your* parents did? Or will you choose your own style?

There are several theories on meeting the needs of infants, including responding on demand, crying it out, and scheduling. (We will look at each of these methods more closely in chapter 6.) Although I believe that you can never spoil a baby, I also believe that the calmest, most content babies are those who come to rely upon some type of schedule. And the most content moms are the ones who follow the baby's schedule too!

The best basic baby schedule I have found goes like this: awake, feed, change, sleep, awake, feed, change, sleep. At this age, the timing isn't as important as following the basic order. In other words, it doesn't matter if your baby nurses at exactly 2:00 p.m. as much as it does that he always eats after he wakes up. Having a consistent routine lets your baby know what is going to happen next. Talking to your baby about what comes next is also a great way to bond. Although he may not understand what you are saying, he loves to hear your voice and interact with you.

In later chapters, we will cover in depth the importance of a structured routine and how it changes as baby grows. But for now, relax and be confident in your abilities.

Show Your Toddler Who's in Charge

Showing your child who is in charge is even more important when she becomes a toddler. It has always bothered me to hear people talk about going through the "terrible twos" and the "treacherous threes." Children are never terrible or treacherous—though, at times, their behavior can be.

One of the most important bits of advice I can give parents is that discipline starts at birth. Webster defines *discipline* as "training expected to produce a specific character or pattern of behavior, especially training that produces moral or mental improvement." If this is true, then (as covered more thoroughly in chapter 4) we *discipline* our children, in the purest sense of the word, when we teach them to depend on us for their basic needs.

The first time you do something—anything—starts a pattern. If you don't want to have a tyrant toddler on your hands, then the most important rule is this: *be consistent.* Even if you are consistently wrong, be consistent. For example, when I first started out as a nanny, I insisted that no toys be allowed in the car, because I did not want to keep track of, search the floor for, or get hit with toys while driving. This worked well because the kids knew what to expect: toys do not belong in the car. There was never a fight about it, and I never had to endure repetitive pleadings on the issue because they knew the rule. *Yesterday, toys didn't come in the car; today, toys won't come in the car; and tomorrow, toys won't come in the car either.*

Looking back, I now know that allowing the kids to bring toys into the car would have been a great way to teach them responsibility (and keep them from bickering!). It is one of the few rules that I no longer enforce. But I was consistent with the boys in their early years, and that was more important overall than the rules I chose to set. The same is true for you. Your kids probably won't end up in therapy because they couldn't bring a toy in the car, but they might end up in a counselor's chair someday if there is a long-term pattern of radical inconsistency in your parenting style.

So if the house rule is "We only eat in the kitchen," the first time you allow your toddler to eat outside of the kitchen, he will begin to doubt the validity of that rule. Obviously, it is not a crime to eat in the living room, and some families are comfortable with more flexibility. The point is, whatever your rules and routine, keep to them. (If you realize that a rule is no longer working for your family, there are ways to change your mind without giving up authority. But those special circumstances will be covered in detail in chapter 2.)

Say What You Mean, and Mean What You Say

Follow-through is also essential at this age. For example, if your daughter misbehaves at a restaurant and you tell her, "If you do that again, we are leaving," and she does it again and you do not leave, you are teaching your child that you do not mean what you say. Only tell your child, "We are going to leave" if you are prepared to follow through. This means you *are* leaving—even if you are in the middle of your meal and are still hungry! (Have the waiter pack up your meal, and you can enjoy it in peace later.) The first time you do not follow through with what you say, you open the door for doubt in your authority. I can guarantee this, although it may sound extreme. It only takes once to teach a child that you don't mean what you say.

Children are unpredictable. You never know what inconsistency they're going to catch you in next.
—Franklin P. Jones

I remember when one of my charges was three years old, he had a pair of plastic toy pliers that were part of a building kit. One day he used them to snip at a friend's nose—hard! I warned him, "Pliers are for building. If you use them to hurt again, they are going in the trash." Sure enough, he did it again. I took the pliers, broke them in half (so I wouldn't be tempted to give them back), and threw them in the trash. He cried and cried. I felt like a horrible nanny, but I knew that if I did not follow through, especially on a safety issue, the next time he would doubt that I would do what I said.

Looking back, I have to admit, I didn't anticipate that I'd have to throw the toy in the trash; it probably would have been better for me to say, "I will put the toy in time-out." But the lesson on follow-through was worth the momentary tears and extra drama. My charge is now almost in grade school, and he tells that story to everyone. He is so proud that when he got a new pair of pliers for his fourth birthday, he knew how to use them appropriately and never hurt anyone with them again.

> *All children behave as well as they are treated.*
> —Anonymous

The boys are confident that I am a person of my word, whether it is while disciplining or making a promise. I always follow through. What trust and security this has built into our relationship!

Have Realistic Expectations

If you expect your child to do as you wish, you need to be very specific. If you do not clearly state your expectations, how can your children ever live up to them? You can tell your son, "Be a good boy." But what does that mean? He doesn't know how to meet that expectation. Tell him instead, "I need you to listen and cooperate today. This means I want you to come with me without throwing a fit when it is time to leave the playground." There is no room for doubt in that expectation.

Expectations also have to be age appropriate and realistic. You can't expect a three-year-old to sit on an airplane quietly and read a book. Knowing this, you board the airplane with lots of toys and treats in your carry-on bag and say to your child, "We are going on an airplane. If you can keep from kicking the seat in front of you for five minutes, Mommy will take something special out of her bag for you to enjoy."

You really *do* know what is best for your child. It may seem easier at times to say yes in the moment ("Yes, we can stay at the playground as long as you like") to avoid a tantrum, but in the long run, you're not teaching your child to know who is in charge. If you listen to your God-given inner voice of parenting wisdom, you really do know when your child is tired and needs to go home to rest—so why would you let her stay at the playground until she's tired and cranky? You would only be stalling the tantrum, not eliminating it.

> *It is better to bind your children to you by a feeling of respect and by gentleness, than by fear.*
> —Terence

At some point, expect that your child will say something like, "You aren't the boss of me!" When she does, be ready to affirm that you are *indeed* the grownup in charge—and that someday, when she is a mommy, she can be the boss.

Allowing your child to make decisions that you should be making undermines her sense of security. If you currently have a toddler, up to this point you have been making the decisions. She has trusted you to meet her needs, and she's likely arrived at toddlerhood happy and healthy. But just because she is one foot taller and starting to speak in short sentences (many of them punctuated with the word *no*) doesn't mean she is ready to take over the home. In this book, you will learn to empower your child by giving her appropriate choices that you, the boss, can live with. Each year, you will be able to loosen the reins, but no loving parent gives their preschooler the keys to the car and permission to drive it.

Who's the "Best" Boss?

There are several schools of thought on which parenting style works best. Child research psychologist Diana Baumrind has identified three basic parenting styles: authoritarian parenting, permissive parenting, and authoritative parenting. Which style of parenting is right for you?

Authoritarian parents use force to emphasize obedience, and they usually end up raising children who are withdrawn and fearful. These parents are overly aggressive, and their children tend to be unassertive and moody.

Permissive parents believe in freeing their child from restraint, allowing them to rule the roost. The children tend to be rebellious, self-indulgent, and impulsive. Children raised in this style often are subject to peer rejection due to the lack of discipline in the home.

Authoritative parents seek to "direct their children's activities in a rational manner, encouraging discussion, and also exerting firm control when children disobey, but without being overly restrictive. These parents recognize their children's individual needs and interests, but set standards of conduct. These children are the best-adjusted of the three groups; they are the most self-reliant, self-controlled, self- confident, and socially competent."[1]

In short, the happiest and most secure kids on the planet have the winning combination of loving and authoritative parents—that is, parents who discipline consistently while letting their children know they are deeply loved.

I know it may seem odd, or maybe even old-fashioned, to talk about being the boss in such black-and-white terms—especially when parenting often feels more like varying shades of gray. Remember, you do not have to be a perfect person to be a fabulous parent. You don't have to do everything just right. We all make mistakes, even us nannies who usually have the advantage of a good night's sleep and who can more easily distance ourselves from emotion to see what is really best, long term, for the child.

There will come a day, not so far off, when you can communicate your own foibles and failures to your child to let him know you are human. The ultimate goal is that someday your adult child will be one of your dearest friends. I've heard so many moms and dads say, in wonder, how amazing it is when their children become enjoyable friends when they arrive at adulthood. That day will come. And it will come in stages. If your kids are preschoolers, that day is not here. Trust me.

At this young age, your child is better off with simple, clear lines of authority. The less fuzziness at this age, the better. You are the boss; your child is not. You are not on a campaign to be his best buddy.

Does this role as boss scare you a little? Think of all the times of transition in your past—when you had to rise to an occasion of leadership (ready or not), when you found yourself having to fill shoes that seemed too big for you at the time. What did you do? More than likely, you took on a role and then faked it until you made it. So imagine someone who represents a model of assured, kind authority to young children. Mary Poppins, perhaps? Maria von Trapp? Mrs. Doubtfire? Act as *if* until you *are*.

And pray, pray, pray for God's reassurance along the way. You need to be who you are, but sometimes it is so nice to pray something like, "Lord, I'm tired of being the grownup in charge. I feel like a little girl myself today. Thank You that You are bigger than me, that You are the Ultimate Boss of this family and my life. Empower me, teach me, and give me wisdom and courage to be a good representative of You by the way I parent my children today."

Knowing that stories are worth a thousand sermons, let's revisit the playground—this time with a mom who is comfortable with her role as a loving authoritarian and who doesn't use her adult-size power to intimidate her child but instead expresses empathy while remaining firm. See if you can guess some of the practical Nanny Tips she is using to build trust in her daughter, with loving authority, while teaching her child that, for this time of her young life, Mommy, indeed, knows best.

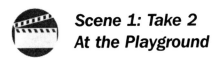

Scene 1: Take 2
At the Playground

MOM. Allie, we're leaving in five minutes. Just want to give you a little fair warning.

ALLIE. I don't wanna go!

MOM. I understand you don't want to go, and I'm sorry that we have to go when you are still having fun. But that's always the way it is with fun, isn't it? None of us ever wants it to stop. Don't worry; we'll come again soon. But here's the deal: we are leaving in five minutes.

(Four minutes pass.)

MOM. One more minute, Allie, to finish up what you are doing.

ALLIE. Mommy, do I have to?

MOM. Yes. You know the rules. When I say we need to go, we need to go. No fussing.

(One minute passes.)

MOM. OK, Allie, let's go.

(Allie stands and walks toward Mom, taking her hand to go. She's not happy, but she's not pitching a fit or being disrespectful.)

MOM. I'm really proud of how you came with me without a fuss. What a big girl you are becoming! *(Allie smiles.)* Tell me what you liked the best today, and we'll put another play-in-the-park day on the calendar when we get home, OK?

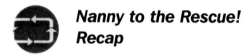

Nanny to the Rescue!
Recap

Did you figure out some ways to show your child who is boss without losing your cool or acting like a dictator? Here are a few suggestions—along with some other reminders from this chapter—to chew on and try out!

1. *Show love often.* Using endearing terms lets your child know she is special.

2. *Give warnings before transitions.* Preparing your child for transition lets her know what to expect. Would you prefer a mall-closing announcement to sound like this: "The mall is now closed! Put that cute pair of shoes down, and leave immediately!"? Of course not. The announcement usually goes something like this: "Attention, shoppers, the store is closing in five minutes. Please bring all your purchases to the counter." Enough said.

3. *Respond to your child's whines with empathy and firmness.* Not giving in to your child's tantrums is hard but necessary. You might offer a practical reason if she asks, "Why?" but do not get in the losing battle of reasoning with a preschooler. After giving a brief reason, just say, "Because I'm the mommy, and God put me in charge of you. Someday you'll get to be a mommy and make more choices. But for now, I'm in charge."

4. *Affirm acceptable behavior.* Catch your child doing something right—even if it is a small improvement—and tell him how proud you are of his good behavior.

5. *Address unacceptable behavior.* Remember, a child is always good; it's his *behavior* that can be bad at times.

6. *Be consistent.* Being consistently wrong is sometimes OK, but be consistent.

7. *Follow through.* Say what you mean, and mean what you say.

8. *Set age-appropriate, realistic expectations.* Clear, realistic expectations build self-esteem as long as you don't set up your child to fail.

9. *Allow your child time to "relive" her fun day with you in happy conversation, and then follow up on your promise to return and enjoy more fun another day.*

Real Kids, Real Funny

"How can I be only three, when my feet are growing so tall every day?"

—Meghan, age three

When four-year-old Andrea heard that Alan Shepard, who had walked on the moon, had died, she asked, "Did he fall off?"

"Cows are made of hamburgers," one mom overheard her daughter patiently explain.

And from my personal nanny diary this week, one of my charges said, "I asked God to help me sleep, but I still couldn't go to sleep. Do you think I was up too late and He had already gone to sleep for the night?"

CHAPTER TWO

THE FIVE Cs OF SUCCESSFUL PARENTING

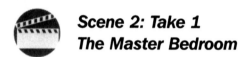 **Scene 2: Take 1**
The Master Bedroom

WIFE, *falling on the bed.* Ugh! It was such a rough day. Jenna was really off the wall.

HUSBAND. Uh-huh . . . Um, can you hand me the remote?

WIFE, *clearly irritated.* Didn't you hear me? She was really, really bad today!

HUSBAND, *fiddling with remote.* Oh, I'm sorry . . . I just . . . It's just . . . Oh, look! The game is on!

WIFE, *sighs loudly.* You don't understand. I need your help. I don't know what to do.

HUSBAND. Look, I don't know anything about child psychology. Why don't you check out a book or ask your mom or something? *Yes!* Go, Pats!

WIFE, *muttering to herself.* I can't handle this . . . God, if You are listening, please help! *(She grabs her pillow, rolls over, and faces the other way.)*

Have you ever felt lonely in your marriage when it comes to raising the children? I've heard many moms (although I'm sure it is also true for some dads) bemoan, "Sure, I'm married; but I feel like a single parent."

If you or your spouse feels this way, consider these questions: What blueprint for family life are you following? What is your purpose here on earth? What are your top priorities in life? Are they the same as your spouse's? Do you even know?

> *When someone deeply listens to you, it is like holding out a dented cup you've had since childhood and watching it fill up with cold, fresh water. When it balances on top of the brim, you are understood; when it overflows and touches your skin, you are loved.*
> —John Fox

Communication

Once you have laid a spiritual foundation for your marriage and family, how do you build and maintain a beautiful, loving home together? *By communicating effectively.* Communication is the key to success in any relationship. Unless you, your spouse, and your children are all mind readers, you have to develop healthy ways to communicate with one another in order to become a happy, healthy family.

As it has been said, we have two ears and one mouth for a reason—to listen twice as much as we speak. When I was in eighth-grade marching band, I learned an important life lesson. As we would stand in formation, awaiting direction, our band director would say, "Listen with your eyes." He wanted to make sure we were visually connecting with him before he gave us any more verbal instruction.

I still carry those words of wisdom with me to this day. Good listening takes effort. You have to concentrate on what the person is saying, you have to process what he is saying, and you have to respond to what he is saying in a way that shows you were actively paying attention. Hearing what someone says is one thing, but deeply listening to what someone is saying with his voice, tone, words, body language, and eye contact is another.

One of my pet peeves is when I am telling a story and cannot finish it because my friend is too busy waiting for her turn to talk to pay attention to what I am sharing. Have you had a conversation like that? It's frustrating, to say the least!

Train Your Kids to Be Good Listeners

Teaching your kids to wait their turn, in deed and in conversation, is a valuable tool. One way you can practice this with your child is to use a prop, such as a decorated toilet-paper roll, to illustrate how a conversation flows. (This exercise can work with adults, too, and is often used in business training seminars.) Each child is given the prop for a predetermined amount of time. The child holding the prop is the only one allowed to speak during his or her turn. The other children have a very important job as well: to be the "listeners."

It is also important to teach kids how to enter into a conversation. Teaching a child to say, "Excuse me" before speaking will be a great diffuser of the communication battles to come. However, you have to follow this lesson with another important one: saying, "Excuse me" does not give your child permission to speak immediately.

You can teach your children to be good listeners by modeling good listening as a parent. Here are five ways to be an active listener to your child:

1. *Give your child focused attention.* If you can't completely focus on your child at the moment, say, "Honey, let me finish this; then I'm all yours." Then follow through! Turn from what you are doing, and focus your attention on your child.

2. *Look your child in the eyes.* Look directly into your child's eyes when he talks—no looking at the TV or computer.

3. *Use physical cues to affirm that you are listening.* Smile and nod, or show empathy and nod, to let your child know you hear him at an emotional level.

4. *Make sure your child finishes before you respond.* Ask, "Is there anything else?" before you dive in to give an answer or feedback.

5. *Ask permission to share your thoughts.* For example, you might say, "I am so sorry you are feeling hurt. Can I give you some ideas that might help you feel better?"

She has to wait until you look at her and ask, "Yes, honey, what would you like to say?" (Unless it is a big emergency. Make sure you clearly define *big emergency.*)

When you teach a child to politely wait her turn to talk, you are teaching her several life lessons. Not only does she learn patience and respect, but she's learning how to break the cycle of instant gratification. Whew! That's what I call loaded learning, and I love these moments of high-impact learning with my charges.

Pay Attention to Verbal and Nonverbal Cues

We all share our thoughts and feelings at some level, but effective communication doesn't always come naturally. There are two types of communication: verbal and nonverbal. When our words and our actions (or tone or body posture) don't match up, problems and confusion arise.

For example, let's say that you ask your child, "How was your day?" He grins and responds, "Great!" That's verbal communication expressed in an excited tone. Message given and received, loud and clear. Now let's replay the scene, this time adding some powerful nonverbal cues. Let's say your child looks down at his feet, purses his lips, and turns his face away as he enthusiastically says, "Great!" Those mixed signals let you know that his day wasn't really all that great. His body language communicates that he's hiding something.

You have to pay attention to both verbal and nonverbal cues to truly understand your child. And it takes real work—trust me, I know! This is especially difficult when you are tired or juggling multiple little ones.

Now let's reverse the lesson. If tone and body language are keys to your child's communication with you, then they are also keys to your communication with your child. Your verbal and nonverbal messages have to match when speaking to your child. For example, when speaking to your preschooler and desiring her full attention, what should you do with your body? You should get down to his level, even on bent knees, and look him right in the eyes. Sometimes it helps to gently hold his hands or shoulders as you prepare to speak.

If you are disciplining your child, use a disapproving expression and a firm voice. If you are communicating positive reinforcement, use a proud voice and a pat on the back. When your body language and your words match, deciphering the true message becomes a much simpler task for your children.

Clarity

How can your children learn to abide by your rules and expectations if they don't understand them? You need to be absolutely clear with your children about exactly what behaviors are acceptable and unacceptable. You should clearly explain your family's "house rules" and expectations to your children in a clear, age-appropriate manner and in simple terms they can understand.

For example, if your toddler doesn't yet speak, when she pulls the plug out of the outlet, get down to her level, look her in the eyes with a disapproving glare (I call this the "nanny no-nonsense look"), and say firmly, "No. Plugs are not for pulling." She will know right away that her behavior did not please you, even if she didn't understand your words. Your body language and tone of voice were clear and left no room for confusion: *Mommy is definitely not happy. I do not pull plugs out of the wall if I don't want to see Mommy's mad face again.*

A little girl came home from school and told her mom she got a great part in the school play: "I was chosen to clap and cheer!" Listening is much the same way. Sometimes we get to take center stage; sometimes it is our job to listen actively—to internally clap and cheer!

Create Your House Rules

Just like a good sports team has a playbook, a good family has a rulebook. The most important thing when setting house rules is that you choose only the rules that you will enforce regularly.

How do you determine which rules get included in your family rulebook? First, sit down with your spouse, and each of you make three lists: the "must haves," the "would be nice to haves," and the "no big deals." The "must have" list includes all safety and respect rules. These are the nonnegotiables—no hitting, no biting, no jumping on the furniture, no back talk, no swearing, no screaming. You get the drift. These are the essentials that need constant reinforcement to maintain sanity and order in your family.

The "would be nice to have" list may include things that are negotiable. These will differ by family but may include things such as keeping toys in the playroom, sitting properly at the dinner table, not eating outside the kitchen, or not wearing shoes in the house. These aren't really major issues; they're more "lifestyle preferences." If these rules were broken, the household wouldn't necessarily fall apart; but having them in place may make things run more smoothly.

Finally, you have the "no big deal" list, which includes all the other things that may be nice but not worth the effort of enforcing consistently (in other words, the success of the household isn't rooted in them). These are more minor annoyances than major infractions. Maybe this list includes things like folding socks Mom's way or putting the toilet paper on so it rolls over instead of under. These are nitpicky items that are not really worth fussing over in the grand scheme of things.

Once you and your spouse have each made your lists, compare them. Why? Because there is no sense in creating a house rule that is not going to be enforced by both Mom and Dad (or any other adult in the home, for that matter). Once you have compared lists, hopefully your "must have" list includes most of the same rules as your spouse's list. You can include all of these in your family rulebook. In the second column, you and your spouse each pick your top two "would like to haves." Then you can basically throw out the "no big deal" category to make life easier. (Yes, I realize this may be a relative term. You may need to compromise if a "no big deal" on your list is a really big deal to your spouse.) You should be left with a family rulebook consisting of no more than ten house rules. The fewer the better.

Once you have your "top ten" family rules, it's important to phrase them short and sweet so there is no room for misinterpretation. Here are ten rules that I have used as house rules:

1. Keep your hands to yourself.

2. Be respectful to others.

3. No screaming.

4. No jumping on (or off) furniture.

5. Adults only in the fridge and in the cabinets.

6. Wash hands after use of bathroom and before meals.

7. Sit properly at the table.

8. No playing ball in the house.

9. No toys to hurt someone.

10. Only age-appropriate toys and TV shows.

These rules are the nonnegotiables. The kids know that breaking these ten rules won't be tolerated.

Make a Family Covenant

Once you have settled on your house rules and have worded them clearly and concisely, it's time to sit down and go over the family rulebook, play by play. Gather everyone around, create a list on poster board, and go over the rules one by one, stopping to address any and all questions to ensure that the meaning of the rule is clear. Once you've finished reviewing the rules, make a family covenant. This is an irreversible contract that states, "We will do our best to follow the house rules." Then tack up your house rules and get ready to enforce them. You will be tested!

What do you do when one of the rules is violated? Ideally, you will have covered this during the family meeting so your children clearly understand the consequences. We'll talk more about discipline and punishment in chapter 4.

Consistency

Consistency plays a *huge* role in creating a smooth-sailing family environment. Having predictable, unchanging responses to undesirable behaviors will result in the change of behavior. Both parents need to consistently enforce the house rules and the age-appropriate consequences for breaking those rules. Giving in or bending the rules—even once—without a good reason and clear explanation sets you up for a brand-new battle each time the same situation arises. The child thinks, *I cried for five minutes last time, and Daddy gave in. I bet if I cry a little bit louder and a little bit longer, he'll give in again this time.*

If you don't want to lose your mind, keep one step ahead of your children—with clarity and consistency.

Cooperation

Now that you have clearly defined your house rules, effectively communicated them to your children, and been consistent in implementing them, cooperation will be the determining factor of your success.

One help in getting your spouse to cooperate with you is to agree to this wonderful bit of wisdom: "Praise in public; criticize in private." You and your spouse are a united front—one team of two—or at least you must appear to be at all times when within earshot of your children. This is why you want to make sure that you and your spouse agree on the rules for the kids and that you are both willing to reinforce these rules. You don't want to be arguing over what's best for your children in front of them. Instead, your conversations in front of your children should look more like this:

"Mommy, I want to watch TV."

"Honey, you know the rule: no TV while we are eating at the dinner table."

"Daddy, I want TV."

"What did Mommy say, honey? TV is not for the dinner table; that's our family rule."

The rule is clearly defined. *We don't watch TV at the dinner table.* The rule is clearly communicated. *No TV at the dinner table.* The rule is consistent. *Our family rule is always no TV at the dinner table.* The rule is reinforced by the team. *Mommy and Daddy both agree: no TV at dinner.* Now isn't that simple?

Enter a new issue: you want TV to be allowed occasionally during dinnertime. As you know already, this discussion cannot take place in front of the kids, at the location of said issue. Timing is everything, and standing in front of the TV with your children watching you is not the time or place to share your brilliant new idea with your spouse. The time is later; the place is in private. Then and there you can openly communicate, discuss, and reevaluate the house rule. If you both decide to change the rule, the pattern repeats itself, and the five Cs apply.

Dad says, "Kids, we have some news we think you will like. Mom and I talked it over and have decided together that for every night we have good behavior at the dinner table—meaning no throwing food, no talking during the blessing, and no getting out of your seats—you will earn a point toward dinner-table TV time! Five points, and you can watch a video while eating dinner! What do you think?"

"Yeah! Cool!"

You were united in this decision. You changed your mind without giving up your parental authority. The kids didn't manipulate a change in the rules. Everyone is on the same page of the same book. Your new expectations and goals for your family are clearly communicated, clearly defined, and clearly presented to the kids by two parents on a team of one.

Centering Faith

One day, it dawned on me that all the people I know who have had successful, long-term, happy marriages and families are those whose faith is central and active—not just with one of them, but with both husband and wife. Their faith is not just a religion they check on a form, but a belief in a God who hears their prayers and stands ready to lend aid and comfort. They can turn to God for help together, even if they express their faith in Him in different ways. The happiest marriages I've known—Auntie Pat and Uncle Ralph, Auntie Angela and Uncle Frank, Ginger and Tom, Alicia and Paul, Colleen and Scott—are all couples who go to church and pray together regularly.

When I was young, Auntie Angela and Uncle Frank were my mom's best friends. Their daughter, Alicia, mentioned above, is also my best friend. In fact, as the story goes, our parents planned to have us at the same time! Anyway, Alicia says that one time her parents didn't talk for three days, because Auntie Angela wanted to go to a Baptist church and Uncle Frank wanted the family to go to a Catholic church. According to Alicia, that was the only major fight they ever had. (With kids, there are no secrets!)

You know what? Fifteen years later, Auntie Angela and Uncle Frank still go to separate churches, and they still have the most loving model of a marriage I have ever seen. And here is the kicker: their daughter also has the same type of loving marriage.

The moral of this personal observation? First, I don't think a happy marriage depends so much on which church you attend as long as both of you are being filled with the love of God regularly and pour it out, in liberal doses, on each other. Also, the love and faith shared between parents spills over to the kids and gives *them* a better chance at a happy marriage.

Many families have discovered that the Bible provides a great blueprint for marriage and family life. Inside its pages are real stories of real families (including plenty of dysfunctional families!) and God's plan for how a husband and wife can love and serve each other with faithfulness, patience, and a healthy interdependence through the ups and downs of life. The Bible gives clear instructions about raising children, helping them grow according to their giftedness, and shepherding their hearts when they go astray.

I know some of you reading this may have suffered abuse or neglect or feel as though you were "beat up with the Bible" by parents who claimed to be Christian yet never demonstrated the kind of love that Jesus Christ modeled and asked us to share with each other. But a funny thing usually happens when people who were turned off by past faith experiences become parents. They start asking themselves, "How am I going to explain God to my child? How will I answer their questions? How can I give them something solid to believe in, when the world can be so harsh?" Having young children in our care is often a time when we begin to seek out faith, reexamine church, and long to be part of a community of people who are seeking the same thing. If this is the case with you, I urge you to go after God with your whole heart—ask Him to lead you to a balanced, loving group of believers.

I think one reason that spiritual books are becoming blockbuster bestsellers is that they are touching a nerve and meeting a giant need across our country. They tell us that God wants to use us and bless us, that our life on earth matters, and that God loves us individually. Isn't that a message we all want to pass on to our kids as well?

A centering faith is an anchor to your marriage and to your family. It is worth taking time to talk through your beliefs and determine how you'd like to share those with each other and your kids. Statistics show that couples who pray together regularly have markedly fewer divorces and happier marriages. "Few things comforted me as a child more than when my mom or dad came into my room and prayed for me," a good friend of mine shared. When you are out of words or confused, praying with your children to ask God for answers or for peace can be very powerful in teaching them how to soothe their emotions.

If your family begins to implement the five Cs of successful parenting—communication, clarity, consistency, cooperation, and centering faith—you'll soon be giving each other high-fives instead of cold shoulders!

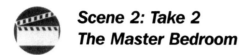

Scene 2: Take 2
The Master Bedroom

WIFE, *falling on the bed.* Ugh! It was such a rough day. Jenna was really off the wall. She bit me when I told her she couldn't watch *Sesame Street* because it was naptime.

HUSBAND. Oh, that's not good. Were you OK? It's probably something all kids do at least once, but we really need to take care of this before it becomes a habit.

WIFE. Yeah, I agree. I got down on her level and told her, "Biting is not OK" in my firmest voice. Then I gave her a time-out. After she apologized, I put her down for her nap.

HUSBAND. That seems reasonable. She knows what time-outs are for, and she hates that voice, so I'm sure she got that biting is not OK.

WIFE. I could use some help with reinforcing it, if she does it again. Any other ideas on how to handle it?

HUSBAND. Hmm . . . I think you handled it perfectly for a first offense. If biting becomes a habit, let's check out some books on what to do when kids bite or ask Paul and Laura—they've raised three great kids. I promise to jump in and help you with Jenna if it continues, OK?

WIFE. You have no idea how loved and supported that makes me feel. Have I told you lately that I love you?

HUSBAND. Enough to watch a football game together right now? *(Chuckles.)* We can see some real aggressive behavior—grown men fighting over a ball. Then the biting may not seem so bad!

WIFE, *laughing as she leans over to give him a kiss.* You always make me laugh. And because you are such a great husband and dad, you can control the remote for the whole game—if you promise not to bite. *(Laughter and snuggling, and the Patriots game, commence!)*

Nanny to the Rescue!
Recap

Were you able to catch the Nanny Tips that turned this fictional family from frenzied to functional?

1. *Communicate effectively.* Clearly state exactly what the problem is so there is no room for misunderstanding. How can your spouse help solve the problem if he doesn't know exactly what the problem is?

2. *Address the action, not the child.* All kids are great gifts from God; it's their behavior that stinks sometimes. Instead of saying, "Good boy!" praise your child's behavior by telling him, "Great work!" or "What a polite thing to say!"

3. *Listen; don't just hear.* Show that you are paying attention to what is being said and that you are working to process what you are hearing. How? Give your child focused eye contact, stop what you are doing, and get down on her level, if possible.

4. *Be supportive.* You are two parents on one team. Show empathy for what your spouse is going through. Offer suggestions, kind words, and support to each other.

5. *Reinforce each other.* Tell your spouse things like, "I believe in the action you took. I support your decision."

6. *The family that prays together stays together.* If you and your mate are comfortable doing so, praying aloud is a wonderful "glue" to hold your marriage and family together. Don't know where to start? Check out Stormie Omartian's series of books on prayer: *The Power of a Praying Wife, The Power of a Praying Husband,* and *The Power of a Praying Parent.* They'll prime your prayer pump for sure! And for the whole family to enjoy a ritual of praying at meals, see *Table Graces for the Family.*

7. *Be on the same page.* Make sure that you and your spouse are on the same page of the same family rulebook, which you wrote together.

8. *Laugh loud and laugh often.* Laughter can cure almost anything, or at least lighten the load.

9. *Show appreciation for each other.* Acknowledge each other's efforts, dedication, and work.

10. *Never go to bed angry.* End each night with "I love you" and a kiss. (My mom taught me that one.) In fact, some families always end conversations with "I love you!" I like this idea because no matter what happens in an uncertain world, you can always be sure your last words to each other were "I love you."

CHAPTER THREE

MOM & DAD, INC.

 Scene 3: Take 1
Kitchen / Family Room

MOM, *shouting from kitchen to Dad in family room.* Jack, can you take the
   kids to swimming lessons today?

DAD. Sorry—I have a golf game.

MOM. Come on; they're your kids too! I need you to do your part!

CHRIS, *entering family room from kitchen.* Hey, Dad, can I have a cookie?

DAD. Yeah, sure.

(Chris goes back into the kitchen and grabs a cookie out of the cabinet.)

MOM. What do you think you're doing, Chris?

CHRIS, *grinning.* Dad said I could have a cookie.

MOM. Didn't I just tell you no when you asked five minutes ago?

CHRIS. Yeah, but Dad just said yes.

MOM. Jack! Why did you tell Chris he could have a cookie? He asked me
   first, and I said no! You know lunch is almost ready!

I f it took one team of two parents to produce a child, why would the responsibility of nurturing and raising that same child lie with only one team member? You and your spouse are a team, and you need to share responsibility for parenting your children.

In today's world, most households need two incomes to live comfortably, which leaves parents juggling marriage, kids, household chores, and careers. Even families who are fortunate enough for one parent to stay home face the dilemma of meeting everyone's needs without sacrificing their sanity.

Good Parenting Takes Teamwork

In parenting, as in a dance, it takes two to tango—though it might take some practice to keep from stepping on each other's toes. Parenting is much easier and more enjoyable if both parents are equally committed to each other first and then to working together as a team to navigate the parenting waters.

What a Good Parenting Team Is Not

Parenting as a team *doesn't* mean you have to draw rigid black-and-white lines to divide everything 50–50, with specific roles and duties for each parent. For example, wouldn't it be every mom's fantasy to choose her own parenting roles and forever hand off the yucky ones to Dad, and vice versa? "I'll take rocking them to sleep (when they are tired and limp) and kissing them good morning (when they are in a good mood), and hey, because I'm feeling generous, I'll even change an occasional damp diaper. How about *you* get up with them at night, change all the dirty diapers, and handle teething and temper tantrums. Deal?" Dream on. It takes two to tango, and it takes two to handle teething and tantrums.

You probably have an idea of what a good parenting team is not. It isn't a team where Mom does all the discipline, while Dad gets to be the fun guy who lets the kids get away with stuff. It isn't a team where Dad is perceived as cool and Mom as a fool. It isn't a team where Dad says no to sweets, but Mom is the Secret Sugar Santa.

What a Good Parenting Team Is

A successful parenting team is comprised of two relatively sane and loving people who share a common goal: raising happy, healthy children. They work together to achieve their set goal. And work it will be! Here are some traits of good parenting teams.

Both team members realize that they have strengths and weaknesses and are ready to pinch-hit when one's strength is the other's weakness. Maybe Mom has a hard time putting the kids to bed at night because she hates hearing them cry. Maybe Dad can handle the crying better than Mom, but he has no patience for the details of getting the kids ready for bed. So Mom reads a bedtime story and says good night in the living room, and then Dad brings the kids up to bed, piggyback style. This is teamwork at its best.

Grab two pens and notepads, and sit down with your spouse for this easy exercise. Make three columns on your notepad. Make an A list—things you really enjoy doing as a parent with your kids. Then make a B list—things you don't mind doing fairly often. Finally, create a C list— things you just dread, the chores and duties that make you want to run away from home when the thought enters your mind. Compare lists, and let this be a starting place for how one parent's dreadful chore might be the other's dream job . . . and let the trade-offs begin!

> *A group becomes a team when each member is sure enough of himself and his contribution to praise the skills of the others.*
> —Norman Shidle

Team members encourage, support, and learn from each other. They hold hands on this roller-coaster ride called parenthood because it is both exhilarating and scary. They rejoice together in their victories and cry together in their momentary parenting defeats. As the Swedish proverb says, "Shared joy is double joy; shared sorrow is half a sorrow."

How does this look in a real-life scenario? Imagine you and your spouse have agreed, together, to use a kind, safe, time-proven method of getting your kids to sleep through the night. Dad walks through the living room and sees that the first night of hearing them cry it out is harder on Mom than it is on the kids. She's fighting tears and desperate to go to them. He puts his arms around her and soothingly says, "Hey, honey, you are a great mom. I know you don't want our kids to be unhappy, and hearing them cry is tough. But I'm glad you understand the importance of having them learn to fall asleep on their own—in their own bed. We've checked on them and know they are fine, and this won't go on forever. I feel bad too, but I'm happy that we agree that this is the best method to handle bedtime, and the payoff will be worth this temporary pain." (Don't worry: in chapters 6 and 7, you will learn all about my tried-and-true method of getting your kids to sleep, and why it works.)

Team members are both willing to sacrifice, to be inconvenienced, and to contribute whatever it takes if it is truly in the best interest of their family. Mom may want the kids to be on separate sports teams so that each child can come into their own, on their own. This beautifully meets one of the family goals: fostering independence in siblings. But, boy, does it take sacrifice, dedication, and inconvenience to be in two places at once! Both parents are going to have to chip in to make this work, and they need to decide as a team that the sacrifice is worth it.

> *No one can whistle a symphony. It takes an orchestra to play it.*
> —H. E. Luccock

Single Parent, Double Load

Let's be realistic. In today's world, half of the marriages in the United States end in divorce, leaving one parent carrying the childrearing responsibilities of two. There are also other situations in which the parenting team is reduced to one: single moms, another family member raising a child, a spouse away in the military, widows or widowers, and any other nontraditional family structure that leaves children with only one parent actively involved in their lives.

Though it may be tempting to indulge your children because they have suffered the loss of a parent in some way, you must be firm and consistent in your parenting. For one, you may not have others to back you up and take over when you need a break. Hopefully, you have some family and close friends who provide support when you need them. However, unlike the old days, families are often separated by many miles.

If you are a parenting team of one, fight the urge to do it all yourself. Instead, reach out and find every available parenting resource. Many communities provide support for single parents, including childcare share, parenting classes, and a host of other resources designed to provide you with the support you need to be the best parent you can be.

Instead of sticking to a two-member-team mentality of parenting, creative single parents add group mentoring to their parenting efforts. Perhaps an uncle can teach your son to pitch, a trusted grandparent can guide him as he comes to a major decision, and a fellow single-parent family can be your vacationing buddies. All of these people are mentors who will round out your creative but very real family. The downside is that gathering mentors for your children takes a lot of work, and you are on your own much of the time. The upside? You get to *choose* your children's mentors—and as many of them as you feel your children need. Think of how wonderful it would be for your children to feel loved and cared for—even partially "parented"—by a wide variety of grownups who taught them all sorts of skills and who were there for them

Nanny Tip

To be a successful and strong single parent, you have to nurture the family nurturer—you. Be sure to take extra care of yourself, so you can have the energy it requires to be a good parent.

- Get as much sleep as you can, guilt free! (Yes, this means letting all the nonessentials go. You can keep the house spotless when your kids are eighteen.)
- Exercise with your children for a two-for-one deal: you get your muscles moving, and you get to spend quality time together.
- Soak in the tub when the kids are in bed, and treat yourself to candles, music, and a good book.
- Fill your fridge and pantry with healthy, energy-promoting snacks. (Be sure to treat yourself with some good dark chocolate too. You've probably heard the news that dark chocolate is full of antioxidants!)

Take care of your body, mind, and spirit, so you can be a full cup from which to nourish your child. Of course, this advice is great for all parents, but you single parents are tackling double duty and have no spouse to tell you to slow down and pamper yourself a few minutes. So that's what I'm here for today!

on many levels through many years. You, as a single mom or dad, can create a rich heritage of adopted extended family for your children if you choose to be proactive.

Children need unconditional love, structure, and consistency. You can provide all those things!

Kids Play Their Parents Against Each Other

Let's say you are now parenting as a team—Mom and Dad. That's a great start. But remember: kids are smarter than you think. At times they seem almost like kittens, cute and adorable, snuggly and sweet. But they almost always have their whiskers out, looking for an opportunity to fit in any space, however small, that has been left open by the parenting team in order to get what they want, when they want it. Maybe it's a special treat; maybe it's a toy. Trust me: when the peewee team sees an opportunity to penetrate the parenting team, they will quickly take advantage of it. Ask your mom. Didn't you do the same thing when you were a kid?

As in football, to maintain team unity, your parenting team must have a strong offense and a strong defense. Your offense? Having a set of family rules and expectations that you communicate clearly to each other and implement consistently with the children. Your defense? Having faith in your teammate that, no matter what, your spouse will adhere to the family's rules and mutual goals.

Gettin' good players is easy. Gettin' 'em to play together is the hard part.
—Casey Stengel

So when your child asks, "Can I have a cookie?"—as in the scene that opened this chapter—neither parent will be taken off guard. The family rule has been set, just like the rules in any sports game. Referees can't change the rules just because the other coach is yelling about a bad call. Refs simply enforce the rules that were agreed upon long ago. (This, by the way, is a great way to explain family rules to your kids who enjoy sports.) So if the family rule is "No sweets before lunch," Chris can be sure that when he asks Mom, she'll say no and Dad will back her up.

Chris can also be sure that there will be a penalty for his attempt to gain team interference. Like any other team, when you experience a momentary defeat (say, giving in to your child's demands when you know that you shouldn't), you and your spouse regroup, reassess, and resume team play. Call a time-out and explain what went wrong. "Chris, I said yes to you because I didn't realize how close it was to lunch. First of all, I should have paid more attention. Second, you should never have asked me for something that your mom has already declined. So no cookies at all today, buddy."

Then you get back in the game and play your best.

Don't Let Yourself Get Traded to the Peewee Team

When the unity of the parenting team is broken, one member becomes at risk of being traded to the peewee team. When this happens, a child is allowed to manipulate the parenting team, resulting in conflict and confusion. We've all seen cases where a kid plays one parent against the other, so that one becomes the "good guy" and the other the "bad guy." The movie *Mrs. Doubtfire* shows a classic case. The father never disciplined the kids; instead, he gave signals that he was really on the kids' team—the team that was "against Mom." As a result, chaos reigned on several levels.

Teams share the burden and divide the grief.
—Doug Smith

The mother resented her position as "the heavy"; she longed to be fun too. But her husband stole that joy from her. Though the kids had a good time with their father, who was definitely the "fun parent," the end result was tragic. The parenting team was broken, the family was torn, and the parents eventually divorced. What started out, perhaps innocently, with a dad who just wanted to have fun ended up in such imbalance that everyone suffered.

I can't help but smile when I see how peace began to come into this family once the father took on the imaginary role of kind but firm nanny. If you can't seem to get distance from your parenting role, imagine yourself to be Mrs. Doubtfire. Adopt a "nanny" mind-set and ask how a calm, kind, and firm nanny would handle the situation at hand. You may be surprised how well this mental trick works.

With a unified team, there is no room for confusion or manipulation. When a child asks, "Who's in charge?" the answer should come from both of you, without hesitation, "We are. Together. Any more questions?"

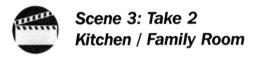

Scene 3: Take 2
Kitchen / Family Room

MOM, *shouting from kitchen to Dad in family room.* Jack, can you take the kids to swimming lessons today?

DAD. Hmm . . . I have a golf game at three. What time is swimming?

MOM. One thirty till two o'clock. If you can bring the kids to swim class, I'll meet you there by two, and you'll be able to tee off by three, no problem. I really need a long, relaxing bubble bath today.

DAD. Sure, I'll be glad to do it.

CHRIS, *entering family room from kitchen.* Dad, can I have a cookie?

DAD. I think I hear your mom making lunch in the kitchen. Did you already ask Mom?

CHRIS. Man, how come that never works anymore?

DAD. Because we smartened up. Nice try, though. For your good effort at manipulation, you win the grand prize of no cookie after lunch. Buddy, you'll wise up soon.

(Later that evening.)

MOM. You get two big husband points today, Jack.

DAD. Really? What did I do?

MOM. You stood up for my authority with Chris over the cookie-before-lunch thing. And you were gracious to work with me so I could relax without the kids.

DAD. So is there a reward for my good behavior?

MOM. Want a cookie?

DAD. I had something sweeter in mind . . .

(Mom smiles slowly and winks.)

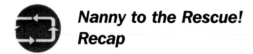

Nanny to the Rescue!
Recap

Were you able to figure out the game plan to create a win-win situation for a team victory?

1. *It takes two to parent.* Share the responsibility of parenting equally. Do your part.

2. *One team of two is stronger than two teams of one.* Be unified and be united.

3. *Clearly identify your parenting goal and establish how you will get there.* Develop rules together. Communicate the rules to the family. Implement the rules consistently.

4. *Trust that your teammate is always trying in good faith to do what's best for the team.* Commit to each other to do your best in achieving the team goal, and commit to following the same game plan.

CHAPTER FOUR

DISCIPLINE IS NOT A FOUR-LETTER WORD

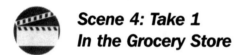

Scene 4: Take 1
In the Grocery Store

JAMES. Mom, can I have a candy bar?

MOM. No, James. How many times do I have to tell you no?

JAMES. Please, please, please! I'll be good!

MOM. I said no. You're being a bad boy. Stop asking.

JAMES, *crying*. But I said please. Mommy, please!

MOM. Stop it right now, or I'm taking you home!

JAMES *crying louder*. Please! PLEEEEASE!

MOM. OK, fine. Here is the candy. Now be quiet!

JAMES, *giggling*. Yippee!

I once saw a cartoon where one kid, who was gobbling up a huge candy bar, was telling another child, "How'd I get it? I got it the old-fashioned way. I whined for it."

Can you relate? Sometimes it seems so much easier to just give your kids what they want to shut them up, especially when you are running on empty yourself. Have you heard about the HALT technique, which is used with great success in Alcoholics Anonymous? I think it applies to parenting beautifully. When you are most tempted to toss good parenting out the door and let the kids run over your common sense, ask yourself if you are Hungry, Angry, Lonely, or Tired. Most likely, you'll find that one or more of these feelings are lowering your guard.

In an ideal world, wouldn't it be great to be able to really halt life for a while? Maybe you could press some imaginary Pause button on an aggravating scene with your child—and then, while he is in animated suspension, you could take care of your personal needs, eat a nice lunch at a lovely sidewalk café, go bowling, take a guilt-free nap, or spend some time with your spouse or best friend. Then, once you are refreshed and ready to roll, you could press the Start button and handle the parent-child conflict like a pro.

It is nice to dream, isn't it? In truth, this dream can become reality. As your kids get older, it gets easier to push that imaginary Pause button. You can say to an older child, "Honey, I'm just too tired for this decision right now. I'm going to take a nap, and then we'll discuss it once I'm rested and in my right mind." But if you are a parent of preschoolers, that dream quickly fades. You'll find it is wiser—and easier—to just work hard on the front end of parenting and develop a good discipline system that operates smoothly so you and your child can both avoid impromptu emotional meltdowns.

Here's the deal, like it or not: teaching your children the dos and don'ts of life is a responsibility you were commissioned with the moment you said, "Welcome to the world, my precious baby!" It would be a great disservice to your children if you approached discipline with a laissez-faire attitude. Early discipline lays the foundation for your children's immediate future (handling family life with ease) and their long-term good (when they transition to self-discipline in the real world).

The Four-Ingredient Recipe for Effective Discipline

Disciplining a child is an act of love designed to equip your children with an internal compass that will guide them through life. When your kids are ready to walk out the door into the real world, you want to make sure you've given them everything they need to be self-motivating, self-disciplining, empathetic, and productive adults. A huge part of their preparedness for life starts with how you train them early.

Here are the four ingredients that are necessary for effective discipline.

Know the Difference Between Discipline and Punishment

One of the most common misunderstandings I've discovered as a nanny is that parents do not know the difference between discipline and punishment. These terms are often used incorrectly or interchangeably, yet discernment between the two is the first ingredient in the recipe of getting in firm control of your child training.

Discipline is defined as "training expected to produce a specific character or pattern of behavior, especially training that produces moral or mental improvement." When we are disciplining children, our goal should be to train by instruction and practice in order to teach self-control, which in turn will help prepare our children for life in the big world.

According to Webster, *punishment* is defined as "a penalty imposed for wrongdoing." Often, punishments are simply reactions—and not necessarily well-thought-out ones. If a child throws his food at the dinner table and gets a whack on the hand, what is he going to remember most: that we don't throw food or that Mommy slapped him on the hand and it hurt? Of course he is going to focus on the physical pain and emotional hurt from the slap—and these feelings may be so overwhelming he may not connect the "punishment" to the "crime." He's just trying to recover from the momentary sting, rather than being trained and taught.

Give Your Children Clear Rules and Expectations

How can a child learn to abide by the rules and expectations of his parents if the rules and expectations are not clearly defined? As we said in chapter 2, your children should have a clear understanding of desirable and undesirable behaviors as well as your house rules. As parents, you should first discuss and decide these rules and expectations together. Then as a team, share your house rules with your children.

Keep in mind that your family rules and expectations should be age appropriate. For example, you cannot expect an eighteen-month-old to load and unload the dishwasher, but you can expect him to leave his cup on the table (instead of throwing it on the floor) when he is done. The child should also have a clear understanding of the age-appropriate consequences that will result if he doesn't cooperate or meet the expectations. An eighteen-month-old may lose his cup if he throws it on the floor, while a three-year-old may be removed from the table to a time-out and told, "Dinner is now over."

Consistently Correct Bad Behavior and Affirm Good Behavior

I can't emphasize this enough: consistency plays the biggest role in determining the effectiveness of discipline. Having a predictable, unchanging response to the undesirable actions of the child will result in a change of behavior. This is equally true for positive reinforcement. If a child consistently receives praise for a desirable action, that action will eventually become a default behavior. So in addition to giving your children consequences for wrongdoing, you must also catch them being good and give them praise at these times. ("You were so kind to your baby brother just now. See how gentle you are!")

When your definition of acceptable and unacceptable behavior is clearly defined and presented to your children, you need to be consistent in implementing it. Your rules should be something your kids can depend on, day in and day out, at least until your children have reached an age where they can begin to utilize the top-of-the-line internal compass that you lovingly helped provide, set, and program for them.

When consistency is absent, confusion arises. The child never knows what to expect, which is much more overwhelming to a child than being told no. Children feel most secure when they know exactly what to expect. In fact, I'd go so far as to say that children *thrive* on parental predictability. They want the reassurance that Mom and Dad know what they are doing—and by being consistent, you are giving them the gift of feeling safe. Sure, they may show disappointment at being told no at the time; but in the long run, children who feel secure within the boundaries of consistent rules in their home are happier and healthier emotionally.

Treat Your Children with Consideration

Make sure that you are condemning the *behavior*, not the *child*. Remember, you never want to deem a child good or bad. As I've said, all children are gifts from God and are inherently good. When you label a child "bad," you destroy the child's self-esteem. When you address the behavior, however, you are fixing an action or attitude. To successfully discipline your children, they must know they are unconditionally loved and respected as a member of the family—no matter what.

Also, and this is so important, evaluate the sensitivity level and personality of each child, and discipline the child in a nonthreatening way. Maybe all it takes with Abigail is to give her "the look," and she stops the unacceptable behavior. Maybe with Matthew it takes a time-out. Perhaps Denise responds better when you take away TV time or a favorite toy. Each child has his own threshold for accepting discipline, so it is important to be considerate of his sensitivity levels. What might be absolutely needed to train one child could break the heart and spirit of a more emotionally fragile one.

Saying No Without Guilt

What is so bad about saying no? Nothing! Teaching your children the meaning of *no* is one of the best gifts you can give your child. And believe me, it is much easier to teach the meaning of *no* to a two-year-old than a twelve-year-old—or even a thirty-year-old. We've all seen grown men and women react inappropriately when they have been told no or experienced a setback. Anyone who has been in a long line after a plane is delayed usually gets to see one or two angry, disappointed adults acting like preschoolers. Or perhaps you've seen grown men throwing a golf club or tennis racket in a temper tantrum. It's not a pretty sight (or a good example!).

Why do these adults embarrass themselves in such a way? My guess is that they were never taught how to deal with hearing, much less listening to, the word *no*. In the real world, adults have to deal with being told no all the time. We must teach our kids how to deal with the feelings and emotions that surface when someone turns you down—and this needs to start from an early age. Here's an example:

"Mommy, can I have a cookie?"

"No, honey."

The child cries. "Why not, Mommy? I want a cookie!"

"I understand you want a cookie, and it makes you sad that you can't have one. It's OK to be sad, but we are not having a cookie right now."

By saying no in a clear fashion and also acknowledging your child's feelings ("I know you are sad"), you are letting her know that you are listening to her and responding to what she is trying to communicate. It also lets her know that no means no.

This may sound unusual, but there are times I practice saying no to my charges. Here's an example:

"Shell, can I brush your hair?"

"Hmm. Let me think about it. No."

"Why not?"

"Because sometimes I have to practice saying no, and you have to practice listening to it."

How mean! you may be thinking. *Why did she say no when there wasn't a good reason behind it?* I practice saying no to the boys because I'm equipping them with the tools to handle the minor defeats life throws at them. I also believe it's best for children to experience their first defeats in a loving, safe environment—one in which they can learn to deal with the defeats productively, rather than out in the real world without a trusting parent (or caregiver) to guide them. After I told Fraser he couldn't brush my hair and he handled it well, I followed up by complimenting him and promising him that he could brush my hair at another specific time.

How many adults do you know who are overwhelmed in life because they never learned how to say no—or how to respond to it? Consider the poor sportsmanship by professional athletes or disgruntled employees on the nightly news. You don't want your children to behave like that when they are adults. Why would you let them behave like that now?

Good Fences Make Good Children

Would you let your two-year-old daughter play alone, unsupervised, in the backyard if your property had no fence? Of course not! Why? Because she does not have enough life experience to make safe decisions on her own. She is not yet able to think ahead or realize future consequences. She doesn't know that if she leaves the yard, her safety could be at risk; she doesn't yet have the self-control to stay in the yard even if she wanted to. (Kids learn by exploring, which comes from natural, unbridled curiosity!) She cannot yet make a judgment call about where the safe part of the yard ends and the dangerous part begins. She would also have no one to pick her up if she tripped over a rock and got hurt.

You cannot give children too much freedom too soon. But how do you know when and how to progress from your children totally depending on you, to becoming emotionally interdependent, to becoming fully independent? There are several psychological, emotional learning steps or stages between infancy and middle childhood that I find both helpful and fascinating. You are better equipped to train a child when you understand their learning, reasoning, and empathetic limits and milestones.

Four Stages of Cognitive Development

Swiss biologist and psychologist Jean Piaget was quite interested in cognitive development. After observation of many children, he posited that children progress through four stages and that they all do so in the same order. These four stages are described below.

The Sensorimotor Period (Birth to Two Years)

During this stage of development, an infant begins to discover his body and his relationship to their environment. He relies on his sensory issues (touch, taste, smell) to learn about himself and to discover the world around him. At this stage, children also begin to realize that objects are separate from themselves, rather than an extension of their being. Piaget called this the "sensorimotor period" because early intelligence can be seen as children use their sensory perceptions and motor activities. Ever wonder why your eighteen-month-old doesn't fall for the "Where did the ball go?" trick anymore when you hide it under the pillow? It is because he has made the connection (after repeatedly experiencing the same scenario) that although he can't see it, the ball is still there.

Preoperational Thought (Two to Seven Years)

At this stage, in simple terms, a child thinks the world literally revolves around him. At this stage, he believes that everyone thinks as he does, and he cannot put himself in another's shoes. Language development begins, but it is self-centered. A child in this stage will parallel play (do an activity side by side without interacting), and he neither knows nor cares that the friend next to him is doing something different. As children grow older, they begin to understand the difference between fantasy and reality and have a basic idea of the roles we have in society. Don't get mad when your four-year-old demands you do as he wishes; he truly has not made the connection yet that there is a bigger vocabulary than "me, myself, and I." Egocentricity has to be trained out of a child. It takes time and patience, and it will happen much more naturally as children mature in other ways.

Concrete Operations (Seven to Twelve Years)

This is the stage where you can actually begin to reason logically with your child about actual things (not to be confused with abstract things) and he will finally understand! By this age, a child can organize and sort items. For example, he can group animals together or identify a group of characters as letters. Children also begin to lose that "it's all about me" mentality (although I am sure that never completely goes away). As their language skills continue to grow, they begin to catch how conversation between two people works. Occasionally, at this age, kids even begin to understand that some truths are reversible. In other words, they will finally understand that one plus two and two plus one both equal three.

Formal Operations (Twelve Years to Adult)

Children at this stage are capable of thinking logically and abstractly. They can also reason theoretically. This is the highest level of cognitive development, and Piaget believed not everyone reaches this stage. If reached, the development of this stage continues throughout adulthood. A child who has reached this stage can form his own hypotheses and systematically test them to get results. It is at this age when you ask your child, "What would happen if . . . ?" and your child can imagine and give you an answer (one that actually may make sense!).

The main point in sharing this theory with you is to demonstrate that we can't treat children like miniature adults. They simply don't have the logical ability to make wise choices at an early stage, as they will when they've had time to go through the natural maturing process.

Discipline Dynamics

As any seasoned teacher or coach will tell you, it is much easier to be very strict with inflexible rules at the beginning of the school year—and then, if it seems right, to relax them a bit later on. In his best-selling book *Dare to Discipline* (and its two subsequent revisions), James Dobson advised high-school teachers not to smile the first semester. He was, of course, exaggerating a bit—but probably not much! It's easier to go from tough to tender-hearted than from tenderfoot to trying to be tough.

Any child can tell you that the sole purpose of a middle name is so he can tell when he's really in trouble.

—Dennis Fakes

I distinctly remember being a high-school junior when we got a new choral instructor midyear. At first, it was great. She tried to be our best friend, letting us have a grand old time. Then, as concert season approached and we continued to goof off, she grew quite frustrated and would often blow up. I remember actually telling her that it was much easier to start off with tight reins and loosen them than the other way around. It is nearly impossible to restore order in a classroom if chaos and inconsistency have been reigning for months.

Parents, it is much the same way for you. Think of yourself as the family fence builder. You are better off starting out with a strong fence made out of close slats and then slowly removing one slat at a time to create a less restrictive fence. Trust me: you don't want to have to turn a weak fence, with wide gaps, into a strong, solid fence in a moment's notice. Make less work for yourself by setting firm boundaries for your children and then relaxing some of them as your children mature and are able to handle more freedom.

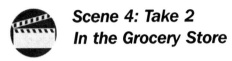

Scene 4: Take 2
In the Grocery Store

JAMES. Mommy, can I have a candy?

MOM. No, sweetie. We don't have candy at the grocery store.

JAMES. Please, Mom? I'll be good.

MOM. Thank you, James. You are always good, but you could do great by listening to Mommy in the store while we are shopping. That would be very helpful.

JAMES. OK, Mommy. But if I do good listening, can I have some candy?

MOM. I said no, James. If you ask again, you will get a time-out. Would you like a time-out?

JAMES, *sighing*. No, Mommy.

MOM. Great. Let's finish up then! Good cooperation.

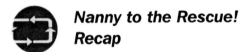

Nanny to the Rescue!
Recap

Could you count the Nanny Tips that transformed this toddler from terror to tamed?

1. *Say what you mean and mean what you say.* No means no!

2. *Discipline helps your kids; it doesn't hurt them.* Discipline is done out of love; punishment is done out of anger.

3. *The parent is in charge.* You are the boss, and you have the right and responsibility to set limits and rules . . . and to implement them.

4. *Consistency is the key to success.* Follow-through builds trust in your word. It lets your child know, without a doubt, that you will do what you say you will.

5. *Keep your cool.* Discipline your children without lots of emotion. Address the action, not the child. All children are gifts from God; it's their behavior that sometimes stinks.

6. *Be a good communicator.* Listen to your child. Acknowledge and validate his feelings, repeat back to him what you are hearing, and communicate to him effectively by clearly stating your expectations and the consequence if your child disobeys.

7. *Praise positive behavior.* Praise is a great way to reinforce an acceptable behavior.

8. *Don't give in to your child's demand.* Saying yes keeps him from learning the more valuable long-term lesson of delayed gratification or how to handle a small disappointment. By automatically giving in to a request, you are showing your child that you're not in control, unsure of your decision, and not committed to doing what you say.

9. *Give choices that you can live with.* Say to your child, "Do you want a time-out or not? The decision is yours. If you behave, we can zip along with our fun day. If you do not behave, we have to stop the fun and wait for you to finish your time-out." This gives the child the power to affect his temporary destiny and is another step to building a good, strong internal moral compass.

10. *Remember the HALT technique.* Are you (or is your child) hungry, angry, lonely, or tired? If at all possible, delay your answer to a difficult question until you—or your child, as the case may be—are rested and refreshed, with an emotionally calm tank.

CHAPTER FIVE

BE POSITIVE, PRACTICAL, AND PROACTIVE

 ### Scene 5: Take 1
In the Car Going to Grandma's House

KERRIE. I don't want to go!

MOM. Me either, but we're going.

KERRIE, *crying.* I want Teddy!

MOM. Sorry, but we can't turn around now; we're late!

DAD. I knew this was too much to do today. We really shouldn't try to go right now.

MOM. We don't go to your mother's, and you get mad. We do go, and now you don't want to! You're impossible!

KERRIE, *starting to scream.* I want my teddy bear!

MOM. I am trying to drive, Kerrie. Stop whining!

KERRIE. Mommy, please—I really NEEEED Teddy. *(She cries loudly.)*

MOM. Fine. We'll go back and get him, but you better be a good girl at Grandma's.

KERRIE. OK . . . *(sniff, sniff)* . . . Mommy. *(Her sobs begin to abate.)*

DAD. Let's just stay home.

MOM. We are going, and that's that. One way or the other, we are going to get there.

A positive attitude is quite easily achieved in a positive environment. If this sounds overly simplistic to you, stay with me. Sometimes the most profound truths are the simplest ones.

How do you create a positive environment in which to raise your child? Think of your five senses when creating an environment conducive to positive feelings. I once heard a pastor say that if you have uplifting music playing in your house, the atmosphere does not allow for negativity. I tested this by listening to music that I love on the way to work. I started walking into work refreshed and in a joyful mood, and others noticed my upbeat attitude.

A positive environment contributes to positive feelings. Why do you think love scenes in the movies have romantic music playing in a dimmed room? These environmental cues set the mood. Most adults instinctively know how to create an atmosphere for a romantic evening (good food, nice lighting, soft music, aromatic candles), but how many of us stop and think of how to "set the scene" in other ways? With a little forethought, we can set the perfect scene for waking up, going to bed, going on errands, doing chores—for ourselves and our kids. Try jotting down common events in a typical day. Next, think about how you could help your kids transition from one activity to the next with a little creative mood setting.

When you choose to be pleasant and positive in the way you treat others, you have also chosen, in most cases, how you are going to be treated by others.
—Zig Ziglar

Setting the Sleepytime Mood

Need some idea starters? Let's take bedtime, for example. How can you create a positive environment for kids going to bed? Would you leave the lights on, bright as can be? Of course not. If you have a dimmer switch, you can transition by dimming the lights or turning off the overhead lights and keeping one small bedside lamp on. For auditory clues, slow your speech down a bit, and speak calmly and more softly. Put on some soft music, a CD of lullabies perhaps. To use your children's sense of touch to get them ready for bed, a warm bath is wonderful. Or toss their pajamas, socks, blankie, or stuffed toy in the dryer a few minutes with a fabric softener sheet to give them something warm, soft, and fragrant to sleep in or snuggle with.

Another fun thing to try is aromatherapy. Smells of vanilla or lavender or chamomile are relaxing. A bedtime story, prayer, or lullaby can be part of a positive routine. Milk or warm cereal as a bedtime snack may also induce sleepiness. You wouldn't expect adults to sit quietly at a rowdy rock concert while all others are jumping around singing with the music. So how can you expect a child to have a calm attitude when everything around her says things aren't calm? If you set a correct tone and environment, your child will more naturally and happily move from activity to sleep.

What are some other creative ways to set the mood for your child? How about when it is time to wake up? How can you help your kids greet the day with positive energy? Natural light (sunshine if possible, through open window shades), music that starts soft and then gets peppy, energizing citrus smells (perhaps a glass of fresh orange juice to start the day)—the possibilities are endless!

Positive Reactions to Small Setbacks

Children look to adults to gauge their reactions. Have you ever noticed that when a child falls at the playground, she often will first get up and look around? As soon as someone approaches her, slightly panicked, and asks, "Are you OK?" the child seems to experience a delayed reaction. *Oh*, she thinks, *something bad happened, and I'm supposed to be upset about it!* And the crying commences.

I have a policy never to go up to my charges when they fall down in play (unless it happened from a dangerously high perch!) until they react first. That way I can gauge the severity of their injury, if any, rather than have them gauge the severity of their injury based on my reaction.

Even infants pick up on the feelings of the adults around them. A positive attitude communicates that you are content with what is happening—that things are OK. The kids can relax—they are safe, and life is good. Since so much of optimism is caught, rather than taught, it is important to ask yourself, honestly, if you have a pessimistic personality. If so, I suggest that you read books or listen to audiotapes that will help you see life through rosier eyes for your sake and for the sake of your kids.

Norman Vincent Peale's classic, *The Power of Positive Thinking*, is as helpful today as it was dozens of years ago. *The Power of a Positive Mom* by Karol Ladd is also an excellent resource. If you are feeling brainy and want to read some research on the subject, try Martin Seligman's *Learned Optimism*; Daniel Amen's *Change Your Brain, Change Your Life*; or Dan Baker and Cameron Stauth's *What Happy People Know*. All are fascinating books on how our thoughts affect us and why.

If you've spent a lifetime in a toxic or negative environment, you will have to really work at learning optimism as a way of life and passing it on to your children. (Children are so often the best motivators to change or improve our own behaviors, aren't they?)

When dealing with life's small disappointments, point out as best you can the silver lining that is usually behind every dark cloud. "Honey, I know you don't want to leave the playground, but look on the bright side—the sooner we leave, the quicker we can come back next time." You are validating your child's sad feelings while being positive about what is to come.

> *Fix your thoughts on what is true and honorable and right. Think about things that are pure and lovely and admirable. Think about things that are excellent and worthy of praise.*
> —Philippians 4:8 NLT

Teach your children some simple, heart-lifting songs to sing when things are glum. You could sing the classics "Keep on the Sunny Side" or "High Hopes." And children love "My Favorite Things" from *The Sound of Music*. By helping your children think the best of any situation, and by giving them tools to comfort themselves when they are down, you are teaching the skill of self-soothing. This is a powerful life skill that will serve them well through childhood and on into adulthood.

Practical Plans for Pleasurable Adventures

When you plan ahead, you are thinking in advance about how to deal with any major obstacles that may arise. For example, you would never leave the house without making sure that the diaper bag is loaded with diapers. Why? Because you don't want to get stuck in a "stinky" situation.

When you have a structured environment for your family and a clear, set schedule that you strive to adhere to, you are able to plan your day around your children's needs. For example, if you know you have to take a long car ride to visit Grandma, the best time to take the ride isn't when your toddler is just waking up from a nap, hungry, with tons of pent-up energy. It is best to take a car ride when she is ready for her nap, so she will fall asleep in the car. You are planning to accommodate her schedule, rather than interrupt it. I am not saying that you should live in an inflexible world without room for spontaneity. I'm saying that when it's within reason, take the steps possible to stick to your schedule.

Your child's schedule not only should be planned but should reflect a well-rounded, balanced routine. His day should consist of mealtime, naptime, quiet time, creative playtime, active playtime (outdoors, if the weather is nice), and family snuggle time. This schedule gives your child balanced experiences and allows him to express his creative side and his physical side. It also allows for him to learn to be alone, with his family, and with others in a group setting.

It's like when you are on a sports team. You get to practice your skills individually, and then you bring them to the team. Then your team plays games with other teams. The alone practice time is just as important as the team practice and the game. How can a child know his role in the family if he doesn't know himself? A child needs to learn to play alone, to think alone, and to realize that he is an individual as well as part of a family. If you don't provide him with an opportunity to learn to be alone and enjoy being alone, how else will he learn?

> ♥ **Nanny Tip**
>
> Write down ten healthy pleasures or calming activities that you use to soothe yourself when you are feeling blue (such as a hot bath, a good book, a funny movie, etc.). Now plan to do one per week!

It is also important to allow children time, within their daily routine, to develop their life skills. Their large motor skills are developed while playing outside and running with a ball. Their fine motor skills develop when they are learning to hold a paintbrush. Their reasoning and logic skills develop when they are presented with a problem, such as sorting shapes and putting them into the appropriate slots. Their affection skills develop when they snuggle with Mom and Dad. And their creative skills develop when they make their teddy bears come to life in imaginary play. A well-balanced day makes for a well-balanced child.

Such a well-balanced routine provides great experiences, but how do you get from one experience to the other? In a word, transitions. Kindergarten and early childhood teachers are all familiar with the term *transition*. In fact, they usually sing little songs to help little ones move from one activity to another. "Clean up! Clean up! It's time for us to clean up!" or "It's time to get quieter, quieter, quieter . . ." (and as the teacher sings this, her voice gets softer and softer).

You can also plan verbal transitions, such as these:

"Finish up, honey. Five more minutes, and we are leaving."

"OK, start cleaning up. We are leaving in two minutes."

"Great job! Thanks for cleaning up. Time to go."

> *When you engage in systematic, purposeful action, using and stretching your abilities to the maximum, you cannot help but feel positive and confident about yourself.*
> —Brian Tracy

You prepare the children for what is coming next. If you already have a routine in place, they will know that what comes next is not (or usually not) negotiable. Giving children environmental cues, such as turning over an egg timer, showing them that you are looking at your watch, or putting on your coat, helps set the atmosphere that says, "Playtime is over." When in doubt, remember that kids love consistency and thrive with structure.

Providing a balanced variety of positive experiences for your child helps him build a positive attitude toward life and all it has to offer.

Proactive Parenting

Proactive parenting plans ahead to prevent (as often as possible) things from going off course. On the contrary, reactive parenting responds *after* things have indeed gone off course. In life, especially in the parenting years, things are not always going to happen the way you planned. (What new parent hasn't left the house without an extra outfit for her infant, sure that baby had pooped his last for the day, only to find out he'd been saving it all up to release on your special outing?) To de-stress your life, you'll need a few preplanned strategies for coping with potential problems. Remember, be prepared!

Preparedness Techniques

Here are some typical scenarios and how I've learned (often the hard way) to prepare in advance for them.

You anticipate that the kids and their guests will argue over toys. If a large group of children is coming over, do a bit of preplanning by setting up stations so that the children can rotate and take turns. Have some kids cook their favorite fantasy recipe in a pretend kitchen, while others build a castle with blocks (for eating the pretend "dinner" in later), and still others play the roles of the diners, ordering and awaiting their orders. Have an arts and crafts table ready to go with an easy project for all to participate in. Homemade play dough and cookie cutters set out with dull plastic knives and vinyl place mats keep them occupied a long time. Having structured playtime with larger groups seems to work best.

You experience a sudden change in weather when on an outing together. Create a "weather kit." Keep an old sweater or two, plus an umbrella, packed in a bag in the trunk of your car.

You are stuck in traffic and the kids are starving. Keep an emergency snack container filled with crackers, water, or other shelf-stable snacks in the glove compartment.

You fear being caught without a pacifier or losing one. Buy pacifiers in bulk, a dozen at a time. Leave one in every room, one in every car, two in your purse or diaper bag—and even leave a couple at Grandma's house.

Someone has a boo-boo! Keep the first-aid kit handy in the car. Band-Aids, amazingly, fix almost anything (kudos to my charges' mom for that one!). You can even put one over a "hurting heart" when a child has wounded feelings or is sad about having to leave the fun of a play date.

You've had a fender bender and are shaking so badly you can't remember your name, much less all the information the police want. Keep a list of all emergency phone numbers, doctors' information, and medical information in the car along with a copy in your purse. A laminated index card works really well for this purpose. People often have a hard time recalling this information during times of stress.

Your kids are a chocolate mess, and you are miles from a clean bathroom. Always keep a few water bottles, paper towels, and wet wipes in the trunk. This makes for easy cleanup of the kids—and the car.

Now it is your turn. Take some time today, if you can, to jot a list of ways you could prepare for problems ahead of time. Then prevent future stress by having a backup plan or putting together appropriate "emergency kits" for those just-in-case scenarios.

Scene 5: Take 2
In the Car Going to Grandma's House

KERRIE. I don't want to go!

MOM. Oh, sweetie, I know you are tired and it is naptime—so why don't you try to close your eyes and nap in your comfy car seat?

KERRIE, *crying.* I want Teddy!

MOM. I thought you might. Daddy, can you get Kerrie's teddy bear out of the "Going to Grandma's" bag?

DAD. See, Mom's got all the bases covered.

MOM. I figured she'd nap on the way over, so she'll be wide awake and happy to visit your mom. You know how much your mom loves to dote on Kerrie, and Kerrie just eats it up! It's going to be a fun time.

(Kerrie falls fast asleep in the backseat.)

DAD. She's out like a light.

MOM. That was the plan!

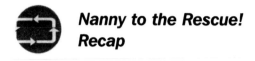

Nanny to the Rescue!
Recap

Can you see how being positive, practical, and proactive made the trip to Grandma's go up rather than down?

1. *Positive.* Mom approached the situation with a positive attitude. She reminded the family of the joys that come with seeing Grandma. She assured Kerrie it was OK to go to sleep in the car, and she used endearing terms.
2. *Practical.* There is a method to Mom's madness. She knew Kerrie's schedule, so she went on the adventure when it was the most sensible time to go. Do what makes sense, and save yourself stress!
3. *Proactive.* Mom thought ahead and knew that Kerrie might "need" her teddy, so she was prepared to respond to her need. Either she packed the stuffed toy ahead of time, or she had an exact replica in the car, just in case.

PRACTICAL HELPS FOR COMMON PARENTING CHALLENGES

CHAPTER SIX

GETTING YOUR INFANT TO SLEEP

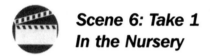 **Scene 6: Take 1**
In the Nursery

MOM, *rocking four-month-old Adriana.* Hush, hush, it's OK. Go to sleep, sweetie. Mommy is here.

(Adriana wails loudly.)

MOM. What's the matter? Please stop crying, baby. I'm holding you. I'm right here.

(Adriana continues to scream.)

MOM, *tearful.* Honey, come help me. I've been holding Adriana for twenty minutes, and she won't stop crying. I don't know what I'm doing wrong or what's the matter with her, but she just won't calm down.

DAD, *taking Adriana from Mom.* Here, let me try.

(Adriana screams louder.)

DAD, *shouting above the wailing baby.* Honey, I think she wants you!

MOM. What do we do? Just let her cry it out?

DAD. Well, she's got to be crying for a reason.

MOM. But I've tried everything! I'm at my wit's end!

s anything as unnerving as a crying baby who is obviously tired but will not go to sleep? Toss in parents who are also sleep deprived from middle-of-the-night feedings, wakings, and changings, and you have a formula for insanity.

For moms and dads (and overnight nannies) to be able to handle the additional stresses of raising small children, they need—at minimum—a decent night's sleep. Sleep deprivation is probably one of the biggest but least recognized causes of impatience, fogginess, and general malaise in young parents.

Are you spending your nights half-sleeping, half-sleepwalking toward the cries of your child? Do you sometimes feel like a red-eyed zombie, day and night, just going through the motions of surviving kids, too exhausted to enjoy them—or yourself? Chins up, drowsy parents! In this chapter, I will share practical tips that will leave your whole family more rested and able to handle the big and small challenges of parenting.

"Bedtime" Doesn't Have to Be a Bad Word

Why is bedtime often approached as something negative? From birth, bedtime is a necessity. We don't force babies to sleep; they sleep on their own, because they need it! Why is it, then, that as a baby grows into a toddler, bedtime turns into a negotiable activity, something we allow our child to have control over?

Bedtime is a battle that can be avoided if it is approached, from the get-go, with a relaxed attitude. Instead of looking at bedtime as the end of the day, teach your child that it is the beginning of the next! Sleep is needed so that we can have the energy to thoroughly enjoy tomorrow. I often tease my charges by saying, "Tomorrow won't come if you wait up for it."

Most new mothers have a cradle, bassinet, or portable crib next to their beds for the first few weeks and months of life. This allows for easy feeding, easy access to check if your child is still breathing, and a nice transition from the womb to independent sleeping. But there comes a time—and it comes quickly!—when parents have to implement a sleeping arrangement that works best, long term, for the entire family.

Methods of Putting Baby to Sleep

There are several schools of thought on the best way to put a baby to sleep, but a few methods rise to the top of the basic sleep choices. There is the family bed, with the baby staying in bed with Mom and Dad through the night. There is the popular Ferber method, which involves among other things letting your baby "cry it out" for a night or two. And finally, there are hybrid approaches, such as the new and popular methods of the "Sleep Lady" (Kim West), described in her book *Good Night, Sleep Tight*.

Which sleeping method is right for you? I can't necessarily tell you, but I can tell you the pros and cons of each so that you can make the right decision for your family.

> *There was never a child so lovely but his mother was glad to get him to sleep.*
> —Ralph Waldo Emerson

The Family Bed

In the mid-1970s, a book called *The Family Bed* sparked an interest in the benefits of having children sleep in their parents' bed. The authors pointed out that for centuries, mothers have been sleeping with their infants. Many health advocates responded by saying that this practice, with whatever advantages it may have, resulted in a much higher risk of infant suffocation.

Today, the baby-in-bed battle continues. The most recent and probably most popular book on the pros of co-sleeping (along with scientific research that answers some of the most common objections) is called *Good Nights: The Happy Parents' Guide to the Family Bed (and a Peaceful Night's Sleep!)* by Jay Gordon and Maria Goodavage.

In a chapter called "Baby Knows Best," the authors present the argument that babies who sleep with their parents have less chance of falling victim to sudden infant death syndrome (SIDS). They base their argument on the fact that babies sleep in a faceup position when in their mother's arms. Because this style of sleeping promotes a lighter (and possibly safer) sleep, SIDS is less likely to occur. The advantages of this method are obvious: more skin-to-skin contact, less crying for baby, and no getting out of bed to feed or nurse during the night.

I have found that there are different parenting personalities, and it is important for each family to evaluate their individual as well as team parenting styles. Keeping an infant in your bed may be just the solution for you and your mate—but therein lies an important piece of information. If you choose the family bed, Mom and Dad really must agree together that this is their method of choice and be united in the decision. Why? Because there are many drawbacks to the family bed arrangement.

Baby may sleep well, but how about Mom and Dad? Many parents find they're being awakened too often during the night to feel they are getting a solid night's sleep. Is the sacrifice of sleep worth the extra cuddle time with your baby?

Sex and intimacy between spouses may be interrupted. Although there are creative ways to get around this issue (outlined in the previously mentioned book *The Family Bed*), it is an issue. Even if you enjoy intimacy in another room and save sleep for the family bed, there's an interruption in spontaneity. There's more of a "family" mood than a "romantic" mood to the bedroom. Some couples can handle this interruption for long periods of time when their children are small; others cannot. More than any other method, this one requires total buy-in from both husband and wife to make it work without damaging your marriage.

Your child may not have a chance to develop independent and secure sleep habits. How can a child learn to self-soothe or put himself back to sleep if Mom or Dad is always there to do it for him?

There are legitimate safety concerns about co-sleeping. These risks range from a child being suffocated with bulky blankets or pillows, an adult rolling on top of a child, a child falling off the bed, or even a child getting wedged between the bed and the wall or the mattress and the headboard. These risks are realities that cannot be overlooked.

The Ferber Method

Dr. Richard Ferber, director of the Pediatric Sleep Disorders Clinic at the Children's Hospital in Boston, wrote the book on sleep problems, literally. His book *Solve Your Child's Sleep Problems* is recommended reading for any parent ready to implement the "cry it out" sleep method.

For the Ferber method to work successfully, you have to have your child in another room—and if you choose to use this method, once you put your child in bed, that's it. The pro of this scenario is that children learn to fall asleep on their own. The con is that it can be quite a loud and traumatic experience. It is hard to know who feels more traumatized during this period: the baby or the tender-hearted parents (or both).

Some feel that with this method, the child loses the sense that Mommy is there to reassure and meet needs. Others believe that there is something to be said about the short-term suffering that results in lasting positive sleep habits. If this short period of feeling abandoned seems too difficult to you, rest assured that any "damage" done won't put your child into therapy. Most of us functioning adults were probably taught to sleep through the night through the "crying it out" method, as this has been the most common method of getting a child to sleep for the last few decades.

Dr. Richard Ferber is a proponent of crying it out, but there is a progressive method to doing so. Dr. Ferber stresses the importance of not applying his method blindly; he acknowledges that parents must be willing to let their baby cry for the method to work. He says, "Circumstances are not always the same. When the baby cries, if he or she has a scary dream and wakes up frightened, [the baby] will respond differently than when asking for the fifth glass of water. Figure out what is happening and why. You cannot jump right into treatment."[1]

Dr. Ferber notes, for example, that if a baby is frightened, it is not good for the parent to let the baby cry and leave the room. What the baby needs is reassurance. Or if a baby is crying because he is in pain or sick, do not leave him on his own; he needs assistance.

Many parents have found tremendous relief and help from the Ferber method, but just as many others have pronounced themselves "Ferber failures" because they just couldn't handle the crying bouts, however contained and limited. I empathize.

The Sleep Lady Shuffle

Though you must make your own conclusions after doing a bit of research into the alternative approaches, I am encouraged by a third, increasingly popular method of helping your baby sleep through the night. This method meets the needs of the parent (getting some sleep) and the baby (learning to fall asleep) with less crying and less trauma.

Social worker Kim West (known to her clients as the Sleep Lady) promises a kinder, gentler way to get your child to sleep through the night in her book *Good Night, Sleep Tight*, one of the current best-selling books on children and sleep. In this book, West emphasizes that sleep is a learned skill and explains how parents can teach children to sleep, even at an early age. She starts with newborns, showing parents how to avoid sleep problems from the beginning. She then gives solutions for older babies and children who have developed poor bedtime, nighttime, or naptime habits.

Key to the program is what she calls "The Sleep Lady Shuffle," which begins at around six months. This is a progressive method in which the parent puts the baby in the crib at night and stays nearby (sitting in a chair) to soothe the child. Then over a period of several nights, very gradually, the parent moves the chair away from the crib until he or she is out in the hall.

People who say
they sleep like babies
usually don't have them.
—Leo J. Burke

You can check out Kim West's routine from her book or Web site: www.sleeplady.com. Many readers of her book are comforted by her empathetic, "nonpreachy" tone. A mom (and a nanny) has enough problems without a finger-wagging child expert in her face, so this book makes for a relaxed reading experience.

Nanny Shell's Mix-and-Match Method

I tend to mix and match the above methods of getting children to sleep, depending on the family's preferences and the child's personality. Keep in mind that teaching your children to soothe themselves is a skill they'll use their entire lives. It allows them to put themselves back to sleep if they awake in the middle of the night. Here's my method:

1. You start out the first night by staying close to your baby, gently rubbing her back until she falls asleep.
2. The next night, you put her in the crib, wait for her to fuss, and then rub her back.
3. The night after that, you give her a few minutes longer to cry, then go in and reassure her by whispering, "It's OK; Mommy is here. Go to sleep, little darling." And on and on until baby slowly loses the dependence on your presence to comfort her and adjusts to falling asleep on her own.

You will probably find a combination of systems that works best for you and your baby. This is a general guide. Consistency is key in getting your children into a sleep routine, just as it is in developing a daytime routine, so whatever method you choose, give it a chance by being consistent.

To Rock or Not to Rock?

You're sitting in the rocking chair, warm and snuggly as your baby drifts peacefully to sleep. As she is sleeping, you put her in her crib, thinking she will remain in peaceful slumber during the transfer from your arms to her crib. Then reality sets in. As

Nanny Tips

Here are some practical helps for a pleasant night:

- *Make sure your children's physical needs are met before you put them to bed.* If they have already been fed, changed, and dressed seasonally, you don't have to ask, "Are they hungry, wet, or cold?" if they cry.
- *Keep the room temperature slightly cool.* Babies sleep best when the thermostat is set around sixty-eight degrees.
- *Put children down with confidence.* Your words and actions should communicate, "This is just what we do." Talk calmly and soothingly.
- *Put children down in their beds while they are still barely awake.* This gives them the opportunity to adjust to the surroundings rather than waking up and wondering how they got there.
- *Keep the room dark.* Experts suggest that night-lights can cause harm to the developing eyes of an infant. On a future note, consider this: how will an older child be afraid of the dark if he's never slept in the light?

soon as you put her down, she screams, you pick her up, and the process starts over again. And again. And again . . . until finally you both fall asleep so deeply that an eighteen-wheeler driving by and honking its horn wouldn't wake you up.

The positive outcome of this scenario is that baby feels good and Mom feels good, initially. There's something very satisfying about holding a baby until she is deep in slumberland. But the negative outcome is that your baby isn't learning that it's OK and necessary to fall asleep on her own—and you aren't getting the beauty sleep you need either.

I suggest that instead of rocking your baby all the way to sleep, you put your baby down right before she falls asleep. Sounds impossible, does it? This technique combines a little of everything to create a method that has worked for me.

The steps to success are as follows: You create a peaceful environment, hold your baby comfortably and securely, rock your child until you are sure she is calm, then put her in the crib. She may fuss, but you can pat her on the back and tell her, "It's OK." Whatever you do, don't take your baby out of the crib. Repeat: *don't take your baby out of the crib!* This technique teaches your baby that the crib is a safe place that she can enter even while awake. It also teaches her to fall asleep on her own—with, of course, a little reassurance from Mom at first.

Putting baby to bed in her crib while awake also lets her know where she is, so she is more aware of her surroundings when she wakes. Would you like to fall asleep in your bed, only to wake up in the kitchen? No, it would be disorienting. Allowing your baby to fall asleep in her crib makes it easier for her to fall asleep on her own when she wakes up in the middle of the night because she won't be disoriented by her environment.

Choose a Sleep Method That Works for You

Sleep habits are built pretty quickly. On average, a baby should be sleeping through the night around three months of age. But many children have trouble sleeping through the night (and thus, so do Mom and Dad) even at a much older age— even three or four years of age! If this is the case for you, don't despair. It's never too late to help your child sleep peacefully through the night. Both Ferber and West have detailed sections in their books on helping an older child with sleep problems. Since the scope of my book is so broad, I cannot go into all the details of sleep coaching or training, but if this is a big issue with your family, I've given you some great places to start to get immediate relief! Also, we'll deal with bedtime rituals for toddlers and preschoolers, as well as naptime hints, in the next chapter.

Whatever method you and your spouse choose—the family bed, the Ferber method, the Sleep Lady Shuffle, Nanny Shell's mix-and-match method, or your own family combo—remember to employ the consistency rule of thumb. Pick a method—whichever method works with your personality, your emotional limits, and your child's basic needs—and then stick with it long enough to give the method a fair and reasonable chance to work.

A final word to you moms and dads of newborns: until you establish a routine, you may not sleep well for the first couple of months. Realize that sleep deprivation is a huge drain on your energies, so do all you can to play catch up. Here are a few tips:

- *Take turns doing the "night shift."* Even if Mom is breast-feeding, Dad can change diapers and bring the baby to Mom.

- *Take power naps whenever possible.* Dr. James B. Maas's book *Power Sleep* is a great resource on this subject.

- *Enlist some backup care.* Ask family and friends to watch the baby while you nap.

- *Let some things go.* Release your need for an immaculate house or complicated meals, and make your motto Keep It Simple. Do all you can to make your routines easy so when the baby is napping, you can catch up on zzz's without feeling guilty about what isn't being done.

Whew! We've spent a lot of time discussing baby's sleep habits, but as parents will tell you, the issue is huge. In fact, it's big enough that I've decided to spend another chapter on describing bedtime rituals for toddlers and preschoolers, along with some naptime hints.

In a recent interview for *Baltimore Magazine*, Kim West gave these tips, which are both accurate and practical:

- Most sleep problems in children are behavioral, not medical. Even so, if your child is having trouble getting to sleep or staying asleep, check with your pediatrician to rule out any physical causes.
- Install room-darkening shades if your child wakes up very early or has trouble napping.
- Try using a white-noise machine in your child's room to block out noise from the rest of the house or outside.
- If you aren't ready to take away your baby's pacifier, leave several in the crib so you don't have to get up at night to retrieve a lost one.
- Establish a morning ritual as well as a nighttime ritual. A morning ritual helps reinforce children's understanding of wake-up time versus sleep time. West recommends a "dramatic wake-up": throw open the blinds, switch on the lights, sing morning songs, and start the day.
- Though West counsels against picking up or snuggling your baby during the night (she encourages soothing and patting instead), this edict does not apply to a child who is sick or who has had a nightmare or a fright.
- Both parents should be able to put the child to bed. Though Mom and Dad don't need to have identical routines, the routines do need to be similar.[2]

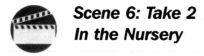

Scene 6: Take 2
In the Nursery

MOM, *rocking four-month-old Adriana.* Hush, hush, it's OK. Go to sleep, baby. Mommy is here.

(Adriana wails loudly.)

MOM. OK, let's see here. I just fed you, so you aren't hungry. I am holding you the way you enjoy. Why are you crying?

(Adriana continues to scream. Mom remains calm, going through mental checklist.)

MOM. Ah . . . I think you may have a wet diaper. Mommy forgot to change you, honey. Let's get a clean diaper and see if that helps. This is definitely your "I'm not comfy!" cry. *(Shouts down the hall.)* Honey, would you come hold Adriana? I need to run and get some fresh diapers from downstairs.

DAD. OK. Come to Daddy, baby girl.

(Adriana continues to cry.)

DAD. Oh, sweetie, Mommy's getting you a clean diaper. Is that what's going on? You don't like to be wet? We're going to fix that in a jiffy.

MOM. Here we go! *(She changes the baby.)*

(Adriana starts to calm down and even begins to giggle, loving that "freshly diapered" feeling. Mom bundles her up, turns on some soft lullaby music, dims the light, rocks her until she's sleepy, and then places her in the bed. Adriana fusses just a wee bit. Mom quietly and softly pats her back. Adriana relaxes, sucking quietly on her hand to soothe herself, and drifts off to the Land of Nod.)

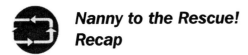

Nanny to the Rescue!
Recap

What did this mom do to end her nursery nightmare?

1. *She remained calm.* She kept her emotions steady as she went through a mental checklist.

2. *She objectively analyzed what was going on.* She took inventory. Was the baby fed? Dry? Hot? Cold?

3. *She tuned in to her baby.* The mom focused on the sound of her baby's cry. Babies have different cries for different problems. Eventually, you'll discern what each cry means.

4. *She spoke to her baby reassuringly.* Both the mom and dad let their baby know what was happening. They told her it was OK; they were solving her problem. Your child may not understand all you are saying, but by speaking words in a calm and reassuring voice, you are teaching her that when you talk this way, help is on its way! (Also, you may end up calming yourself in the process.)

5. *She took action to problem solve.* She changed her baby's diaper, resolving the discomfort before proceeding with bedtime rituals.

6. *She used soothing bedtime rituals.* She turned down the lights, put on soothing music, bundled her baby up, rocked her just until sleepy, and stayed nearby (but didn't pick her up) until she finished putting herself to sleep in the crib.

In a recent interview, Dr. Ferber shared some of the most common reasons that babies have trouble sleeping through the night. Those reasons are as follows:

- Inappropriate associations with falling asleep
- Inappropriate sleep schedule
- Too much feeding at night
- Problems setting limits
- Fears at night
- Sickness

He also offered the following helpful suggestions for creating a good bedtime routine:

- The baby should be on an appropriate sleep schedule for his age.
- The baby should fall asleep under the same circumstances that he wakes up to; things should not change. If possible, the baby should not fall asleep in the living room (or car seat) and wake up in the crib.
- Don't let your baby associate television with sleep. The baby should not go to sleep with it on or turn it on as the first activity after waking up.
- Quiet and a relatively dark environment are best for sleep. No bright lights![3]

CHAPTER SEVEN

SLEEP ISSUES FOR TODDLERS AND PRESCHOOLERS

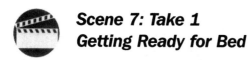 **Scene 7: Take 1**
Getting Ready for Bed

MOM, *to three-year-old Charlie, who is watching TV.* Charlie, time for bed.

CHARLIE. No! I don't want to!

MOM. In your room. Now! I'm not going to argue.

CHARLIE. But I'm scared.

MOM. Go, Charlie. Now!

CHARLIE. I'm hungry.

MOM, *picking up Charlie and carrying him into his room.* I told you to get in bed ten minutes ago. Now I have to carry you like a baby.

CHARLIE, *kicking.* No! I don't want to go!

MOM, *putting Charlie on his bed.* Good night. Be a good boy. *(She shuts the door.)*

CHARLIE, *pleading.* Mommy, please! *(Gets out of bed and follows Mom down the hall.)*

MOM, *picking up Charlie and bringing him into his room.* In bed!
(She shuts the door.)

CHARLIE, *hysterical.* No! No! NO! *(Gets out of bed and runs after his mom.)*

MOM. Argh! Fall asleep on the floor, then. I'm too tired to care!

O K, now that you are well rested and recovered after the last chapter, let's talk about sleep issues with toddlers and preschoolers.

The Toddler Bed—Coming to a Bedroom Near You!

You will be surprised how soon after your baby learns to fall asleep in his crib, on his own, that the toddler bed begins making its way to a bedroom near you. Once your child can crawl out of the crib (usually around eighteen months to two years old), he is ready for a toddler bed. How do you prepare for such a transition? The same way that you taught your baby to fall asleep. You are clear, confident, and consistent.

Nanny Tip

If you have young ones who can crawl out of the crib (and you still want to buy more time until you find the right bed), you can invest in a "crib net." This dome-shaped net goes over and securely attaches to the crib rails, with a zipper for easy access. This is especially useful for families who have cats (or other pets) and for children who share the same room. I still can't figure out how two sixteen-month-old twins could start out asleep in separate cribs at night and end up in the same crib the next morning. It was cute; but for their safety, I found that the crib net kept them from risking injury during the great nighttime escapes.

Having a toddler bed poses a new set of obstacles, but rest assured, you will overcome them. One practical thing you can do to help make this transition smooth is to allow your child to help choose his new bed. Also, help make his environment familiar (and comfortable) by transferring his favorite crib blanket to the new bed, using the same color sheets, and putting the bed in the same location as the crib.

I will also let you in on a secret: if your toddler doesn't know it's OK to get out of bed in the middle of the night, he won't. I swear. I know it sounds crazy, but it is true. If you make it clear that bed is where he belongs, he will not get out. He won't know that he can! But this only works if the first time your child attempts to get out of bed, you address it clearly. "Excuse me, John. We belong in bed during bedtime. We don't get out of bed unless there is an emergency." (Be sure to define *emergency* very clearly so there is no misunderstanding. Our definition includes fires as well as using the potty—if you're sure that you are going to wet the bed.)

Don't argue, negotiate, or nag your child. You tell it like it is, in a clear, non-emotional way: "Sleeping is just something that we do, and this is how we do it." Children will live up to the expectations you set for them. If you expect them to get out of bed, they will, again and again and again. If you expect them to stay there, they will.

When helping your child move from the crib to his first toddler bed, you can use the same methods you used when he was a baby to get him to sleep alone. The first night, you sit on the edge of the bed, rub your child's back, and assure him that this is the new place for sleep. The next night, you move to the floor and use your voice to whisper assurances . . . but do not engage in conversation. The next night, move a little farther away. No talking is needed, just your presence. On and on each night, until you have scooted out the door with it shut behind you. Your toddler may fuss and cry some, but if you are sure he is not ill, be consistent with your sleep method, and you will prevail.

> *Any kid will run any errand for you if you ask at bedtime.*
> —Red Skelton

The Bedtime Routine

"Just one more story!" "Just one more drink!" "Just one more hug!" So the bedtime chorus goes until you are ready to scream for relief. What can you do to solve the bedtime stall?

First, *create a clear, concrete connection that the bedroom is for sleeping.* Don't play in the bedroom, don't have time-outs in the bedroom, and don't do anything overly active but sleep in there. This way, the child makes a clear connection between the bedroom and bedtime. Even if you live in a small home or apartment, you can still make this work. Think creatively. Make a corner of your family room (or any other room where you have space) the "toy area" by putting down colorful foam floor pads to designate play space. Arrange your furniture so it acts as a divider to a play area. Whatever you do, the idea is to reinforce that the bedroom is for sleeping, not for playing.

Second, *develop a routine that addresses all the possibilities before bed.* For example, our bedtime routine starts at dinner. Each night, we have dinner at five. After dinner, the boys take their showers. Then they get in their pajamas and put their dirty clothes in the hamper. After that, we come back downstairs to have a drink of water. We then brush our teeth.

Third, *allow your child a half-hour age-appropriate video or a book of their choice, to be watched or read in the living room.* With this "treat" to look forward to, there's no problem getting through with showers or teeth brushing, or even getting into pajamas. They know once they are clean and in their pajamas, they have something fun to do before bed. If possible, try to make a stack of designated sleepytime books and videos for them to choose from—books that are soothing and movies that are softer and less intense in tone.

Finally, *take the children to the bathroom and then to bed at your established bedtime.* I take the boys to bed at seven fifteen, prompt. They get tucked in, and they get a hug and a kiss. They are told each night, "Do not get out of bed unless there is an emergency or you need to go to the bathroom." The lights go off, the doors are left ajar, and they are told again that they are loved.

Some parents add a time to pray with their kids as a soothing end to the day. I heard of one man speak of how his father would toss the children's blankets in the dryer each night to warm them, tuck the kids in nice and tight, say a prayer of blessing over them, and then kiss them good night. This man is nearly fifty years old, and his eyes still mist over with this tender memory of his father. How do you think this dad (who became a father in his forties!) now tucks his own children into bed? Never underestimate the power of consistent, loving routines to give a child security, a good night's sleep, and memories to last a lifetime.

Our bedtime routine rarely changes. The kids can recite it back to me. They know what to expect, without surprise. Of course, they may test me now and again. Whenever I put the kids to bed and their dad gets home first, he always says, "I cannot believe they are in bed sleeping. It's only eight o'clock!" I try to tell him that it's because the kids know not to get out of bed when I'm on duty. The boys understand that getting out of bed is not something that they do when I am there, and if they do get out of bed for anything other than an emergency or the bathroom, they will lose a privilege. How do the boys know this? Because the first time they tested me, I followed through.

I remember one night in particular when the kids were giving me a hard time about going to sleep. I said firmly, "Boys, the next time someone gets out of bed, we will not go to Hannah's house tomorrow as planned." Five minutes later, I heard the footsteps, went upstairs, informed them we would not be going, and left the room. The next day, I followed through. I think it was more painful for me, but they certainly got the point that I mean what I say and I say what I mean.

The other day, the boys' mom asked Austin, "Why do you go to bed so easy for Shell and not for Mommy?" His response was, "Mom, she is even meaner than you think." *How awful,* I thought, listening to the conversation. Then she asked him, "What does Shell do that is mean?" He responded, "If I get out of bed, she takes a privilege away."

"What did she take away?" his mom asked.

"I don't know," he replied. He'd totally forgotten!

What we did learn was that Austin's definition of *mean* really meant that I would consistently make sure there were natural consequences for disobedience. He knows without a doubt that when I say, "If you get out of bed, you will lose a privilege," I will follow through on what I say. That is not being mean; it is being consistent.

Things That Go Bump in the Night

Children often have a hard time going to bed because their parents have a hard time putting them there. Parents are afraid that their child is going to be afraid, so they do things to prevent him or her from being afraid. Have you ever asked yourself what there is to be afraid of? The answer should be nothing!

Kids are sometimes afraid of the dark. Why? I'm sure there are a variety of reasons, but sometimes I think they are afraid because they have been unwittingly taught to be afraid. Perhaps Mom or Dad was afraid of the dark as a child, and to prevent any possibility of darkness fear, the parents leave bright lights on when the child sleeps. You can help your child be confident in the darkness if you associate darkness with sleep and make it a peaceful experience. Now, of course, a little night-light is OK and can add to the ambiance of a calming environment. But make sure it is a *little* light, not a floodlight posing as a bedside lamp. Show your child it is safe to be in the dark by turning off the lights with confidence. Say, "We need light to play; we need dark to sleep." It's really that simple.

Another idea to help a child adjust to sleeping in the dark (which will help him sleep deeper and longer) is to invest in a dimmer switch or a light with a dimmer on it. Each night, gradually turn down the lights until they are off or barely glowing. Approach this new "change" with confidence. Tell your child, "Now that you are so big, we get to turn the light off." Perhaps you can even use it as an occasion to celebrate. Tell him, "This week, we are going to do something fun. Every night, I'm going to turn the lights in your room down just a little bit, and by day seven you'll be a big boy, sleeping in the dark all by yourself! When that night comes, I have a special nighty-night treat for you to sleep with!" Then give him a special sleep-only stuffed animal to cuddle with or new pajamas.

Another idea if your child is still afraid of the dark is to give him a small flashlight with batteries. Tell him it is a special light and that when the batteries get weak, the light will get dimmer. (Be sure to keep it on.) Eventually the flashlight will be out of "light juice," and that will be the special time when he is ready to sleep in the dark all by himself!

Praise your child for accepting the change, and encourage him in his abilities to do and try new things.

Mean Monsters and Other Imaginary Friends

Just like putting baby to sleep, there are a few methods in dealing with monsters and other imaginary friends that "visit" our little ones in the night. You have two choices: you can ignore the fear, or you can acknowledge the fear. I have tried both. Both work, and both have pros and cons.

Ignore the Monster

When your child says he is afraid of monsters, you tell him simply that monsters do not exist. You assure your child that it's OK to be scared about real things, but "Monsters didn't come into the house when you were one year old, they didn't come when you were two years old, and they won't come when you are three, because monsters are not real." The pro to this method is that you are teaching your child to trust you and rely on your word. You are also teaching him the difference between real fears and imaginary fears. The con is that your child may get the idea that it is not OK to be scared, something that we never want to convey to a child. To prevent this from happening, be sure to say, "Honey, it's OK to be scared, and we all get scared sometimes. But we do not need to be scared of things that are not real. And monsters are not real."

Acknowledge the Monster

Depending on the stage of reasoning, the above method may or may not work. If your child is still convinced that there is a monster in the room and logic isn't working, I've found it sometimes easier to follow *his* logic and help him deal with his imaginary monster.

You can fill a water mister and call it "monster spray" that your children spray in various places before bedtime. If they are young enough, they will associate the spray with the "destroying" of monsters and will believe that the monsters are gone. The pros of using this method are that the child gets to bed reasonably easily, feels secure, and feels like he has control and power over the monsters. The con is that you have validated the need to "destroy" the monsters, which conveys the message that perhaps monsters do exist after all.

To avoid confusion, take care of the problem and still tell the truth. I usually say something like, "OK, sweetie, I've told you that monsters are not real, and that's the truth. They come from our imagination. But let's just pretend there *are* monsters in the room. Then all we have to do to clear them out of here is use this pretend anti-monster spray . . . and that will be the end of them!"

Napping Is a Necessity

Many parents believe that if their children sleep during the day, they will not sleep during the night. In my years of experience, I have found that this is not true! In fact, the opposite is true: an overtired child takes much more time to wind down and fall asleep than a well-rested child.

Dr. Ferber's book *Solve Your Child's Sleep Problems* addresses many myths of child-hood sleep (such as the myth that children who nap won't sleep during the night) and provides wonderful charts on how much sleep and what type of sleep (naptime versus nighttime) a child of each age needs.

How Much Sleep Does Your Child Need?

Generally, newborns sleep more than they are awake. On average, they spend between sixteen and twenty hours per day sleeping (or at least dozing)! At around three months, most babies tend to sleep an average of ten hours during the night and five hours throughout the day. Those ten hours we consider "sleeping through the night" do, however, usually consist of a few wake-up calls for Mommy. From six to twelve months, children usually sleep three hours during the day, broken into a morning and afternoon nap, and they sleep through the night for about eleven hours.

Between ages one and three is when naptime dwindles. This is different for each child and for each family. My thought is let children nap as long as they will. Naptime will eventually dwindle from two naps to one, usually lasting from one and a half hours to three hours, followed by a solid nine to ten hours of nighttime sleep. Children age four and beyond have pretty much given up napping altogether (except on those days that you've completely worn them out and they fall asleep on the floor), and they require between ten and twelve hours of good nighttime sleeping.

Take the Stress out of Naptime

Here are some ideas that might help you take the stress out of naptime.

Keep naptime consistent. If you plan your child's naps for morning and afternoon, he will naturally fall into the groove. His biological clock will set to the one you program. You can plan your schedule around naptime, but that doesn't mean you have to be home during it!

Your child does not have to sleep only in the bed. If you are out, let your child sleep in the stroller or plan your long car rides for naptime. Naps don't have to rule your life!

Don't wake a sleeping child. If your child is sleeping, he needs it. Maybe he is in a growth spurt, fighting off a cold, or just really worn out. Let him sleep. Do you like to be suddenly awakened? Not unless it's an emergency!

Don't give the impression that naptime is optional. If your child claims he is not tired, say, "OK," but then insist that he go in for "rest time" on his bed. More likely than not, he will fall asleep.

Find Help for Your Child's Sleep Problem

If, after applying all that I've suggested, you are still having problems with getting a young child to sleep through the night, talk to your pediatrician, follow up with suggested resources in this chapter, check out the recommended books, or search that wonderful modern mother's helper: the Internet. If your toddler's sleep problem is severe and persistent, you can find physicians who specialize in children's sleep problems. Your pediatrician can surely refer you to one. This may be needed if you suspect there might be some breathing difficulties or other physical problems that are impairing your child's sleep.

And now, merry napping to all, and to all a good night!

Nanny Tips

Here are some more ideas for providing a sleep-friendly environment:

- *Don't keep the house too quiet.* When children are sleeping, parents tend to try to keep the house quiet by tiptoeing and whispering. Not only is this unpractical, but it teaches your children that they can sleep only in absolute silence! Talk it up and be normal! Teach your kids to sleep in a real-life setting.
- *Don't go into your child's room.* If your child is a light sleeper and awakes when you go in to check on him, use a baby monitor to hear him or even a TV monitor to see him.
- *Use a white-noise maker in the child's room.* This can be soothing and muffles background noise.

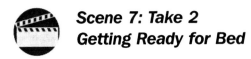

Scene 7: Take 2
Getting Ready for Bed

MOM, *to three-year-old Charlie watching TV.* Bedtime in five minutes, right after they play the *Arthur* song.

CHARLIE. No! I don't want to!

MOM. You know the routine, honey. Dinner, brush teeth, bath time, TV or reading time, potty time, and bed at what time, Charlie?

CHARLIE. Seven fifteen, Mommy.

MOM. That's right, honey. So after the song, we will head to bed. We have about two minutes left.

CHARLIE. OK. *(A few minutes later, he shuts off the TV.)* It's over, Mommy.

MOM, *picking up Charlie and bringing him into his room.* Thank you, love. What a great helper you are, shutting off the TV. Give me a big kiss and hug.

(Charlie hugs and kisses his mom.)

MOM, *putting Charlie on his bed.* OK, hon. Let's get in bed, snuggle with Teddy, and say our prayers.

CHARLIE. And give me a hug and tuck me in like a bug! Give me a kiss like a cute little fish!

MOM. You got it! Have a good sleep, honey. Tomorrow we have a fun day. I love you!

CHARLIE. Love you, Mommy.

MOM. Love you, too, honey. *(She shuts off the lights and exits the room, leaving the door slightly ajar.)*

A good laugh and a long sleep are the best cures in the doctor's book.

—Irish proverb

Nanny to the Rescue!
Recap

What Nanny Tips did this mom use to make the irritating impossible turn into the pleasantly possible?

1. *Have an established bedtime routine.* Having a routine lets your child know the exact order of what is going to happen.

2. *Be consistent in your routine.* Your child will feel secure if he knows what to expect. He has eaten, gone to the bathroom (or has at least tried or put on his Pull-Ups), and brushed his teeth. All the bases are covered before you enter the bedroom.

3. *Be clear about your bedtime expectations.* Let your child know that he goes to bed at seven fifteen (or whatever time you choose). That is bedtime, and it's not negotiable.

4. *Empower your child by giving him some control over the situation.* Allowing your child to shut off the TV, select the book, and choose the color of his toothbrush provides him with age-appropriate choices that empower him and make him feel like he is participating in what is going on.

5. *Praise your child for positive actions.* Say, "Thanks for helping and doing your part."

6. *Have a special something that you do only at bedtime.* Give your child something to look forward to at bedtime. Maybe it's a catchy phrase you both say, a special bear he only gets to snuggle with while in bed, or something that gives him a positive association with bedtime.

7. *Use loving words and actions.* Kisses, snuggles, and hugs are great bedtime primers.

8. *Show that you are confident.* The bedroom is a safe place; the lights *can* go out. Tomorrow is a big day, so rest is needed. Have the attitude that sleep is something that is just part of the day, like eating and playing. It is nothing to get upset about.

9. *Say, "I love you" as the last words before sleep.* I tell my charges, "I love you guys," each night I get the chance to put them to bed. What better last words for the evening are there?

CHAPTER EIGHT

POPSICLES FOR BREAKFAST AND OTHER NANNY NO-NOS

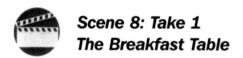 ### Scene 8: Take 1
The Breakfast Table

MOM. Meghan, time for breakfast. What would you like?

MEGHAN. I want Pop-Tarts.

MOM. Pop-Tarts aren't a breakfast food.

MEGHAN. Then why are they on the cereal shelf?

MOM. I have no idea. Meghan, it's time to eat. Pick a cereal.

MEGHAN, *crying*. I want Pop-Tarts!

MOM, *irritated*. Sweetie, please, if you don't pick a cereal, I will pick one
for you. We need to start our day.

MEGHAN. I had Pop-Tarts yesterday! *(Screaming.)* Not fair!

MOM. Fine, have the Pop-Tarts.

MEGHAN. Yea!

(Ten minutes later.)

MOM, *exhausted, noting Meghan has gone from sleepy to hyperactive.*
I wonder what got into that child?

n today's world of immediate gratification, fast food seems to permeate the house. Long gone are the days when moms could afford the hours it takes to prepare three square meals a day. Society has solved that problem: the prepackaged pantry. We don't even need to buy peanut butter *and* jelly. Today we can get it in one convenient jar, already mixed together. We can even get PB&Js frozen, with the crusts cut off, toaster ready. Yummy.

The good news is that we only have to push a button on the microwave to feed our kids. The bad news is that convenience foods are taking an enormous toll on our children. Childhood obesity is on the rise across the globe, and the incidence of obesity in U.S. children has nearly doubled in the past twenty years.

Time for a true confession: I have struggled with a lifelong weight issue. During one of my "diet" phases, I decided to go to the grocery store to purchase food for the day and determined to avoid anything that was packaged. I filled my cart with ripe whole fruits, lean meats, and colorful fresh vegetables in addition to good cheeses, whole-grain breads and cereals, milk, and yogurt. I compared this purchase to my usual shopping receipt and found, to my surprise, that these healthy selections almost doubled the cost! Though families who can buy in bulk and avoid prepackaged food actually tend to save money, in my case, eating healthfully was much more expensive. But 130 pounds of weight loss later, I can tell you it was worth every penny. Not only for my health and self-esteem, but also for the money I saved on the healthcare that my extra weight—no doubt—would have eventually cost me.

I had to relearn, as an adult, how to make healthy eating a lifestyle. It wasn't easy, as habits learned as a child die hard as an adult. Now I see how much better it is for children if we can simply introduce a healthy lifestyle to them from birth.

Sugar Versus Sanity

Although a few scientific studies have "proven" that the consumption of sugar has no effect on the behavior of children, I have conducted my own independent, albeit informal, research. Since I am a scientist by training and a twin child specialist by trade, I am not totally without qualifications. Here is what I've observed: Take two kids playing nicely together, enjoying the day. Input a hot fudge sundae for each child, and you get two kids bouncing completely off the wall. In trial after trial, the results were successfully repeated—*both* kids responded the same way.

If you notice this trend in your own children, then try my tips for surviving sugar insanity.

Teach Your Child the Importance of Nutrition

Simply teaching young children about nutrition is a great place to start. I've found wonderful success in telling my charges that there are different types of foods:

- *All-the-time foods.* These are foods we can eat as much we want! These are foods that are good for us, ones we can and should eat in larger quantities. Fruits and vegetables go in this category.

- *Special foods.* These are foods we save for special occasions, like birthday cake or a warm sugar cookie during the holidays.

- *Sometimes foods.* These foods fall into the middle. And though we can't eat them in unlimited quantities, we can enjoy them several times a day. This category includes meat, cheese, yogurt, and milk. (Remember to give your child whole milk until age four; children need the milk fat to help with brain development.) Whole-grain breads, oats, and heart-healthy cereals also fall into this category.

This gives kids an easy classification system and a positive attitude toward food. As long as there is moderation, all types of food can be enjoyed.

Only Buy What You Want Your Children to Eat

The easiest way to solve battles over what a child is going to eat is not to buy (or at least to keep hidden out of sight) the foods that you don't want your children to eat. If you don't want your child to eat Pop-Tarts for breakfast, do not have them in the house. Consistency also plays a role in nutrition: if you know you absolutely do not want your child to have sugary, prepackaged pastries for breakfast—ever—then never give them Pop-Tarts. Just like any other bad habit, it is better to avoid starting something that may be hard to quit than to risk letting your kids get hooked on empty sweets (and put up with the whining that will surely follow).

> *Toddlers are more likely to eat healthy food if they find it on the floor.*
> —Jan Blaustone

Never ask a very young child what she wants for breakfast. First, the choices are too overwhelming for the child; and second, you may not be prepared to handle your child's answer. (For example, your son may request doughnuts and Dr Pepper.) If you know you want your child to have cereal for breakfast, ask, "Do you want cornflakes or Cheerios today?" If it's French toast, ask, "Would you like your French toast cut in squares or triangles?" If you want to give him some nutrition-packed fruit, ask, "Do you feel like having blueberries or strawberries today?" With this method, you are empowering the child to make a choice while giving him a limited number of choices (count them: two!) that *you* can live with.

Don't Indulge a Picky Eater

Don't start the habit of making separate meals for would-be picky eaters. The first time a child says, "I don't want that" and you prepare something else, prepare yourself for a daily battle over mealtime. If you've given your child two choices of foods you know he likes, then he needs to eat what he has chosen. If he isn't hungry (which is more often the underlying reason he doesn't want to eat what you've served), wrap it up and save it for the next time his tummy is really ready for food.

It is my belief that children are not born picky eaters; the home environment makes them that way. We all know that some kids go through phases when they do not like certain textures, colors, or tastes of foods. Also, children with sensory integration issues or allergies have special circumstances. But in my eleven years as a nanny, I have never cared for a child

Nanny Tip

Did you know that you have the power to give the word *dessert* your own definition? For example, my charges firmly believe that a fruit salad is dessert! They also believe parfait of yogurt, layered with fruit and granola, is a dessert. Ditto for frozen yogurt. Of course, we occasionally (say, once a week) indulge in a more traditional dessert: ice cream, cookies, or fruit snacks. But for the most part, the boys are very happy with healthy, less sugary, natural treats.

who *eventually* wouldn't try everything. (My current charges even eat sushi, something that I myself have just recently tried . . . and didn't like.) *Eventually* is the key word here. Just because a child did not like applesauce yesterday doesn't mean he won't ever like it. After a child rejects a food, give it a break and then reintroduce it a week later. You may be surprised at the results.

I grew up eating meat and potatoes. I am embarrassed to admit that although I am a true New Englander, I had fish for the first time when I was twenty-eight years old! I now love fish and eat it at least twice a week. The reason I was afraid to eat fish is that we didn't grow up eating it in my home, so it was new to me, something I had never experienced. Perhaps I tried it when I was younger and didn't like the way it was prepared. So if one fish dish doesn't appeal, try another kind of fish or another recipe.

When you know certain foods are packed with nutritional value, it's worth the effort to experiment until you find a way to eat and enjoy it. So when it is age appropriate, introduce a taste of a wide variety of foods to children. Variety at mealtime not only allows new experiences for their palates (you may have a little chef in the making) but also makes mealtime a more enjoyable experience.

Cut Down on Unhealthy Snacks

In the kitchens I oversee, I have a policy that distribution of food is for adults only. This is a great rule that can save you hours of battle time. If you have already built a foundation of trust with your child, she knows you will provide for her needs. Don't let her provide for her own nutritional needs before she is ready. Since you don't give a preschooler a set of sharp knives, don't give your child free access to the fridge. Allowing the child to have carte blanche access to the fridge or pantry allows him to have control over what he eats and when. What typically happens is that your child is not hungry when you serve a well-prepared, healthy lunch because he helped himself to nutritionally void snacks at whim all morning.

My charges have never been big snackers, because they have been trained to eat healthy, well-rounded meals by my clock. Each meal consists of a dairy, grain, fruit and/or vegetable, protein, and water. Their meals are also served at the same time, give or take a half-hour, every day. Breakfast at seven thirty, lunch at noon, and dinner at five. (This is a great schedule because it coincides with the school day and after-school activities.) Because of the quality of their meals, the timing, and the portions (an average toddler's portion size is only about one-half of an adult's), their bodies are trained to be hungry at those times.

Plan a Nutritious Menu

A typical breakfast at my charges' home consists of a whole-grain bagel with cream cheese, cut-up fruit, and water or milk. Lunch is a sandwich with whole-grain bread and ham or turkey. (That's a story in itself. I had my first slice of wheat bread when I started this job! This just goes to show that family habits, healthy or not, carry through to adulthood.) And sometimes, of course, the boys get their favorite, PB&J (which is always served with a slice of cheese to bulk up the protein). I add fresh vegetables, such as carrots or string beans, and fresh fruit and give them their choice of milk or water.

Having a well-rounded week of meals is what counts. And naturally, we occasionally eat chocolate-chip pancakes, but then we make sure to balance out the remaining days' menus with less sugary choices. Looking at your child's menu over the course of a week, rather than a day, will give you great insight into what his or her average intake is.

Even though the boys eat well-rounded, good-portioned meals, there are the occasional days they are truly hungry for a snack . . . or so I think. In these cases, they are allowed to choose from the "all-the-time" food group. It is amazing how, all of a sudden, raisins do not appeal to even the hungriest of kids!

Like adults, even young children can learn at an early age that eating together is an important part of family life. For example, each night when Mom returns home from work, Fraser insists he is hungry. Mom's jacket is not even off, and Fraser is in front of the fridge. I smirk in anticipation of what is going to come next.

"Mom, can I have dessert?" Fraser says ever so sweetly.

"Did Shell already give you dessert?" Mom asks.

"Yes, but I didn't like it."

"Oh, I see," Mom says curiously. "Well, did you eat it all?"

"Yup, aren't you proud, Mom?" Fraser grins.

"Yes, Fraser, I am proud."

"So can I have dessert, Mom?" he asks again, snuggling up to her leg.

"Sure, Fraser, you can have some raisins."

(This is where the principles of consistency and teamwork really shine!)

A few minutes later, Mom looks over and says to Fraser, who has gone back to playing, "Fraser, I thought you were hungry."

"Oh, I'm not interested in raisins," he says. "I decided I'm really not that hungry."

The moral of that story is if your child *seems like* he really does need a snack, offer him one from the "all-the-time" food group, and then you will know for sure if he is truly hungry or if he wants to eat for other reasons.

Since my "adults-only" policy for the fridge and pantry has been in effect as long as the kids have been eating solid food, they did not even know that they could open the fridge if they wanted to, because it was something that was simply not done. Scheduling and routine, as we covered in earlier chapters, are of great significance. They are also important when it comes to when and what a child can eat. When kids hit grade-school years and can show they are self-monitoring, you can begin to loosen this rule. But for now, make it easy on yourself and healthier for your kids by keeping the fridge and pantry off limits.

Cut Back on Sweet Drinks

I want to touch on the subject of juice, because although it is a convenient and available beverage, most fruit juices and sports drinks are overly sweet and provide empty calories—calories that could have come from a better nutritional choice. Too much sugar (even fructose) is still *too much sugar*. And the results will be the same: overweight kids bouncing off the walls. "Minimizing a child's consumption of sweet drinks might be one way to help manage their weight," says Jean A. Welsh, of the Atlanta-based Centers for Disease Control and Prevention.[1]

The verdict is also in on the effects of drinking juices and other sweet drinks on oral health. Since these beverages are made up of concentrated sugars, they can lead to tooth decay and enamel erosion. According to the American Dental Association, "When teeth come in frequent contact with soft drinks and other sugar-containing substances, the risk of decay formation is increased."[2]

Juice is classified as a "sometimes" food in our house so that the children do not come to expect it on a regular basis. Water or milk are the two choices they get most often. My charges had juice for the first time when they were four years old.

While one of the boys was recently on his first play date without me, he joined his friend and his friend's mom for lunch at a restaurant. The mom called me from the restaurant because she had ordered Austin some fruit punch, and he had politely refused to drink it, asking for water or milk instead.

"Oh," I responded. "What else did he say?"

"He said, 'I want to have a special food if I eat my lunch. Some ice cream! So if I have ice cream later, I can't have fruit punch now. My nanny says it is too much sugar for me and will make me cranky and wild.'"

I laughed out loud.

"I told him I thought you'd be fine with making an exception for a special outing, but he insists on talking to you first, before taking a sip."

"Oh, how funny!" I said. "Well, let me talk to him."

When I heard Austin's voice on the phone, I said, "Honey, do you still want some punch if I give you permission to have it *and* the ice cream?"

"Yes!" he answered enthusiastically.

"Well, it is a very special day. You can have both!"

I was his best friend for days. But hey, I'm no dummy. I knew the other mom would have to handle the energetic boys after their special lunch, when they'd both be fully loaded with sugar. I had the afternoon off! (Nannies get breaks, too, on special occasions.)

It is really so much easier to have a consistent rule that you bend only for very, very special treats and occasions. Why? It's effective because you are making it clear that you are the boss, without being bossy.

Clear Rules, Healthy Kids

As you can see from Austin's example, kids live up to the expectations you set for them, whether in nutrition or in behavior. You lead, and they are sure to follow. He didn't feel deprived when he refused the fruit juice. He knew that it was a rule made for his own good, and that made him focus on getting to thoroughly enjoy that upcoming bowl of ice cream. He was practicing self-control based on obedience and trust of adult decisions.

In future years, Austin will become more and more internally discerning, not sugar saturated, and ready and able to make his own wise food choices. The ultimate goal is to teach our kids to grow up to be intrinsically motivated; but at this young season of their life, consistent outward obedience to loving authority gives them opportunities to practice delayed gratification and to learn the rewards that come with it.

Now I am the proud nanny of children who have come to trust me and obey me with little or no question. Obviously, this is a trust that has taken time and energy to build. In my book *Nanny to the Rescue Again! Straight Talk and Super Tips for Parenting in the Grade School Years*, I address how to talk to older children about those adults who are not quite worthy of their trust or obedience.

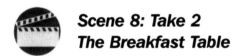 ### Scene 8: Take 2
The Breakfast Table

MOM. Meghan, time for breakfast. Would you like plain oatmeal or apple cinnamon oatmeal?

MEGHAN. I want Pop-Tarts.

MOM. Pop-Tarts? That wasn't one of my choices, dear.

MEGHAN, *pouting*. But I want Pop-Tarts!

MOM. Meghan, it's time to eat. Plain or apple cinnamon?

MEGHAN. Apple cinnamon.

MOM. OK, sweetie, that sounds like a great choice! I may have that too.

MEGHAN. Thanks, Mom.

(Ten minutes later.)

MOM. OK, let's start our day!

MEGHAN. OK, I'm ready!

Nanny to the Rescue!
Recap

Were you able to figure out which Nanny Tips turned this breakfast from sugar saturated to a healthy experience?

1. *Only offer food choices that you are prepared to serve.*

2. *Don't give in to your child's demand when you know it isn't in her best interest.*

3. *Address your child in loving terms while holding a firm line.*

4. *Praise your child for making good choices.*

5. *Don't negotiate when there is no room for negotiation.*

> *Whatever is on the floor will wind up in your baby's mouth. Whatever is in your baby's mouth will wind up on the floor.*
> —Bruce Lansky

Use these simple, quick, and practical ideas to turn the mundane into the insane!

- *Food coloring changes everything.* Pink pancakes? Green eggs and ham? They're all possible with only a few drops of food coloring.
- *Blending for babies.* Babies can eat dinner with you. Take your steamed veggies and meat—unseasoned and unsalted—and purée.
- *Can you say smoothie?* Throw some vanilla yogurt, fresh berries, and ice in the blender for a great healthy treat!
- *Make a sundae.* Layer yogurt, fruit, and Cheerios or granola (depending on what's age appropriate), and top with a cherry.
- *Shred, shred, shred.* Not even Daddy will notice shredded carrots or zucchini in the pasta sauce.
- *Play with the pudding.* This is great for young toddlers: give them some pudding in their high chairs, and let them paint a masterpiece on their tray. If they eat it, it's OK! This is a great, safe way to introduce early art.
- *Try new foods together.* My boys take delight in remembering that I used to be a picky eater, and they are quite proud of my transformation.
- *Be creative with a peanut ban.* When going to places that have peanut bans due to allergies in the family, try sandwiches made with cream cheese and jelly, with a slice of cheese on the side. You still get in your protein, and the kids enjoy this alternative.
- *Rename the named.* Call broccoli "green trees," or call squash "candied potatoes." Sometimes it's the name association that instills the fear of trying new foods.

You can also get some great ideas from the International Nanny Association's cookbook, *Beyond Peanut Butter and Jelly*, available at www.nanny.org. It's filled with creative recipes, crafts, and theme party ideas.

CHAPTER NINE

IT'S MY POTTY, AND I'LL CRY IF I WANT TO!

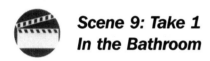

Scene 9: Take 1
In the Bathroom

MOM. Samantha, it's time for bed. Would you please go to the potty?

SAMANTHA. No!

MOM. Come on. You are a big girl now. Go, please. You just had a drink.

SAMANTHA, *crying.* No potty!

DAD. Stop forcing her, honey. Maybe she's not ready to use the toilet.

MOM. She's two years old! Your sister's kid was potty trained at eighteen months. Of course she's ready.

SAMANTHA, *standing in a puddle and crying.* Sorry, Mommy.

MOM. Just listen to Mommy next time!

Y ou may have read (or heard) that most children have the physical and cognitive abilities to use the potty between eighteen and twenty-four months. By the time a child has reached the toddling age, most parents are weary with the joy of changing diapers and anxious to introduce Mr. Potty to their child's routine. However, their child may not be quite as anxious to meet Mr. Potty and, in fact, is enormously content with the convenient (for them) diaper arrangement.

The good news is that your child *will* eventually be potty trained; the bad news is that it may take much longer than you anticipated. Little boys are often not fully trained until they are closer to age three.

So sit back and relax, Mom and Dad. Because rule number one of potty training is that you cannot force Mother Nature. I personally do not know of anyone in high school who wears diapers; and the truth is, no matter what you do, most kids figure it out on their own. It is up to you—the loving, nurturing parent—to provide a positive environment and to have a positive, cheerful attitude about this next step up the stairway through childhood.

Motivating the Motivator

Before you even contemplate putting your child on the potty, you should assess your motive. Getting your child out of diapers as soon as possible may be a realistic desire, but it may not be the right motive. Feeling pressured because a sister's or brother's daughter has been using the potty since she was fifteen months old isn't the best motivator either. The best motivator should be that your child shows interest and readiness to start doing what naturally comes next: moving out of diapers and onto the "throne."

Is Your Child Ready?

Now that you know your primary job is to be the cheerleader when your child is ready to start using the potty, how do you actually know when she is indeed ready? There are several indicators or clues, including

- having bowel movements at regular times;

- pulling her pants up and down on her own;

- imitating others' bathroom behaviors, such as wanting to wear underpants and wanting to watch Mommy (or Daddy) use the potty;

- letting you know when she is going to the bathroom by telling you, grunting, or disappearing into her favorite corner;

- disliking being in a dirty diaper;

- using words for stool and urine;

- having dry periods for three to four hours, indicating her bladder is mature enough to hold and store urine.

The most important indicator overall is that the child is expressing a positive interest in using the potty. The indicators above are not a concrete checklist, but if your child is showing most of these behaviors, chances are she is ready to try toilet training.

How to Start

What I have found helpful is purchasing a plastic potty to put in the playroom when the child begins to show any interest in going to the bathroom. You can bring your child to the store with you and allow her to pick the one that she wants, or you can surprise her. Regardless, make sure it's a model that is easy to clean and easy to transport from one room to the next and that allows her to stabilize herself with her feet when she is pushing to have a bowel movement. You may also want to purchase the kind of seat that attaches to a regular toilet but prevents a child's little bottom from falling through the adult-sized seat. If you do go this route, be sure to also purchase a sturdy stool for the bathroom so she can climb up and have a platform high enough to put her feet on.

Although it may not be Martha Stewart's idea of tasteful décor, having the potty

Second-timers note the facts and take each one in stride: "He's learned to take his diaper off; you'd better step aside."
—Babs Bell Hajdusiewicz

in a room where the child plays most often is least threatening to a child. You are just adding something to an environment that already exists, where she is already comfortable. (Having the potty in a room where the child is at ease will allow her to explore this new addition at her own pace. She probably will, out of curiosity, go sit on the potty with her pants on, since it does look like a chair. That's fine and good. Let it become her own little space where she's not intimidated in any way.) You can also help your child to role-play using her favorite teddy bears or dolls on the potty, which kids usually love to do.

Once your child shows some comfort sitting on the potty with clothes on, the next step is to get her on there without clothes. To do this, you can bring the potty to the place where she normally has her bath. Before her bath, while she is already naked, is an ideal time to introduce her to what it feels like to sit bare-bottomed on her potty. Continue this routine before her bath for a few days.

Potty Time

Once your child is comfortable sitting on the potty, without her diaper, the next step is to show her what goes in the potty. Toilet training is a process. The next time she goes poop in her diaper, take her to the toilet, sit her on it, lift her off it, and then drop the stool from the diaper into the potty. This will allow her to form an association with sitting on the potty and letting the poop go into it. This is also a great time to foster independence by allowing her to flush the toilet (if she wants and is not afraid of the noise) and by teaching her to pull up her pants and wash her hands on her own.

By this time of your toddler's life, her bowel and bladder habits are probably pretty predictable. So in addition to having her sit on the potty before bath time, if you know that she usually poops right after breakfast, this is the next time to begin putting her on the potty, sans diaper, each morning. One day soon you'll hit the jackpot, you will have a nice token for your patient efforts, and the potty party will begin. (In fact, you can even teach your child to do a little happy potty dance to celebrate the occasion!) The main point, at this stage, is to get her used to the potty and its part in the daily routine. If she resists and clearly does not want to sit on the potty, take a step back and wait for her to express interest in trying it out again.

You can also foster independence by allowing your child to use the potty when she wants to, in addition to letting her know that you are there to take her when she needs to go. You can let her run around the house naked and tell her, "You can sit on the potty anytime you want to!"

Once you are truly into the "training regime," you'll want to invest in lots of underwear or cloth training pants. Pull-Ups are great for children who are almost trained and have only an occasional accident, for nighttime training, and for long car rides when you may not be able to pull over with a second's notice. The downside to Pull-Ups is they don't allow the child to feel wet, and that feeling is a great motivator for staying dry.

Toilet training is a process. There is a book called *Toilet Training in Less Than a Day*, but most of the parents I know who tried it ended up flushing the book down the toilet. Potty training is a two-steps-forward, one-step-back process, and it will be easier on you and your child if you accept nature's gradual way of getting your child to the next development step rather than fighting or hurrying it.

That said, expect that your child will have an occasional setback. These setbacks are not a time for punishment or embarrassment; instead, use them as a teaching moment. Say something like, "We all have accidents, and we simply all try again." (What a great life lesson for all ages!) You can gently remind your child that the potty is there for her use, and you can encourage her to help pick up messes or redress herself, but there is nothing to be the least bit angry about. Be generally upbeat and matter-of-fact in your tone. Your child's muscles are still developing, and her body is still adjusting to releasing on command.

There is, however, the occasional child who will intentionally not use the potty, although she is able to do so. The potty issue has become a struggle of power and control, which is not good. One way you can deal with this is to give your child control in other ways related to toilet training. You can allow her to choose her underwear, shop for her special toilet paper, or choose her own hand soap. These may seem like little things to you, but to her, it may be just the sense of power she needs so that she can relax with the process.

Other external factors can also impede the potty-training process. If a new baby comes into the home, sometimes a toddler will regress and want to be the baby. How would you like it if your mate brought home a new spouse, assured you that you'll both be equally loved, and proceeded to cuddle and coo precious terms of endearment to mate number two? In only a slightly exaggerated example, this is what a toddler often feels, emotionally, when a new baby brother or sister moves into her space. It stands to reason that if this new bundle of joy gets all that wonderful attention and wears diapers all day . . . what's the big deal about using the potty?

A move to a different house, family upsets, or any other change in circumstances can also result in potty-training setbacks. For this reason, be sure to begin your first attempts at potty training when you know you won't be traveling and will be set in your usual routine, when you anticipate no major changes in life circumstances, and when you have the time to devote to the toilet-training process.

There are hundreds of different toilet training methods—probably because none of them work.
—Bruce Lansky

The Fun Factor

You can raise the fun factor of toilet training by having some toilet-training-related books in the bathroom. You can also have colorful soaps in the bathroom that smell great, which comes in handy when your child is completely independent and you want to make sure she really washed her hands. There are also some great DVDs on toilet training, such as *It's Potty Time* and *Once upon a Potty*, which feature catchy tunes.

Generally, I am a firm believer in not rewarding a child for what she should already be doing as part of contributing to the family routine. However, toilet-training rewards are great motivators. What has worked for me is to keep a clear jar of M&M's in the kitchen. After the child successfully uses the potty, pulls up her pants, and washes her hands, she gets one (and only one!) M&M. The nutritional value is void, I agree, but the motivation factor of a single M&M is truly remarkable.

Another hint is to let little boys float one Cheerio or a piece of toilet paper in the potty and aim for it. This makes a game out of hitting the target and helps boys practice urinating in the right direction.

The Public Potty

It is not uncommon for a child to want to use only her *personal* potty. This can pose a problem when you are out and about. Often, children have realistic fears about public bathrooms—they're loud, they lack privacy, and the seat is often bigger.

(Although I have one friend who had the opposite problem with her daughter. Her daughter fussed about using the potty at home and would whine to go to the potty at McDonald's!)

You can face this obstacle a few ways. You can bring along a foldable seat meant to fit on the "big potty." Unless you have a newborn in tow at this point (God bless you if you do!), your diaper bag should have enough room to add this fascinating object. To add to the fun, you can also buy some disposable seat covers and place one on a public seat before her use. You can then kneel next to the potty while holding your child's hands. This way she may feel like she has some control over a situation that is new to her and essentially out of her control. If using a public toilet causes significant potty battles, you can try one of several travel seats, ranging from inflatable to foldup, that are designed to use on the go.

Nanny Tip

For boys and girls, summertime is a great time to potty train because clothing is generally easier to pull down quickly. (The laundry load will also be lighter!) Summer months also provide another perk for boys. If you feel comfortable, you can allow your child to run naked in the backyard, put the potty on the porch, and praise him when you "catch" him peeing into it!

If you are potty training in the not-so-sunny months, pull back an area rug, gate the room in, and look for signs that he is ready to go. Have his potty handy, and help him on. Praise him for his efforts!

If your child is outgoing, social, and curious, you may also encounter the opposite problem—the one where your child just has to see *every* potty in the *entire* mall! Although it is irritating at the time, grin and bear it. If it is true that we should pick our battles, we can probably let this one slide.

Night Training

Even though a child may be completely potty trained during the day at twenty-four months, it may be months, or even years, before a child can stay dry through the night. It is not uncommon for a child who is five years old to still wear Pull-Ups to bed. Twelve hours is a long time to hold in urine for growing muscles; and for children who are really deep sleepers, the feeling of having to use the bathroom may not yet be strong enough to rouse them from their sleep. You can cut down on wet nights by limiting the amount of fluids after dinnertime and encouraging your child to go to the bathroom before bed.

If your daytime potty-trained child refuses to wear diapers or Pull-Ups to bed, you can put plastic sheets on her mattress and then use layers of the absorbent fabric squares (available in most baby stores) that make for quick and easy nighttime changes. You can also encourage your child to help with the laundry "the morning after." It is important for her to know that she is responsible to use the potty and responsible to help clean up when she doesn't. Again, you are not mad or angry; this is just the way it is.

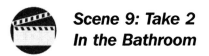 ***Scene 9: Take 2***
In the Bathroom

MOM. Time to go potty, Samantha.

SAMANTHA. OK, Mommy.

MOM. You can watch me, then you can try. OK?

SAMANTHA, *nodding.* Potty!

(Later that night.)

DAD. Do you think Samantha's ready for potty training? She seems to be showing a few signs of being ready.

MOM. Yeah, I do. But all kids train at different times. Your niece was trained at one and a half, my niece at three.

SAMANTHA, *following Mommy to the bathroom.* Peepee!

MOM. OK, sweetie! Just try and see what happens.

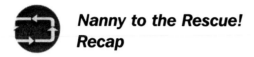

Nanny to the Rescue!
Recap

What did this mom do to change the pity party into the potty party?

1. *Don't force Mother Nature.* You need to wait for your child to show interest in the potty before training.

2. *Start training for the right reasons.* Start when your child shows readiness, not when you are tired of changing diapers.

3. *Use a positive attitude.* Potty training is part of growing up—something that just comes next in a child's development. Be your child's cheerleader, not a drill sergeant!

4. *Make sitting on the toilet part of your daily routine.* Introduce sitting on the toilet as part of your routine right after breakfast (or whenever works for you).

5. *Don't compare your child's progress to others.* Each child potty trains on her own time schedule.

6. *Use encouragement often.* Praise each positive step!

7. *Know that potty training is a process.* Be prepared for minor, momentary setbacks, and use them as opportunities to teach your child that if you don't succeed try, try again.

CHAPTER TEN

THROWING FITS NO MORE

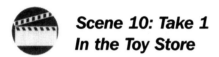

Scene 10: Take 1
In the Toy Store

MOM. Elise, put that down. We are not getting toys.

ELISE. But we're at the toy store! I want a toy!

MOM. Stop it. I can't take you anywhere without you begging for something. Now put it down, or we are never coming back to the toy store again!

ELISE, *sitting on the ground, starting to scream.* I want a toy! For me! I want one now!

MOM, *embarrassed and aggravated.* We are leaving right now. Let's go, or you will not be coming back here, young lady! No more toys for you!

ELISE, *arms flailing, legs kicking, eyes rolling back in the head.* No, Mommy, no, Mommy, no! I want it now! Please! I said, "Please!"

MOM, *walking away.* Fine. Stay here! I am leaving.

ELISE, *full-out hyperventilating.* No, Mommy! NOOO!

MOM, *picking up Elise as she kicks and screams.* Fine, have the toy! Stop being a baby. Just take it and be quiet.

ELISE, *wiping her tears and pointing to another toy.* Can I get that one, too, Mommy?

At one point or another, we have all witnessed a tornado-like tantrum coming from a toddler. Whether you weathered the tantrum through personal experience or observed the trauma of some child having a meltdown in the mall, we've all been through it. We've likely even been sucked into its center! We were either too tired or at that moment lacked the skills to deal with an embarrassing, unnerving situation. And if your child hasn't yet thrown his first walleyed fit in public—because he is still at that precious infant stage—I promise, your turn will come.

However, if you use the information in this chapter, you have no reason to fear. I'll give you some Nanny Tips to prevent, defuse, or repair any tantrum that you may encounter.

A soft answer turns away wrath, but a harsh word stirs up anger.
—Proverbs 15:1 NKJV

A Proactive Approach to Dealing with Tantrums

Proactive measures will, for most children, nip tantrums in the bud. You may be thinking, *Not with my kid! That would never work.* I can assure you, it will. The underlying theme in this book and my philosophy of childrearing is that kids will live up to the expectations, good or bad, that you set for them, as long as they are consistent. What does this have to do with avoiding a tantrum? Everything!

By preparing your child for what is to come, you are setting your expectations. It is like an author writing a novel. You have to set up the scene, define the characters, plan their roles, and think through the upcoming climax so that the story will eventually get resolved.

For example, when you are heading off to the playground, you prepare your child. First, you state the *who*: "Honey, you, Mommy, and Kate are going out." Next, you state the *what*: "We are going to have a great adventure . . ." Then you state the *where*: ". . . at the playground." Then you state the *when*: "We are leaving the house for the playground in five minutes." And at last, state the *why*: "We have some time to spend outside before Daddy comes home." This leaves no stones unturned. The scene has been set. The tone has been defined.

You are at the playground, and your child is having a blast. This is the climax of your unfolding parent-child story. But you have to anticipate what comes next. Once the climax has been reached and it is time to go home, the potential for a temper tantrum is most likely. What do you do to prepare for it? Like a great author, you wind down the story so it can resolve itself smoothly. How? You again answer *who, what, where, when,* and *why.*

"Honey, I need you to listen carefully, OK? You, Mommy, and Kate are going to be heading home."

"But I don't want to go."

"I know! You are having so much fun! But we only have about five more minutes before we need to head out."

"Why do we have to go, Mommy?"

"Remember . . . I told you before we left: Daddy is coming home! He will be waiting for us."

Did you find the answers? The *who* is "you, Mommy, and Kate," the *what* is "leaving the playground," the *where* is "from playground to home," the *when* is "in five minutes," and the *why* is "because Daddy will be waiting." Again, you are also listening to and reaffirming your child's feelings: "I know you are having fun." You are consistent in the way you approach the beginning of the journey and the end of the journey. You are also consistent in your responses. This leaves no room for questions, negotiating, nagging, or manipulation.

What I also like about dealing with tantrums in a proactive way is that it keeps emotions in check. Again, if you approach your child with a confident, "This is just the way it is" attitude, they will respond in kind. If you approach a child with a frenzied, rushed attitude, then that is how they will respond.

It reminds me of encountering a dog that frightens you. If a dog senses fear, he will respond to it. What do you do when you see a dog that makes you nervous or fearful? You turn around and confidently walk away. Why? So that you don't get chased, bitten, or jumped on and licked in the face. The dog gets the picture that you are not interested in engaging in a fight—or in playtime—and doesn't chase you, nip at you, or try to make happy, sloppy friends with you.

A child senses an adult's attitude in a similar way. If you are calm, nonchalant, and assured, the child will sense that you are in control and will follow suit. If you are angry and aggressive, or trying too hard to make every detail of a child's life happy and perfect, kids will sense that vulnerability and take advantage of you.

Disarming a Tantrum Before It Detonates

Here are a few tricks of the nanny trade to prevent temper tantrums.

Give plenty of positive attention. Just like movie stars know that bad press is better than no press, kids pick up that bad attention is better than no attention. Love on your child daily so he doesn't need to seek out other ways to gain your attention.

Take note when a tantrum is most likely to occur. Do the tantrums usually happen after you have had a hard day and do not have the energy to be firm? Do they occur in the morning when you are groggy and grouchy, barking commands like a drill sergeant? Take inventory and see if your mood, perhaps, is setting a bad tone in the home. Play some calming music, sip some herbal tea—whatever soothes you so that you can be in a better mood during stressful times.

Teach your child a way to "pull it together." You can teach him to count to ten, breathe deeply, or even recite the alphabet as a way to calm down. By giving him useful tools, you are providing him with a way to regain his self-control. When he starts to lose it, say, "I see you are upset. Can you try to pull it together so I can understand you better?" He will be proud of himself when he does!

Don't let the child gain emotional ground with you by throwing tantrums. Making statements such as, "When you throw a tantrum, I can't hear you" or, "I don't like watching temper tantrums, so let me know when you are finished and we will talk" convey matter-of-factly that calmness, not tantrums, is the way to gain your undivided attention. We teach our kids (and others) how to treat us by how we respond when they push our buttons.

A calm, assured approach to temper tantrums will work—guaranteed—especially after the first few times you are tested and you come out the winner. This is why it is very important that you come out on top when you have your first test of wills with a toddler.

Defusing a Full-Blown Tantrum

If you have been the type of parent who usually gives in, you can get back in control. But it will likely take a few more times of testing before your children believe your new-and-improved stance is here to last. Take heart; you will prevail. How you react to the first tantrum after you've decided to take charge will determine

Remember, when your child has a tantrum, don't have one of your own.
—Dr. J. Kuriansky

how many more tantrums are to come and how loud they will be in the future.

The best way to deal with a tantrum is to completely ignore it. If your child is having an all-out fistfight with the floor, your first priority needs to be to put her somewhere safe, such as on the carpet with lots of room around her. You need to get her to an environment where she won't hurt herself, because you are not going to attempt to stop the fit. I repeat: the best way to deal with a tantrum is to ignore it completely.

The first time a child throws a fit, your response will determine the child's default behavior in situations where she doesn't get her way. If you don't give in the first time, she may test again, but after the second time she will nearly always get it: *Mommy does what Mommy says she will do.* If you do give in to her screams the first time, the next fit will get louder and longer until you give in again.

If your child will not calm down, remove her from the situation. If your child's tantrum doesn't let up in a reasonable amount of time (particularly in a public place), the best thing to do is pick her up as calmly as you can (without saying a word) and leave where you are and what you are doing. This may sound drastic, but it should

> ### *Nanny Tip*
>
> Taming a child's temper all goes back to being consistent. If you consistently ignore a temper tantrum, your child will come to expect that you will not respond. If you don't respond, she'll eventually think (in toddler terms), *There's no point in getting my Pull-Ups in a wad about this because Mommy doesn't respond to dramatics.*
>
> Say to yourself, "The tantrum lasts a moment; the lesson lasts a lifetime."

only take once to actually drop what you are doing, pick her up without talking, and hit the door before she realizes that Mommy doesn't allow that. Don't get embarrassed or ashamed if "the whole world" is staring at you. If they've had kids, trust me, they've been there! If you handle your child's tantrum calmly and firmly, people will be empathizing with you, not judging you.

This will also work with an older toddler. If she knows that grabbing toys off the shelf is not OK, and you tell her, "If you touch the toys again, we are leaving"—then, when you actually follow through and leave if she fails to listen, you clearly set the stage for the next time around when you say, "I asked you not to touch the toys. Do we need to leave the store?" She will know without a doubt that you will actually leave, so she will be much less likely to ignore your instruction.

When the Storm Has Subsided

Reasoning with a two-year-old is about as productive as changing seats on the Titanic.
—Robert Scotellaro

Don't try to discuss or negotiate with a toddler in the middle of a tantrum unless you want to punish yourself with an exercise in futility. Once your child has calmed down (and what feels like a lifetime has passed) and she has wiped her swollen eyes, has brushed her tangled hair from her face, and begins, once again, to breathe normally—this is the time to get down to her level, look her in the eye, and say, "I know that you were sad that you could not get a toy. It is OK to be sad, but when we are sad, we need to use our words. Having a tantrum will not get you what you want. Mommy wants to hear how you feel, but I cannot listen to you when you are having a tantrum. My ears refuse to work."

Then give her a hug and tell her you love her. This reaffirms that you listened to what she was trying to say, that you understand and cared that she was sad, and that it is OK to be sad—but more importantly, it teaches her a more appropriate way to handle her feelings.

Learning to acknowledge and appropriately deal with emotions and momentary defeats are lessons that are preparing her for healthy adulthood. Learning this lesson early, from someone who she knows loves her dearly, will benefit her for years to come.

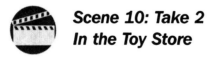 **Scene 10: Take 2**
In the Toy Store

MOM, *while driving.* Elise, we are on our way to the toy store to get a birthday gift. We will be there in a few minutes. (*A few minutes later, she parks the car at the store.*) We have to go into the toy store to get a gift for Ryan. You can help pick out his gift, but today we are not here to buy toys for us.

ELISE. But we're at the toy store! I want a toy!

MOM, *unbuckling Elise from her car seat.* Honey, I understand we are at the toy store and we sometimes buy toys for you here, but today we are shopping only for Ryan. If you see something you really like, when we get home we can put it on your wish list. Are we ready to go in?

ELISE, *holding Mom's hand, walking into the store.* OK, Mommy. If I do really good behavior in the store and don't touch things or run off, can I get something?

MOM, *stopping in front of the entrance.* You know the rules. First, you don't get rewarded for what you are supposed to be doing anyway. Second, you know bad behavior in the store is a bad choice, and if you make that choice, we leave. Ryan would be sad if he didn't get a birthday gift, don't you think?

ELISE. Yes, Mommy.

MOM. OK, let's go! *(They enter the store.)* Can you help me pick out Ryan's gift?

ELISE, *pointing to the Lego section.* Mommy, he would love this!

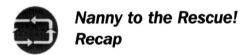

Nanny to the Rescue! Recap

What Nanny Tips did this mom use to change her toy-store terror into a birthday-gift browser?

Speak when you're angry, and you'll make the best speech you'll ever regret.
—Lawrence J. Peter

1. *Be proactive to avoid the tantrum.* Prepare your child with what to expect. Give her the who, what, when, where, and why for the situation so that she has a clear understanding of her role and what to expect.

2. *If avoiding the tantrum is impractical, take your child to a safe place.* If your child is having a tantrum in a public place, calmly take your child to a safe place where she will not get hurt. Then ignore her completely.

3. *Never give in to a tantrum.* Ever. If you give in once, you will be expected to give in again, and the tantrums will get louder and longer each time.

4. *Listen to your child, and reaffirm her feelings.* Tell your child you listened to and understand her feelings, and it is OK to have those feelings. (It is how she handles those feelings that is not OK.)

5. *Empower your child with choices you can live with.* She can't get a toy for herself, but she can help pick one out for her friend. She can also add things to her "list."

6. *Use terms of endearment.* Use special terms such as *honey, sweetie,* and *dear* that will remind your child that she is special to you, regardless of her behavior.

7. *Be prepared to follow through.* Don't make empty threats; make solid promises. If you say you are going to leave, be ready to leave. Likewise, do not say, "You will never get a toy again" when you know you cannot follow through. It only takes one time to pick up and leave the store for the child to realize, *Wow. What do you know? Mommy really will leave!*

8. *Don't reward a child for what he should be doing anyway.* Obviously in special circumstances like potty training or teaching a new behavior, rewarding is acceptable. But in general, if you have taught your child to practice good behavior and know she is capable of doing it, don't continuously reward her. The child will begin to associate good behavior with being rewarded. The reward should be that the child gets a good feeling inside because she made the right choice. This is how we help kids move from extrinsic to intrinsic motivation.

9. *"Please" is not a magic word; it is simply good manners.* Some parents unwittingly teach that when their child says please, he is instantly rewarded with any request. Reinforce that saying please is good manners when asking for something he wants. However, after being told no, all the "pleases" in the world won't change your mind.

Nanny Tip

We have a "list" for the boys—a running tally of all the things that they would like to have (kudos to their mom for this invention!).

It has empowered them to feel like they are doing something about their "wants." I cannot tell you how many tantrums this must have prevented.

Fraser would say, "I want this!"

We would say, "Great! We will put it on your list!"

That was the end of it. He was empowered! We then let him pick from the list something he would like for his birthday, Christmas, or other special occasion; and by the time the day rolled around, half of the things on the list he didn't even remember putting there.

This also worked when the boys would want something that was not age appropriate. We would use the same response. "Great! We can put it on your list for when you are thirteen!" Again, that empowered them. It also allowed them to look at things, see the recommended age on the package, and say, "I want to put this on my list for when I am seven." Sometimes all it takes is letting the kids feel like they have choices and some control!

A lady once came to the evangelist Billy Sunday and tried to rationalize her angry outbursts. "There's nothing wrong with losing my temper," she said. "I blow up, and then it's all over." "So does a shotgun," Sunday replied, "and look at the damage it leaves behind!"

CHAPTER ELEVEN

TAKING A BITE OUT OF BITING

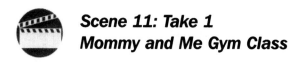 ### Scene 11: Take 1
Mommy and Me Gym Class

TEACHER. Welcome, boys and girls and moms! Are you ready to have some fun?

MOMS AND TODDLERS. Yeah!

TEACHER. OK, let's start out by passing this ball around our circle.

(Kids pass a ball in a circle while on their moms' laps.)

JACOB'S MOM. Come on, Jacob; pass the ball.

JACOB. No, it's mine!

JACOB'S MOM. Come on, sweetie; it's Sarah's turn.

SARAH, *tired of waiting for her turn, gets up off her mom's lap and bites Jacob in the hand as she takes the ball.* Mine!

SARAH'S MOM. Sarah! Get over here! *(Pulls her daughter toward her and bites her hand.)* How does that feel?

(Sarah and Jacob are now both screaming.)

SARAH'S MOM. If your kid would have just passed the ball, she wouldn't have bit him!

f you have a child who is between one and three years old, you have most likely experienced some form of biting. If you haven't, check with your dentist to make sure your child has teeth! Although it is *never* acceptable, biting is most often simply a part of social development in children this age. I don't know which is worse: having your innocent child scream in pain after being bitten by a fellow toddler or discovering that the toothed aggressor is *your* precious child. Neither scenario is pleasant for parents (or nannies), but it's part of life with small kids, and we need to address it. I hope that this chapter will help you prevent dramatic scenes from the toddler version of *Jaws*, playing in a nursery near you.

Babies Who Bite

There are a few common reasons that babies bite. And at least in their wee little noggins, the reasons are all actually logical! Regardless of how logical biting seems to your child, it is important from the beginning to convey that biting is always unacceptable (except in one case—explained at the end of this chapter).

One reason babies bite is that they are teething. Their gums hurt, and it feels good when they put pressure on them. It's kind of like an adult getting a massage for a sore muscle. If this is the case, you can deter your child's biting by offering him a teething ring. A wet washcloth put in the freezer will also work wonders. You can also say to a baby, "Biting hurts! No!" while giving him a stern, disapproving glare. He will get the idea that Mom isn't happy.

Biting is also a way that babies explore their environment. Up until this point, babies have used their mouths to discover everything, and almost everything they have discovered has been great! They've discovered breast milk or formula, solid foods, their hands to soothe them, possibly a pacifier, toys that they have been encouraged to chew on, and so on. At this point, their mouths have been just as important as their hands in learning about their environment.

So it follows that babies would continue their exploration by chewing on—you guessed it!—people. This is where you have to draw the line. A simple, firm "No! We don't bite people!" may be all that is needed, particularly for a sensitive child.

In addition to oral exploration, babies do not yet have any verbal tools to communicate or tools to deal with stress. So they communicate any way they can. (And it is true that champing down on another person's skin certainly gets their attention!)

Babies also may bite out of fear. When a strange person is holding them, they are suddenly flooded with fear and insecurity. If screaming and crying don't work, their instincts tell them to bite. This is a human, instinctual protective act—much like the way a woman who is suddenly grabbed by a strange man will instinctively use her teeth to try to hurt and scare away her attacker.

Sometimes babies just get confused. We may have played those familiar little games with kids, playfully nibbling on their precious toes and hands, saying, "Yummy, yummy, yummy." How can we resist? Babies love this game, and the giggles that follow are adorable. However, we may have unwittingly given them the idea that it is sometimes OK to bite and that biting can be playing, like a game! Babies (and toddlers) will not be able to distinguish between play biting and real biting, so it is probably best to be clear and consistent: biting (even playfully) is not acceptable. Just change the "nibble, nibble" game to giving their fingers and toes lots of ticklish butterfly kisses instead!

Regardless of why your baby bites, try to remember, while biting may be normal at this stage of development, it is also the time to enforce that biting is not OK.

An Ounce of Prevention Is Worth a Pound of Pain

How can you help your child to resist biting others?

- *Communicate clearly that biting is never OK.* (But there is one exception to this rule—read on.)

- *Give positive labels to the purpose of each body part.* For example, lips are for kissing; teeth are for chewing food.

- *The first time you catch your child biting, correct it firmly.* Address the behavior, not the child. Continue to be vigilant in your corrections.

- *Notice what types of situations trigger angry biting in your child.* If you know the triggers for your child's biting, you can try to defuse them before they escalate to the point of no return.

- *Teach your child to respect other people's bodies.* "We don't touch people we don't know unless we have their permission."

- *Give your child verbal tools to express himself.* Simple words like *no* or *stop* can be substituted for biting.

- *Teach your child that it is OK to be mad, but it's not OK to handle that anger by biting people.* Offer him tips to control his anger, such as walking away from situations or getting help from the trusted adult on duty.

- *If your child has a severe biting issue, talk to your pediatrician.* Also, make sure his oral needs are met by providing him with a variety of different textures of food so that he can exercise his jaws.

How can you help your child avoid being bitten?

- *Help your child avoid known biters.* If there is a child in the nursery or preschool who is a known biter, instruct your child to keep their distance from him or her, if at all possible. They can talk and play; just encourage your child to stay an arm's length away.

- *Teach your child to respect other people's words.* Teach your child how to respond appropriately so that he doesn't aggravate a tense situation and possibly provoke a biter. "Don't tease another child if they are not having fun. No means no. Stop means stop."

- *Instruct your child to ask for help.* Teach your child to use his voice and ask or call for help from a grownup when a friend gets too aggressive or makes him feel uncomfortable.

Toothy Toddlers

Biting is most likely to peak when your child is between thirteen and eighteen months old. Why? Because this is the age when most small children enter environments where they are around other groups of kids their age. Picture this: your child begins his first day of group childcare, and he is suddenly surrounded by other munchkins his age—none of whom can yet express themselves verbally, all without the mature skills needed to communicate or deal with anger or frustration in socially acceptable ways. Biting is inevitable, and it is the main reason that children are expelled from group childcare facilities.

One way to avoid "group shock" is to start assimilating your child to other children—slowly—in small playgroups of just one or two other children at first. This gradually teaches them, in their own environment and under close watch, how to interact with other children.

When my charges were infants, we would take a daily stroll to meet the other nannies for coffee by the park. We'd sit in Starbucks and push the strollers together so that the kids could all see each other. (The baristas will usually give your toddler a small squirt of whipped cream in a cup for no cost. Give them a spoon, and they are in baby bliss just long enough for you to enjoy your mocha latte.) Then we would head over to the park across the street. Once there, we'd spread out the blankets and have tummy time with all the babies, who were just a few months old when we started getting together.

Six years later, our "babies" still play with each other regularly! (You should see the scrapbook in which I have photos of the same kids, sitting in the same order, on the same couch—and how they have grown each year!) They learned that there were others in the world, like them, from a very young age. This is especially important when a baby doesn't yet have sibling interaction.

No, not all the experiences were idyllic and happy. Our charges experienced their first bites, hair pulling, and all the other wonderful developmental benefits of mingling with others of their own kind—but they experienced these things in a safe environment with familiar people who could help soothe and train them. We also all had the same rules and firmly enforced "no biting." Their experience with others from a young age limited the number of biting incidents in the older toddler years.

At about twenty-four months, children can make the connection between biting and pain. This is where you can begin to teach empathy and give a more detailed reason of why biting is not OK: "Biting is not OK! Biting hurts." Follow up by saying, "Teeth are for eating food only."

How to Handle a Biting Incident

Let's walk through a typical scenario and how best to handle it. Let's say there are two toddlers fighting over the same toy. (No surprise there.) One toddler decides to get a bit more aggressive and bites the other's arm. Sure enough, the other toddler lets go of the toy, but crying now fills the air. How should you handle the situation? First, address the child who was bitten. Comfort him and ensure that he is OK. Next, pick up the offender, look him in the face, and say firmly, "We don't bite." Then put him in time-out in an appropriate place, perhaps in a chair facing the wall. Again, go back and give all your attention to the "victim," comforting him and giving him all the attention he needs.

After the biter has served his time-out, you can explain to him, "I know you were angry and that is OK, but we need to use our words." Take the child over to the "victim," and show the biter how to say he is sorry and give a hug or a gentle pat as a gesture of empathy. Yes, this exercise may be totally imitation, without sincere remorse or feeling, but it sets an extrinsic pattern that will, in time, turn into intrinsic empathy.

If you notice that a child is biting out of frustration or anger because he is not getting what he wants, you can provide other outlets for him to express his frustration or anger. This can include a special place to draw how he feels or a sign to hold up with a mad face on it. If nonverbal outlets are provided, be sure to use positive reinforcement when the child uses them. You can also praise the child when he starts to bite but stops before he does. You can teach him to cover his mouth if he feels the need to bite. Then praise him if he does!

There's lots of advice floating around about how to handle a biter. In my opinion, biting back is not an effective teaching method. Dealing with an aggressive behavior by demonstrating another aggressive behavior only shows that it is OK to bite, since Mommy did it. It does exactly the opposite of what you hope to accomplish.

Regardless of the situation, it's always important to address the behavior and not the child. "We don't bite." "Biting hurts." "Teeth are not for biting people." "Biting is not OK." These are all phrases that clearly, without question or doubt, convey that the action is not acceptable, but the kid is still good.

When to Be Concerned

If biting behaviors persist after age three, there may be a more serious reason behind them, especially if biting is accompanied by other aggressive behaviors. If the biting is persistent and your child hasn't graduated to using other skills, such as his words, to express his feelings or frustrations, this would be the time to seek professional guidance from your child's healthcare provider.

Special Circumstances

Because this is real life, there is an exception to the rule. We must give our children all the tools necessary to protect themselves. If a child is in fear for his life, or if he is being touched by someone who shouldn't touch him, the first line of defense is to scream, "Stop! Let me go! I don't like that!" (My charges have purple belts in karate and taught me this.)

But if screaming doesn't work, this is one time when you can literally take a bite out of crime. In fact, teaching a child to bite as a method of self-defense may save his life. Of course, the child needs to be old enough to understand when biting is OK and when it is not. But you can tell an older child that if a stranger puts his hand over her mouth, she can bite down as hard as she can on that hand—and then run as fast as she can to a safe place or person.

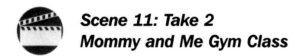 *Scene 11: Take 2*
Mommy and Me Gym Class

TEACHER. Welcome, boys and girls and moms! Are you ready to have some fun?
MOMS AND TODDLERS. Yeah!
TEACHER. OK, let's start out by passing this ball around our circle.
(Kids pass ball in a circle while on their moms' laps.)
JACOB'S MOM. Come on, Jacob; pass the ball.
JACOB. No, it's mine!
JACOB'S MOM, *helping him pass it along.* It's Sarah's turn.

SARAH, *goes over and bites Jacob in the hand as she takes the ball.* Mine!

SARAH'S MOM. Sarah! Biting is not OK! *(Carries her to time-out, sitting her so she's facing the wall.)* Sit in time-out and face the wall. *(Gives Jacob the ball.)* Oh, Jacob, I am so sorry Sarah bit you. Biting is not OK. She is in a time-out for biting. I am so sorry. *(She turns to Jacob's mom.)* When she's out of time-out, I'll have her apologize to Jacob. Anything I can do to help? Some ice or a Band-Aid for him?

JACOB'S MOM, *comforting her son but remaining calm.* Would you mind getting a piece of ice for him? It might help distract him!

(After the time-out is over.)

SARAH'S MOM. Sarah, let's go tell Jacob you are sorry. Biting is not OK, and you hurt him. When you are angry, you need to use your words.

SARAH. I'm sorry I hurt you. *(Pats Jacob's sore arm gently.)*

JACOB'S MOM. Thank you for apologizing, Sarah. Now let's try playing ball again, OK?

 Nanny to the Rescue! Recap

What Nanny Tips were used in this situation?

1. *Address the behavior, not the child.* All kids are all good; it's their behavior that is not acceptable.

2. *Be clear in your expectations.* Biting is not OK.

3. *Be consistent in your response to the behavior.* Use firm words and firm nonverbal cues followed by a time-out.

4. *Don't give in to what the child wants.* If a child is biting because he wants something, don't give in. Doing so will reinforce that biting is effective.

5. *Praise positive behavior.* Praise every step toward victory.

6. *Teach empathy.* "I know you are sad. Biting hurts."

7. *Tell the child that he is responsible for his body.* Teach your child that it is his job to control his body.

8. *Teach tools.* Teach your child positive ways to communicate his feelings.

CHAPTER TWELVE

THE GREAT PACIFIER DEBATE

 Scene 12: Take 1
The Crib

DAD, *putting two-year-old Henry in the crib*. OK, Henry, tonight's the night. You are a big boy. Give me your pacifier.

HENRY, *grabbing his pacifier for dear life and lying on top of it*. No, no, NO!

DAD, *reaching in and grabbing the pacifier from underneath him*. Stop being a baby. You are two years old! A big boy! No more pacifier.

HENRY, *screaming and sobbing hysterically*. No! Mine! Give me! Daddy!

DAD, *walking away to shut the door*. You are a big boy. Go to sleep.

HENRY, *screaming*. Mommy! Daddy! Give it back!

(An hour later; Henry is still screaming.)

DAD, *tossing the pacifier in the crib*. Fine. Here . . . take it!

There is no right or wrong answer to whether you should use a pacifier with your child. If there was, the debate would have ended years ago. Pacifiers have been around for centuries. The phrase "born with a silver spoon in his mouth" is believed to have come from a time when parents popped in a silver pacifier "spoon" in the mouth of a child soon after the baby was born.

The ultimate decision on whether to use a pacifier is yours. With the information in this chapter, you should be able to make a decision that you feel is right for you and your child. There is also room for middle ground in the great pacifier debate. This is one instance in parenting where you can start out doing one thing and later change the rules, if you do so at the right time and with the right attitude.

> *I always wondered why babies spend so much time sucking their thumbs. Then I tasted baby food.*
> —Robert Orben

The Pros of Pacifiers

Babies are born with the natural urge to suck. Many ultrasounds reveal a developing baby in the womb with her thumb sweetly tucked in her mouth. From this, we can gather that a baby sucks not only for food but for comfort—even before birth!

Nanny Tip

If your baby uses a pacifier, purchase several of the same brand and leave them in places you know you will need them. Have a stash in the car, in the diaper bag, in the living room, at Grandma's, or wherever you spend your time with baby. This will eliminate the search to save your sanity when one can't be found.

Most baby stores carry all-natural, child-safe pacifier sterilizer that you can spray on the pacifier and then wipe clean. And always carry a bottle of spring water in your car. Even an eight-ounce size comes in handy for washing pacifiers, preparing a bottle, or cleaning a boo-boo.

The peak time for nonnutritional sucking is between two and four months of age. At this age, a baby's facial muscles are developing, and sucking is familiar, comforting, and soothing.

Using a pacifier as an additional means of self-soothing can be a wonderful boon to busy moms. It also helps to fulfill the baby's natural urge to suck. Using a pacifier can also help a parent tell when a baby is hungry or needs something else. Pacifiers can serve as a sleep aid for a tired or fussy baby.

Pacifiers are also convenient when you need to stall the baby a bit before you can nurse him or get his bottle ready. There is less reason to be concerned over the cleanliness of pacifiers, since most are now dishwasher safe or even disposable.

Nanny Tip

Before automatically reaching for the pacifier to calm a crying baby, ask yourself first if she really needs it. Is she fed, well rested, and in a clean diaper? If so, try to comfort your child in other ways, like with rocking or singing, before you resort to using the pacifier.

The Cons of Pacifiers

The cons of using a pacifier are that, at times, parents can be too quick to plug up the baby, rather than getting to the root of why the child is fussy. Pacifiers can also become a substitute for human soothing or addressing the real, more acute need of the baby. It is also important, especially for newborns, that pacifiers are properly sterilized and dry before giving them to baby.

Bottle-fed babies usually take to a pacifier more easily than breastfed babies since the nipples of bottles and pacifiers are similar. Learning to switch from pacifier to breast can result in nipple confusion, because two kinds of sucking are required— one for feeding from the breast, the other for bottle feeding. For this reason, most professionals discourage the use of pacifiers in breastfed babies until they learn to properly latch onto the breast first. Also, nonnutritive sucking may inhibit the mother's supply of breast milk and affect a newborn's needed weight gain.

Studies have also shown that breastfed babies who are given pacifiers tend to wean earlier than those who do not use pacifiers. A 1999 study reported in the medical journal *Pediatrics* showed that mothers who used pacifiers during the first six weeks after birth tended to wean their babies earlier. This may or may not be advantageous to you, but it is generally recommended that a baby get six months of breastfeeding, if at all possible.

Older babies and toddlers may also come to depend on the pacifier for comfort. They will use the pacifier instead of seeking out their parents or soothing themselves in a variety of other ways. This can especially be a problem if a baby learns to fall asleep continuously with a pacifier in his mouth. What happens when it falls out? (Answer: the baby wakes up sooner than you want him to!) If a pacifier is your child's only means of soothing, then you need to be ready to get up and put it back in. (By the way, never put a child to sleep with a pacifier that attaches to his clothes, because there is a risk of strangulation by the cord or material used to attach it to the clothes. Little fingers can become entangled in the cord, or the clip could possibly break and end up in the mouth of baby, who could choke.)

An older toddler may eventually get teased about her pacifier by other kids; and if she is sensitive, she may get her feelings hurt. Once a child can ask for his pacifier, begin to limit the use of it. For example, you can allow it only during naptime or only in the house.

Pacifier use is also associated with an increased risk of middle ear infections. Prolonged pacifier use in children over age four can potentially cause dental problems, where the permanent teeth fail to come in. Problems also may occur if the tongue and mouth muscles delay in switching from the immature sucking pattern associated with pacifier sucking to the mature tongue movements needed for speech. The results may be distorted speech sounds and delayed swallowing development.

When your first baby drops her pacifier, you sterilize it. When your second baby drops her pacifier, you tell the dog "Fetch."
—Bruce Lansky

The Pacifier Versus the Thumb

Breaking the pacifier habit is much easier than breaking the thumb-sucking habit for obvious reasons: you can eventually remove the pacifier from sight, but you can't remove your child's thumb. Some children, when initially weaned from the pacifier, will begin to suck on their hands or thumbs before falling off to sleep or during stressful situations. This habit will usually cease on its own.

Kicking the Pacifier Habit

Oral habits are hard to break (just ask any adult who has tried to quit smoking!). For an older toddler, sucking on a pacifier has indeed become a habit. After four months, the natural urge for nonnutritive sucking has subsided, and babies are now using their mouths for nutritional needs, such as sucking on a bottle or breast, eating solid foods, and perhaps even drinking out of a "sippy" cup. For this reason, when your child is six months old, you should begin to consider helping him kick the habit. At this age, children are better able to self-soothe or turn to Mom and Dad for comfort. Six months of age is a good time to restrict pacifier use to crib time only, which is an effective way to initiate the weaning process. After about nine months of age, it gets tougher to take away the pacifier because a baby's will is stronger, and he will fight the process harder. The older children get, the more resistance you will face.

Reducing Pacifier Use

For older babies, you can begin to limit when and where they are allowed to use the pacifier. (For example, right before bedtime in the evening or while in their car seat.) Be consistent in the limit setting and enforcement, and reduce pacifier use little by little. Children tend to respond to a more gradual change when they know what is happening.

You can also teach your child that his mouth and teeth are for other things too. Practicing good oral hygiene, such as brushing teeth regularly, can provide him with other, appropriate options for positive oral activities. You can also praise positive behavior often, taking his mind off the pacifier and directing him to other activities where he gains positive attention.

The Final Good-Bye

When you are ready to kick the pacifier habit for good, there are many positive ways of doing it. As long as you have a good attitude, most will work. Here are three tried-and-proven methods of getting rid of the pacifier for good.

The "trading up" method. This method usually provides for a win-win situation. First, you begin to discuss with your child the need to stop using the pacifier.

"Michael, remember what we talked about yesterday? Today is the day we are graduating from the pacifier!"

"Mommy, no. I don't want to!"

"I know it is hard to give away something you like, but remember, I told you that you are a big boy now, and big boys get to trade in their pacifiers for something special."

"But I like it!"

"Yes, I know you do, but I think I have something that you may like a bit better."

"What?" he responds as his eyes widen in anticipation.

"In my family, when boys trade in their pacifiers, they get to go to the toy store and pick out one toy—any toy that they want in the whole entire store!" (You can put a dollar limit on this, moms and dads!)

"Really?"

"Yes, really! Today we will go to the store, and tonight we are having a special party for you with cake and ice cream. Grandma and Grandpa are coming to celebrate too!" (Most grandparents love any excuse to shower love on a young grandchild.)

"Yippee!"

If the timing is right, you can align the letting-go-of-the-pacifier rite of passage with getting a big boy bed or some other milestone that he can equate with getting bigger. Again, a matter-of-fact attitude helps. Getting rid of the pacifier is something that just naturally happens next in your child's development.

The "pacifier burial" method. You can also use the "pacifier burial" method, which is exactly the way it sounds. You have a ceremony in which you allow the child to come up with his own way of disposing of his pacifier. Maybe he wants to throw it into the ocean or lake. (Be prepared to retrieve it when he is not looking. We don't want to be environmentally harmful.) Or perhaps you can bury it in the backyard (help to make sure the hole is deep enough so no animals can get it) or "give" it to a new baby who really needs it (inform the parent of the new baby in advance and be ready with a new one of similar appearance to quickly substitute when your child is not looking). The nice thing about this method is that you are giving the child some control over the situation, allowing him to feel like he has a positive role in his rite of passage.

The "cold turkey" method. Just as some adults need to kick a habit cold turkey (rather than through gradual withdrawal), that may also be true for your child, should the other methods fail. Maybe your child does better with once-and-for-all changes and is more willing to accept a new idea if there is no room for going back. Some children work better handling a situation as it comes rather than preparing too far in advance for it. As long as the cold-turkey approach is initiated with a positive and confident attitude, and this method seems right for your child's personality, it should work.

There are many positive ways to approach "nipping the nip," but what definitely won't work is using put-downs. Saying things like, "Only babies suck pacifiers," or making threats such as, "Stop that whining, or I'm going to take away your pacifier," are not appropriate. This leads to a power struggle where no one really comes out the winner.

What the Experts Say

According to the American Academy of Pediatric Dentistry, sucking is completely normal for babies and young children. The AAPD also believes that because most children stop sucking on their own between two and four years of age, no permanent damage is done to their teeth or jaws. However, when the same finger or a pacifier is sucked on repeatedly, the risk increases for the upper front baby teeth to tip toward the lip and not come in properly (because of the repeated positioning and pressure on those teeth).

The AAPD also advises parents that there is no need to be overly concerned about your child's sucking habits until their permanent teeth are ready to come in. According to the AAPD, sucking on the thumb and sucking on a pacifier affect the teeth in the same way, but the pacifier habit is much easier to break.

Although dental research has shown that pacifiers are safe to use, university researchers in Finland recently published a study that showed "in children less than two years of age, pacifier use increased the average number of annual ear infections from 3.6 to 5.4 episodes. In children between two and three years of age, pacifier use increased the number from 1.9 to 2.7 ear infections per year. Presumably, either the sucking motion associated with pacifier use hinders proper Eustachian tube function (which normally keeps the middle ear open and clean), or—particularly in day care—the pacifiers act as *fomites* (germ-covered objects that spread infection). The authors suggest that pacifiers be used only during the first ten months of life when the need for sucking is strongest and episodes of ear infections are relatively uncommon."[1]

When it comes to parenting advice, go with your gut. When people give you advice on what to do, take away the parts that work for you (if any) and throw out the rest. You know your child best!

Just as with many of the other parenting choices that you are faced with, there is no right or wrong answer to the great pacifier debate. I've simply done some information gathering for you here, and you can mix that with your parenting instincts and your child's personality. Whichever route you chose, I can assure you it won't be a direct route to the psychiatric ward for children recovering from pacifier addiction!

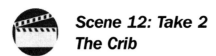

Scene 12: Take 2
The Crib

DAD, *putting two-year-old Henry in the crib.* OK, buddy. Remember, we have been working all week to trade in your pacifier for a surprise. Tonight's the night. I'm ready. Are you?

HENRY, *jumping up and down.* Yes, Daddy!

MOM, *reaching underneath the crib to get something.* Since you are growing up, Henry, we got you something very special. *(She gives him the gift.)*

HENRY, *excited.* For me! Is it mine? *(He hugs his new kid-sized pillow with his name and a picture of a fire truck, his favorite thing, on it.)*

DAD, *giving Henry a hug.* I am so happy you like it! Enjoy your first night's sleep with it.

MOM, *giving Henry a hug.* I am so proud of you!

HENRY, *hugging his pillow.* Good night, Daddy. Good night, Mommy.

DAD AND MOM. Love you.

HENRY. Love you too!

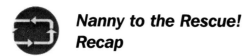

Nanny to the Rescue!
Recap

How did these parents help their son kick the pacifier habit without kicking each other?

1. *The child was prepared, and the expectations were clear.* The parents had a plan, and they followed it through.

2. *A positive, confident attitude builds a positive, confident kid.* You reap what you sow.

3. *Look on milestones as a rite of passage.* Getting rid of the pacifier is just what comes next; it's part of growing up. It is only as big of a deal as you make it.

4. *They didn't give in.* The parents made a plan and stuck to it.

5. *The dad was a cheerleader.* Positive reinforcement and encouragement work!

6. *Use loving affirmations.* Say, "I love you," and use endearing words.

7. *Use a team approach.* Be a parenting team when making changes. Appear united and confident together.

8. *When you close a door, open a window.* Give the child something positive to look forward to when he stops using the pacifier.

CHAPTER THIRTEEN

TAKING TIME FOR TIME-OUTS

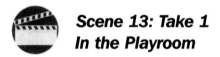 **Scene 13: Take 1**
In the Playroom

(Sarah is smashing her toy truck into the television.)

MOM. Hey, Sarah, stop it!

(Sarah looks up and goes back to playing truck versus TV megawar.)

MOM. Aren't you listening? I told you to knock it off! *(She goes over and grabs the truck out of Sarah's hand.)*

SARAH, *throwing herself to the floor, bawling.* No! I want my truck!

MOM. Stop being a bad girl. This is what happens when you don't listen!

If you haven't already noticed, one of the recurring themes in this book (and in my approach to childrearing) is consistency. There are several ways of reacting to a child's inappropriate behavior. No matter which method you choose, the determining factor in successful discipline is consistency.

If you've decided to adopt a proactive parenting style, you will want to be a responder rather than a reactor. What's the difference? A reactive parent lets her moods or impulses take over when her child disobeys or irritates her. A responsive parent, on the other hand, has a plan in mind that she implements consistently when her child acts up.

One fabulous tool for proactive parenting is the ever-popular time-out. I can guarantee, if applied correctly, the time-out method will be effective.

What Is Time-Out?

Time-out is exactly what the name implies—a designated time apart from the sticky situation at hand. For toddlers, it is a time to take a breather, regroup emotionally, and perhaps stop hyperventilating. For older kids, it is a time to reflect on their actions (or at least a time to pretend that they are doing so). By placing the child in time-out, you are refusing to give any positive reinforcement or attention to the child. You are removing and isolating the child from the current environment and unstable situation.

Where exactly do you put a child for a time-out? There are a variety of places that work well for time-outs: on an area rug, on a short stool, in a corner, or on a special time-out chair. Some parents even decorate this special seat, choosing one that is small, portable, and can be taken on trips. But when you are at home, it is important to use the same location again and again. Just about any location in your home will work, but the two places that should not be used are the bedroom and the bathroom. This is because you do not want to form a negative association between discipline and those areas of the home—believe me, you want your children to *like* their bedroom and the bathroom!

I have to admit, when my soon-to-be six-year-old charges are sent to an occasional time-out, they look really funny squeezing into their handcrafted wooden rocking chairs from when they were toddlers. But they are accustomed to them, and

I hate to mess with a system that has worked so well for so long. In fact, these days, when they realize they've broken a rule, they'll often send themselves to time-out, evidence that outward discipline is becoming intrinsic. (What mom or dad hasn't placed themselves in a psychological "time-out" in order to regroup and act with a better sense of calm? This is a great teaching tool for dealing with anger appropriately that will last a lifetime.)

You know you've lost control when you're the one who goes to your room.
—Babs Bell Hajdusiewicz

The time-out method can be effective for children as young as eighteen months old. The general rule of thumb is that the child is put in time-out for one minute per year of age. So a two-year-old would, ideally, spend two minutes in time-out.

A Typical Time-Out

Let's look at how this method works in a real-life situation with a toddler who is behaving like a tyrant. When two-year-old Sharon takes a toy from her baby sister, Mom should say in a firm but pleasant voice, "Sharon, please give Talking Elmo back to your sister." If she does, great!

If not, go to step two. Mom gets down to her daughter's level, looks her directly in the eyes, and states again, in a firmer but still calm voice, "Sharon, I asked you to give the toy back to your sister. If you do not obey, you will go sit in your time-out chair." If she complies, great! However, if she doesn't obey in the next few seconds, Mom needs to get down to Sharon's level and tell her firmly, "Sharon, you did not listen to Mommy and give back the toy. Go sit in time-out."

It also helps to point a child in the direction of her special time-out place. Being firm, pointing, and giving your child a serious, "I'm not happy" look all send the same signal: the fun has come to a screeching halt because *someone* did not obey the family rules. If your child refuses to go to time-out, you simply pick her up and place her in her time-out location. Determine to stay strong and to ignore all the inner urges to give in to her promises, negotiations, or pleadings. (Think of yourself as a human robot in these moments! "Screaming, whining, crying—does not compute.")

You then say clearly, without wavering, "Stay there until Mommy tells you to get out." Most toddlers don't have the self-control to sit still and be silent, as one can expect from older children. Don't be afraid to help your child stay seated by gently restraining her with your hands and arms. If you let her out just because she fusses and wiggles, this leads the child to believe she is in control of when her disciplinary action will end. It makes your toddler think that she is in charge! Not good. My friends, this situation is one where you "can't let 'em see you sweat." You must stay firm, calm, and in control. If you don't *feel* firm or calm, act as if you are until the feelings come!

I favor the time-out method of discipline because it eliminates arguing, negotiating, screaming, and yelling. It addresses the action and not the child. It is not emotional. The child's actions are neither good nor bad; they are acceptable or unacceptable. (This is an important distinction. It also reminds you that your child's behavior is temporarily not working and needs adjustment but that you have not given birth to "bad seed.") When applied effectively, time-out keeps the child's self-esteem intact while teaching her that there are consequences for her behavior. It also reaffirms that the parent is in charge of the toddler at large.

Effective Time-Outs

For time-out to be effective, you must first establish and communicate your expectations to your child. You must be absolutely clear in your definition of what is acceptable behavior and what is not. Your expectations have to be age appropriate, as well. For example, you cannot expect a two-year-old to willingly share at all times with her baby sister; but you can expect, after teaching her via the time-out method, that she'll understand that hitting her baby sister is not OK and won't get her what she wants. (Unless what she wants is a long sit in a boring place.)

There should be almost no time between the undesirable behavior and the consequence, if at all possible. You need to establish a vivid association between the action and the consequence. Having the consequence follow the disobedient behavior as quickly as possible reinforces the connection.

Before a behavior occurs, talk about the sort of actions that will, unquestionably, call for an automatic time-out. These include biting, hitting, or any other physical assaults on others. Back talk should not be acceptable either. When your three-year-old tells you, "Shut up!" you need to calmly lead her by the hand to time-out and say, "We don't say hurting words to Mommy. Ever. It is an automatic time-out."

Think through some automatic time-outs that are very important to you to enforce, those with no warnings given. Make sure you use general time-outs for outright and continued disobedience and for harming others. Childish forgetfulness, accidents, and misunderstanding a rule should not be punished. These things should be trained and explained instead.

Try to ignore the smaller infractions you can deal with in other ways. Let's say your young toddler says, "No!" when you ask him to put his ball away. Instead of issuing a time-out for that behavior, perhaps a more productive approach would be to say, "I'm glad you used your words and told me that you didn't want to stop playing with your ball. So how about you give your best throw to Mommy this time, and then we can put it away for later together?"

If this lighter approach works, you've saved both of yourselves an unnecessary scene and created a win-win resolution for you and your child. It is generally a good idea with very young children to approach their need to say no with creative alternatives or to distract them with a hearty sense of humor (such as tickling, chasing, laughing, and making a game of putting toys away). Time-outs are for when you draw a line in the sand and the toddler looks you in the eye and puts her darling little toe over the line, daring you to respond. You must respond in that moment, without wavering.

Once you've talked about unacceptable behaviors with your child, be prepared to be consistent in implementing time-outs, and be prepared to give them several times a day, often for the same infraction. Yes, it is tiring, but it is tried and true. Think of how long it takes to train a puppy to learn to go outside rather than on your new carpet—the days, weeks, and months of being consistent. You are training your toddler to follow society's rules of good behavior, and no one ever said it would be quick or easy.

There is no limit on how many time-outs a child can get in a day, so don't worry if it seems that a child is spending too much time there, especially when you are working on a stubborn negative behavior that just takes a lot of reinforcement to break. Be prepared to be tested, but stand strong, stand tall, and you will prevail.

After the Time-Out Is Over

Once the child's time-out is over, she should be encouraged to apologize for her behavior, and then, by your expression of love and relaxed face, the child needs to feel that her slate is wiped completely clean. The previous unacceptable behavior need not be mentioned again (that is, until the next time the incident occurs and the process starts over). Don't use the moments when your child is exiting time-out to lecture her. It's like kicking her when she is down or getting an extra sermon after you've apologized and made amends. She did the crime, she served her time, and now she is free!

Another tactic for time-out success is to catch your child doing a good behavior and praise it enthusiastically. "Wow, Sammy! Thanks for putting your cup on the table instead of the floor. Good work!" Again, you are addressing behaviors, not the child.

For praise to work well, it needs to be specific. Saying, "What a good boy!" means nothing if the child doesn't know what pleased you. Have you heard the adage that when a man praises a woman, he should be very specific? He should not just tell her she is generically wonderful; he should tell her how her ebony hair glows in the moonlight and how her smile lights up a room. We women love to hear all the juicy details when it comes to receiving praise. Kids are no different! So be specific. Rather than saying, "What a good brother you are!" try, "I love how you patted your new baby sister so gently on her arm!"

Parents Need Time-Outs Too

Parenting at times can be overwhelming. Sometimes you may feel like you are on the brink of losing control. If you ever feel like this, you should immediately put your child in a safe place, such as his crib, playpen, or gated area . . . and take a cool-down period for yourself to regroup. Taking a time-out for yourself doesn't make you a bad parent. In fact, it may very well make you a better parent. Just make sure your child is safe while you take your breather.

1-2-3 Magic

I wish I could tell you I invented this great child discipline technique, but I have to give credit where credit is due. Thomas Phelan is the author of an angst-saving book called *1-2-3 Magic*. If you haven't seen a miracle, read his book and apply his techniques.

One great aspect of Phelan's approach is that it centers on nonemotional discipline. It is also consistent, highly doable, and enforceable. It is firm, fair, and balanced. So many methods seem to turn parents into frustrated drill sergeants; others are too permissive. The 1-2-3 Magic method yields good behavior from the child, a less stressed parent, and a higher level of self-esteem for all involved.

Phelan's method is threefold. First, you have the stop behavior technique, which is used to control bad behavior. Next, you have the start behavior technique, used to encourage your child to do what you want him to do. Finally, there are relationship-building actions that strengthen the parent-child bond both before and after the disciplinary action.

Here's a personal example of how I use the 1-2-3 Magic technique.

"Fraser, cars are not for throwing. Please stop."

Fraser throws the car again.

"That's one, Fraser. Put your car on the floor and race it there."

He throws the car again.

"That's two, Fraser."

Yet again, the car gets tossed.

"That's three, Fraser. Give me the car and take a time-out."

Voilà! This method worked well for Fraser. I didn't yell, I didn't nag, and I didn't belittle. I addressed the unacceptable behavior objectively.

You may be asking, "Why do you give the child three chances? Shouldn't he obey right away?" Like adults, children need time to shift gears and to process what is being asked. They are learning, and they aren't going to get it the first time! The 1-2-3 Magic method allows you to teach them and get them to respond without nagging, yelling, or belittling.

1-2-3 Magic has sold more than two million copies and can be found at most bookstores or on-line. It is an invaluable resource for parents of children two to twelve years of age, and it is required reading for any family I work with.

Time-Out Alternatives

Here are some alternatives to time-out when your child can be more simply redirected.

Distraction

Distraction is when you use something to redirect a child from pursuing the unwanted behavior at hand. (The old "Look out the window! What is that? A tractor?" technique often works great to distract a crying toddler immediately. I love windows and mirrors for quick distraction.) The pro is that this technique works well for babies up to the crawling age when they are great explorers of everything from toys to your Aunt Bertha's glass coffee-table knickknacks. When they are very young, they quickly forget what was taken away for something that is newly given.

Here's a typical scenario. Your baby is crawling toward the lamp plug. No need to pick him up and do the time-out routine. Simply intercept him, put him on the other side of the room, and then sit between him and the plug. If you have a ball handy and can distract him by playing toss, all the better!

The con of this technique is that you are not teaching your child why the behavior is not OK. You can say, "Pulling plugs is dangerous and can hurt you." But if the child is too young to comprehend cause and effect, he's not going to understand the logic behind this rule. For this reason, distraction is generally a more practical method for redirecting young babies and crawling infants.

Natural Consequences

I have come to enjoy the occasional use of natural consequences, especially when my charges say they don't want to wear their jacket outside in the middle of winter. The two seconds it takes for them to change their mind is much better than the twenty minutes arguing about why they should wear jackets.

Another situation in which this alternative works well is letting children suffer the natural consequences of throwing food on the floor. If the child throws his food on the floor, he simply doesn't get it back. The consequence is that he may be hungry. The lesson is, "If you throw your food, it's gone." No worries; missing one meal will not make your child starve. (If you take lunch away from a very young child, you can give him a nutritious snack within about thirty minutes to an hour of the misbehavior. This is long enough for the child to experience an unhappy and grumbly tummy, but not long enough to leave him famished.)

When it is safe to do so, sometimes letting a child learn a lesson on his own is a valuable life experience for him. You have to use common sense when employing this method, but natural consequences are often one of life's best teachers—for all of us!

Logical Consequences

Logical consequences are one step removed from natural consequences. In a natural consequence, you just let the consequence happen. (For example, going outside without a coat makes you cold.) A logical consequence takes a bit more thinking. For example, when you ask your child to pick up her toy doll and she refuses, you can do it for her, but the logical consequence is that she doesn't get to play with it. If a child doesn't get up when you call him to breakfast, a logical consequence might be that the child has to wash the breakfast dishes. You are, in some logical way, connecting the offense to the disciplinary action and doing it quickly.

If a young child refuses to sit correctly in her chair at the dinner table and stands up in it instead, you might move her and the chair to a corner where she finishes her meal alone, sitting quietly. There's a logical, rational connection: *If I stand up in my chair, I don't get to eat with everyone at the table.* The natural consequence for this offense might be too high a penalty; your child could fall over in the chair and injure herself badly. Think of a logical consequence as a parentally modified natural consequence.

Think of connecting good behaviors with the most logical rewards as well. In a fascinating book called *Why We Do What We Do*, researchers found that the more logical the reward for a good behavior (and not the most expensive or impressive), the more often kids became intrinsically motivated. The habit of paying kids money for getting a good grade on a math test may not be as effective as giving them extra time to play a fun math game on the computer. When your toddler picks up her toys, a natural reward would be to look around and enjoy the clean floor, and perhaps to take time to lie down there together and read a story on a blanket together—"Now that your floor is all so clean and picked up!"

Ignoring

Ignoring annoying behavior such as whining or tantrums can work if everyone in the household is committed to ignoring the behavior. For this to be successful, everyone must know which behaviors are to be ignored. Healthy human beings usually cease practicing what doesn't work; this is also true with our kids. (You've heard that the definition of insanity is continuing to do the same thing and expecting a different result, right?)

Discipline Methods to Avoid

There are some discipline methods I avoid because they are simply not effective. And in my profession (and for childcare workers and teachers), one method simply cannot be done. That is, of course, the ever-controversial method of spanking a child.

Spanking

Though there are experts who feel that spanking is permissible, even the biggest spanking supporters issue plenty of warnings: Don't spank in anger. Don't spank if you have the slightest tendency to lose control. Then there is controversy over whether to spank with a hand or with a paddle—and which does more or less harm. I believe that spanking comes with too many issues, not the least of which is the fact that it is often a form of humiliation rather than training.

Many believe the logic of spanking is contradictory: *I hit my child so he will learn not to hit another child.* Some Christians use Old Testament verses, many times out of context, to support the thought that God supports corporal punishment. I'll leave this debate to the theologians, but I think the heart of the New Testament Jesus always leaned toward the most loving response: "Let the little children come to me, and do not hinder them, for the kingdom of heaven belongs to such as these" (Matthew 19:14).

The context of Christ's approach to children was one of embracing love balanced with teaching truth in nonviolent ways. (Well, there was that incident of Jesus driving the moneychangers out of the temple of God with a whip. But look at the context: Jesus had just had it with grown men taking advantage of the weak and poor, in God's most holy place. Righteous anger flowed from Him in the same way a parent longs to protect a child from a bully, or worse. There is a big difference between this scene, and the motivation behind it, and an adult taking a paddle or belt to a smaller, weaker child.)

Reasoning

Another method that is mostly ineffective with babies and toddlers until they reach a more advanced mental stage is trying to reason with a child. Try telling a two-year-old who doesn't want his fun to stop something like, "Sugar, now, you need to stop and be reasonable about this. If you don't take a nap, you will get tired and grumpy. Your young body needs lots of rest, and that means that you need to put your toy down now, hop in bed, and go to sleep. OK?"

It's a lovely speech. But it is usually a waste of breath. Better to tell a child that it is time for a nap, followed by, "Off we go to beddy-bye!" and be done with it.

Different Methods for Different Children

Since we know that all children are different and have different personalities and different levels of development, it is important to individualize your approach for each child. Whichever method or combination of methods you choose, it will be effective if you are consistent, keep your emotions in check, and stay focused on training out bad behavior, not on demeaning or disheartening the child.

Does discipline sound complicated? All these methods! All these theories! Trust your gut, Mom and Dad, in choosing a method that works best for you and your kids. (By the way, you will likely have to adapt your discipline methods for each child. Each child comes with a different temperament, so rarely do the same methods applied in the same way work for all of your children.)

After you've read about the various methods, if you'll listen to your heart, stand aside from the emotion of the moment, and follow common-sense parenting, you are going to do what is right for you and your child.

I believe in you!

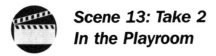

Scene 13: Take 2
In the Playroom

(Sarah is smashing her toy truck into the television.)

MOM. Sarah, trucks are for driving, not for smashing. Please stop smashing the TV with the truck and play with it on the floor. That's one.

(Sarah looks up and goes back to playing truck versus TV megawar.)

MOM, *getting in front of Sarah and making eye contact while using a firm voice.* Sarah. Mommy asked you to stop smashing the truck. That's two.

(The smashing continues.)

MOM. Sarah, that's three. Put the truck down and go sit in time-out until I tell you to get up. Trucks are for driving, not for smashing. *(She points to Sarah's time-out stool in the corner of the playroom.)*

SARAH. No, Mommy! I'll stop now.

MOM. Sarah, go now or I will put you there.

(Sarah walks over, pouting, but sits on her stool for two minutes.)

MOM. OK, Sarah, you can come back to playing now.

Nanny to the Rescue!
Recap

Did you find the steps that this mom used to let her toddler know who was really in charge?

1. *Address the behavior, not the child.* "You are a good girl; what you are doing is not."

2. *Be clear about what your child is doing wrong.* Use the stop behavior technique—tell her exactly what you want her to stop doing. ("Stop smashing the car into the TV.") Use the 1-2-3 Magic warning system. ("That's one.") Redirect her clearly on the start behavior—the behavior you want her to begin. ("Put the car on the floor.")

3. *Do not be emotional.* No screaming, pleading, nagging, or yelling.

4. *Once you begin the time-out cycle, do not give in to her pleas—even if she promises to stop the behavior.* She needs to learn that after "That's three," consequences will happen quickly—no exceptions.

5. *Enforce the time-out, even if you have to physically "help" the child stay there.*

6. *Once the sentence is served, it's over.*

7. *Catch and reward the acceptable behavior; don't just respond to the unacceptable behavior.*

8. *When using consequences and rewards (instead of, or in addition to, time-outs), try to make them as natural or logical as possible.*

CHAPTER FOURTEEN

IS THERE SOMETHING WRONG WITH MY KID?

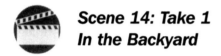 **Scene 14: Take 1**
In the Backyard

SUSAN. Michelle, do you think there is something wrong with Jack?

MICHELLE. No, Sue. Why?

SUSAN. Because he is so wild! Look at him running around and yelling like Tarzan. He's so active. Is this normal?

MICHELLE. Susan, first of all, you are Jack's mom; you have known him for six years. Second, I'm a nanny, not even his nanny. Third, I think you'd know if there was really something wrong with your child. And fourth, they are boys playing baseball for the first time this season. Running and yelling are part of the game!

SUSAN. But your kids are so well behaved. I'm afraid you'll never have us over again.

MICHELLE. Sue, keep it up, and I'm going to think something's wrong with you! Relax. They're kids, and all kids have different energy levels and different personalities. You've got a little tiger out there, but this world needs tigers.

Too often parents seem overly insecure. With the media highlighting the disorder of the day, it's no surprise that many parents wonder if their child is going through a stage, has a personality difference (or disorder), or truly has something wrong with him.

Just today, we had a play date. The above scenario was actually a real-life example. The kids were having a great time in the spring weather enjoying a game of backyard baseball. Since most parents from the kids' school know that I am a nanny, I often get asked questions by parents who probably have lots more experience and knowledge than I do. I'm sure, in part, the rise of nanny TV shows has made all nannies sound like the perfect combination of Mary Poppins, Dr. Phil, and Maria von Trapp.

So, being a real human-being-in-progress myself, stories like the ones above never fail to amaze me. Austin and Fraser (and their mom) taught me that kids have bad moments, not bad days. I take that to heart, especially when evaluating their behavior and development. I must say here that I have learned as much about raising kids from Austin and Fraser's mom as she has learned from me, if not more.

Most moms and dads out there, to tell the truth, are doing a really good job of parenting. And that includes you. It's not that parents don't love their children or aren't trying their best, but sometimes they just don't have the tools to implement. Probably what I do most often is teach parents new techniques and provide them with that extra boost of reassurance: "Yes, you are doing great!" "No, you aren't a bad mommy for making your child obey!" "Yes, your kid is a beautiful, unique, and special child . . . who occasionally acts like a spoiled brat and needs redirecting. But that is true for most of the human race, isn't it? Myself included."

Competitive Comparison

I think that one of the reasons parents are overly concerned with constantly evaluating their children is that they are spending too much time comparing the children to others. Each child, even a twin, is an individual who cannot be systematically compared to another. Of course, there are general developmental milestones that children are expected to reach by certain ages, and these do help us identify whether a child is on track; however, for the day-to-day aspects of life, there is no room for competitive comparison among children.

What is competitive comparison? It is when you consistently seek out other children in your child's age range so that you can observe that child and see how your child measures up. For example, let's say you are at a baby playgroup. Moms are sitting around with babies on their laps.

"Is little Kerrie teething yet?" one insecure mother asks.

"Oh yes, she has five teeth already!" another responds, as if her child has just won first place in the dental race.

"Oh, Kyle has none. Hey, Jeanie, does Allie have any teeth yet?" The worried mom continues her investigation.

"You know, she just started cutting her first tooth!" Allie's mom responds.

"OK, I'm officially worried now. Do you think I should call the pediatrician? Annabel has no teeth yet, and she is the oldest one here by two weeks."

Allie's mom (who has three other children) grins and says, "Kids grow teeth at their own pace and time. I promise you, Annabel will get teeth in plenty of time. You may wish for her toothless days again after the first time she bites down on your breast during a feeding."

The tension dissolves in laughter.

New moms are especially prone to the comparison trap. Moms who have more than one child have generally learned to relax with the process, and they usually have several children who are as different in personalities and progress as they can possibly be.

In the early days of sending Fraser and Austin to preschool (I later found out), the teachers were scared when they heard that "the twins" were coming. Apparently, they'd had a previous experience in the school with twins who weren't very tamed. Before anyone had met the boys, rumors had spread about the arrival of the dynamic duo. The parents were nervous, and teachers were overwhelmed by the thought. The preconception of how this "new set" was going to behave was based entirely on what they had experienced on their first wild go-around with multiples.

The individuality of the incoming children, or even the dynamics of the new "twin set," was not acknowledged. The teachers based their expectations on observing the behaviors of others. Fortunately, the boys had an awesome mom and a nanny on their side, advocating for them, ensuring that they would be judged based on the individual children they were, not the twin terrors they were expected to be. We got a small taste of prejudice and preconceptions, and it wasn't pretty.

My heart goes out to moms throughout the nation and history who've had to cope with much worse, outrageously unfair prejudice based on rumors, false beliefs, or skin color.

Yet I ache to observe some parents react in less obvious ways with prejudice to their own children, pronouncing one child "rebellious" or "slow" and making his sibling appear to walk on water. Ouch. When you compare your child to another, you are automatically setting up one of the children for failure. You are basing your evaluation of your child on unfair preconceptions and observations. So either your child isn't up to par, or the other child isn't up to par.

As long as your child is meeting the general standard developmental milestones outlined by your pediatrician (or unless she says otherwise), relax—your child is OK. He or she is a precious and unique human being. According to the charts, the average baby starts crawling between seven and ten months, but also remember that each child is an individual. Some babies are scooting along the carpet at six months, some start crawling at thirteen months, and some go straight from sitting up to walking!

If your child is under or over the "standard developmental milestones," there's no reason to panic. God created your child with a unique pattern. Calmly learn from reliable sources what you can do to help your child progress, and then take a mental chill pill and relax. If another mom asks why your child isn't sitting up yet, you can say, "We're on top of that. He's fine."

While you shouldn't compare your child to others, you can certainly compare her to herself as a way to gauge her mental and physical and emotional progress. You can evaluate her behavior based on previous patterns, her appetite based on previous meals, and her ability in school or in sports based on her past performance level. If you notice that your child is suddenly losing her appetite or acting very differently (for example, if an easygoing baby becomes frantically fussy), your mom instincts will probably kick in right away—especially if the new behavior lasts for a while. Doctors are beginning to value the "mommy instinct" that knows that "something is wrong with my baby"—even if it doesn't appear so to the physician right away. Doctors used to say, "All babies fuss at times. Don't worry!" But more are learning to ask more detailed questions to get a more accurate assessment. "Is your baby normally laid back? Is fussing a normal part of his day?"

Different Isn't Right or Wrong

Kids are all different. (Thank God!) They have different genes, different person-alities, and different life experiences that help shape their being. But just because kids are unique doesn't mean that they are right or wrong. Kenny may love baseball; Kevin may love cooking. Does one deserve more accolades than the other? No. Differences in children should be embraced. Parents should also remember that just because Kenny loves baseball now and Kevin loves cooking today, who's to say that won't be reversed tomorrow?

Kids also have different talents and levels of abilities. This is where things can get really ugly among parents. When Susie can do a somersault at fifteen months and your child can't do the same thing at twenty-four months, you might (incorrectly) assume that something is wrong. Forget that Susie is double-jointed; the fact that Susie can outperform your child hurts the ego of the insecure parent. Generally, it won't faze the child. The child is really too young to care. But some parents live their lives through the successes of their children, and it starts—believe it or not—at this young age! Kids often pick up the insecurity from their parents' subtle vibes of worry or tendency to compare.

Of course, we all want our kids to be champions, but being a champion is more than getting the gold medal in tumbling. It is learning to work within your abilities and talents to do the best that you can do. Your kid isn't going to be the best at every-thing, but she will be the best at something—even if that something is being the best encourager on the sidelines.

Boys Will Be Boys

Although all kids are different, there is definitely a subgroup of boys that stands out among them all. You know who I mean. This group is made up of boys who are early walkers, love trucks and balls, and love to wrestle with other boys, run around, and let go of energy. They are the ones at the playground, tearing it up on all fours. Someone who has not had a boy of this subgroup in his or her home and is used to quiet, compliant children may think these "go-go-go" youngsters have something inherently wrong with them. They are often labeled as "wild" or "out of control" when they are just active kids, exploring their environment. Unless a go-getter boy is in physical danger of hurting himself or others, give him freedom to explore at his own pace (which will be, most likely, "fast forward").

I remember being at the playground when my charges were about two years old. I was never one to dote on their every little action. It was my philosophy to take the boys to a safe place so that they could explore in freedom without getting (seriously) hurt. Sure they were going to fall and get bumps and bruises, but that is part of growing up. As a nanny, I knew I was in the right job when my boss said one day, "Hey, we have twin boys. If we only go to the ER once a year, we will consider that a success." She may have been exaggerating some, but the truth is, you can only do so much to totally protect a child from minor scrapes and bruises without wrapping him in bubble wrap and only allowing him to play indoors surrounded by padded walls. (A side note for parents of twins: once a year in the ER wasn't much of an exaggeration!)

There are some wonderful advances in playground safety that all parents appreciate (not to mention the ER doctors). Most cities have cushioned, fenced-in playgrounds with child-safe equipment that provide a great outlet for energetic kids. Remember that just because we don't have the energy to keep up with these Tigger-like toddlers at times doesn't mean there is something wrong with them. I once heard that if a typical adult went through all the movements of a typical two-year-old on any given day, that adult would have to be in top Olympic athlete condition. I, for one, believe it!

So let your wild-and-woolly boys be active boys or your "go-get-'em" girls be energetic girls. It's the way God made them!

Removing Labels

Since I am a firm believer that children live up to the expectations you set for them, I believe that if you label a child at a young age, he or she will live up to that label and all that it means.

One famous and heartbreaking study was done with kids who were smart and well behaved. However, the teachers were told ahead of time to expect slow learners and poorly behaved kids to come into their classroom. Sure enough, those good, bright kids soon adapted to their teachers' low expectations. The reverse proved to be true as well. Teachers were told that they were going to have a class of especially talented, original, and bright children coming in. In reality, these were kids from previous "slow-learning classes" whose IQs were well below average. The children performed exceptionally well, as was the teachers' expectation.

If there is one cry of my heart to parents, it is this: *do not label your children*. Not unless that label is "unique and beloved," and then I give you permission to give this label to all of them, in equal doses.

You may not call your child a hurtful name, but labeling can be as simple as telling a child that she stinks at coloring, even in jest. All this does is lower the child's self-esteem while implying she is a failure. Not only will she lose confidence in any artistic ability that she has, but she will probably end up completely avoiding the activity. In fact, I know a man, now in his forties, who remembers the day his mother saw him delightfully painting a picture. He looked up at his mom and said, "I love this! I want to grow up to be a painter!" And she said, "Be sure to get another day job. Painters don't make any money, and you aren't that good at it." Something died inside him that day; he put down his paintbrush and never picked it up again.

Remember when I mentioned Kenny and Kevin? One loved cooking and one loved baseball at the ripe old ages of four and six. By labeling Kenny the "baseball player" and Kevin the "chef" at this young age, you are imposing limits on what they might try tomorrow and who they might become next year. Who's to say tomorrow their interests will be the same? Don't limit with labels.

Labels also affect behavior. If you tell your son he's a brat, he will eventually become—surprise, surprise!—a royal brat. Kids look to their parents for guidance. They also like to please. If you tell your child, "You are a brat," watch out! Your child will subconsciously think, *If I'm a brat, I'd better be a good one.* So goes the mind of a toddler.

There is another reason I really hate labels. They stick—especially when given by someone in authority. Once a child is labeled, that label goes with him wherever he goes unless you pull him totally out of the labeling environment. For example, if you have a preschooler who is labeled as "hyperactive," that label is going to follow her to kindergarten, oftentimes without having her professionally assessed or evaluated. (The teacher grapevine can be amazingly quick to transfer information—be it true or false.) The truth is, your child may be high energy, or she may be going through a high-energy phase. Before allowing someone to stick a label on your kid, make sure that you know the teacher's or psychologist's or doctor's training, experience, and expertise. Then seek a second opinion.

Another important point: I have heard so many parents worry about their child growing up to be defiant or rebellious, perhaps even ending up as a juvenile delinquent. Inevitably, when I ask how old their child is, they will say that he is two or perhaps three. (Threes are, in my opinion, much more challenging than twos.) And I laugh and say, "Nearly all two- and three-year-olds are defiant and rebellious at this stage. That's why child experts often call it 'the first adolescence.'"

Let your child progress. Many parents will tell you that their most defiant toddler turned out to be their most easygoing kid. It ain't over till it's over. And it ain't over until we reach heaven's gates. We, like our kids, are always growing, always evolving and learning, and, hopefully, becoming more and more "real"—like the Velveteen Rabbit. Wouldn't it be frustrating for you to give every effort to make a personal or life change, only to have your family members continue to label you as you once were? It would be like trying to run a race with a boulder tied to your shoe. But if your friends and loved ones were able to encourage your change and visualize you becoming better and better, it would be like running with wings on your shoes.

Labels are for things, not people.
—Michelle LaRowe

Give your kids the wings to fly and become the best they can be. However tempting, do not stick a label on them that might weigh them down the rest of their lives.

Therapy at Age Three?

Most pediatricians I've known don't even want to think about diagnosing a child with a learning or mental disability until the child is at least six years old. (Exceptions to this are covered below.) Often in young children symptoms that may mimic behaviors associated with these conditions are coming from something or somewhere else. Maybe a child is worried about climbing the ladder in baby gym class, and that is why he is extra clingy. Maybe his neighbor just gives him the creeps. So before you worry too much about your child having dysfunctional climbing problems or inordinate separation anxiety, you should relax. Then investigate the specifics surrounding the behavior and read up on what is normal for your child's age and stage.

It is generally believed that most learning takes place between birth and age five. These are the most developmentally important years of a life. I am not a doctor and do not claim to be, but again, I would urge any parents who have been told that their preschooler has something psychologically wrong to seek a second and possibly third opinion. Before giving any child a medication to help with behavioral problems, I'd really want to make sure there is a professional medical and psychological consensus.

Recently, we had an issue with one of my charges. He didn't like to go poop. During his annual physical, we mentioned it to the doctor, who was quick to label him "severely constipated" and prescribed medication for this condition. I was not a happy camper. When we got home, I sat down with my boss and said, "I guarantee he doesn't like to poop because he doesn't want to miss something, not because he is constipated. Let's increase his fiber and have him sit on the potty twice a day." She agreed to give me a week with my method before giving him the laxative. I took him grocery shopping, where he picked out his own high-fiber foods (a bonus to give him some control), and ta-da! Every day (or at least every other day), he's going—and he is proud! I'm also proud because we used our heads first rather than an unnecessary prescription. You know your kid best!

As always, exceptions do exist; and in some cases, prescribed medications are a lifesaver for all concerned. Still, I urge you to discuss any concerns you have about your child with a trusted doctor, preferably a specialist in the field of concern. There are more and more alternatives to problems with ADD and hyperactivity (two of the most commonly diagnosed brain disorders in children) that are nonmedical routes, including some good success with biofeedback and self-soothing techniques. Perhaps these might work for your family. Whatever the case, it is my belief that until that golden age of six, you cannot accurately distinguish if outward expressions of inner feelings are coming from an environmental root or a psychological root—or if it is simply the age and stage. In the end, you know your child best. Never forget that.

Today, especially in some wealthy sections of the country, taking your child to therapy has almost become a new rite of passage. Some parents talk of "waiting for the right age" to send their kids to therapy in the same way they discuss what age they should send their child to preschool or get their child on a sports team.

This isn't to knock the need for good therapy when a child has been traumatized or shows signs of significantly troubling behavior. However, if you are an empathetic parent who is willing to listen to, encourage, and love your child through the bumps and bruises of life, that is really all most kids need to grow up as secure, happy, functioning adults. You are probably your child's best therapist. I once read a book by a professional adult therapist who said that he would probably be out of a job if his clients simply had one empathetic friend who would really listen deeply to the pain in their heart, hold their hand, and walk with them through the pain and into the light of living again.

You know your child best. You are able to observe your child. I believe if you have read the beginning chapters and have learned to parent objectively and to be a kind, empathetic human being, you are your young child's best counselor.

I remember being called in to consult for a family with twins who were a little more than one year old. They were not verbal and were not eating solid foods. They were still on the pacifier and still only on bottles for the nutrients they needed. The first few days I was there, I must have seen four different specialists come into the home! There was the speech therapist, the occupational therapist, and the swallowing specialist. It was like a pit crew for babies.

One of the first things I did with the mom was to help her evaluate why each expert was there. Having heard her out, the next thing I did was ask her to let them all go. I deeply believed this particular mom was feeling so inadequate, so stripped of confidence in her ability to parent, that she called in the troops in sheer desperation.

So I encouraged her and taught her how to parent effectively and objectively. I helped empower her to step into the role of mom with confidence and to believe in herself. I taught her how to have mealtimes that were not pressured or focused on each bite of food swallowed. I taught her how to wean the babies off the bottle gradually. I taught her that it is OK for kids to cry, that it was not her failure—it is what babies do sometimes! I taught her how to approach mothering in an unstressed manner, and guess what? Things improved! Sometimes the truly simple answers, the most obvious ones, really are the most profound.

When I left this family, she felt like she was a better mom, and the kids were eating fine and gaining weight. I still visit this family, and it pleases me to say the kids are growing up happy and healthy. This family is going to be OK—and they are now OK with being OK.

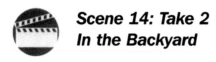

Scene 14: Take 2
In the Backyard

SUSAN. Michelle, do you think there is something wrong with Jack?

MICHELLE. No, Sue. Why?

SUSAN. Because he is so wild! Is this normal?

MICHELLE. Sue, come on now. They are behaving like boys enjoying the nice weather. I wish you could stop comparing Jack to the other kids and appreciate him for who he is, not how he compares to others.

SUSAN. I never thought of it that way.

MICHELLE. Kids are individuals. Love them for who they are, not who you wish they'd be.

Nanny to the Rescue!
Recap

What Nanny Tips can you use to stop the comparison game?

1. *Stop comparing your child to others.* Realize your child is a unique individual, and love him for who he is.

2. *Never label a child.* Children will live up to a label that you give them.

3. *Therapy isn't a milestone.* Use caution when seeking out specialists for your child, and make sure you aren't doing it because it is just "in vogue" to do so. More often than not, you can read a bit about your child's problems and comfort him by listening, holding his hands, and even praying together.

4. *You know your kid best.* Never underestimate the power of a mother's instinct.

5. *It's OK to be OK!* Perfection is not required—not for you, not for your child. Don't look for something to be wrong with your child. Like anything else, if you look hard enough, you will find it. Practice noticing what is right instead, and enjoy that!

CHAPTER FIFTEEN

TEACHING CHILDREN TO SHARE

 Scene 15: Take 1
On a Play Date with Friends at the Park

(Two-year-old Katie is playing in the sand pit with two-year-old Max.)

KATIE. That's mine! Give it back!

KATIE'S MOM. Yes, honey, it is yours. Take it back; it's OK.

MAX'S MOM. Katie has three buckets; can't she let Max use one?

KATIE'S MOM. No. They are hers, and she is playing with them.

MAX'S MOM, *as kids are screaming and pulling on the bucket.* But she isn't playing with all three!

KATIE'S MOM. Well, you should have brought your own. They are Katie's, and she doesn't have to share if she doesn't want to.

MAX'S MOM, *picking up Max.* It's OK, honey. I'll bring your sand buckets next time. Let's go swing.

f you haven't already encountered a scene like the one above, you may. When it comes to their kids, parents' tempers really can escalate as protectiveness, rather than rationality, takes over.

Isn't it odd that our human nature really does think in a scarcity or hoarding mode unless we are trained in generosity and abundance thinking? One has to wonder how many wars have been started by middle-aged land-hungry adults acting like stingy toddlers in a nursery! Since sharing is an important life lesson, it is best to teach kids how to share from a young age. But you have your work cut out for you!

Realistically, kids cannot grasp the concept of sharing until about age three. However, you can begin to nudge them out of their grasping mode and teach the principle of sharing so that when they reach the right age, they will more easily be able to master the concept on their own. This is just another example of how following a pattern (just because Mom or Dad says so) will eventually lead to an ability to show real empathy from the heart.

Modeling Sharing

From birth, children learn to mimic. Have you ever stuck out your tongue at a four-month-old baby? What happens next? She copies you and sticks out her tongue at you. Before you know it, you and baby are competing in a full-fledged sticking-your-tongue-out tournament. Babies observe, and then they model what they observe.

This principle can be applied to sharing. Here is an everyday situation that you can turn into a modeling experience.

"Mommy, I want some," your child says.

"How do we ask?" you reply.

"Mommy, can I please have some of your water?"

"Sure, honey. That was nice asking. Here is a sip. Isn't it nice when Mommy shares with you?"

"Yes!"

You can also model sharing with young toddlers by helping them to share. When a sharing situation arises, you can talk a child through it while physically helping her to share an item.

"Give me that," Sammie says to his sister.

"Honey," Dad interrupts, "how do we ask?"

"Kay, please give me truck."

"No!" Kay responds. "It's mine!"

Dad gets down on one knee and meets little Kay eye to eye. "Kay, you have been playing with the truck for some time now. Can Sammie have a short turn?" (Dad then helps by taking her hands gently in his and guiding the toy toward Sammie.) "Don't you like when Daddy shares his ice cream with you?"

"Yes."

"Good! Then let's share with Sammie. And then in a little while, he can share something with you. Deal? Can you pass this over to him all by yourself?"

(She passes the toy.)

"Great sharing, Kay." (Dad turns to Sammie.) "Sammie, can you say thank you?"

"Thank you."

This whole affair is now followed by lots of praise, perhaps even some clapping of approval.

Each opportunity for sharing that you encounter should be used as a teachable moment. When you see other people sharing, point it out and praise their behavior. For example, when you are at the playground and one child shares his shovel with another, praise that child in front of yours. When your spouse gives you a sip of his coffee, point it out. "Thanks, dear, for sharing your coffee. That was kind and courteous." Let your child see you share with others and others with you, and talk about it. "Watch how your brother is sharing a piece of his notebook paper with Mommy. Thank you!" If you are constantly encouraging children to share graciously, that will come to be their default behavior.

Nothing brings out a toddler's devotion to a toy she has abandoned more quickly than another child playing with it.
—Robert Scotellaro

First Forms of Playing

Young children's first form of playing is parallel play. This is when they play next to each other, doing similar activities, but do not really interact. In these situations, it is nice to have a variety of similar toys so that their first experiences with other children are positive and nonthreatening. Who likes feeling as though someone is invading their turf? So before your young one has a play date, you might consider putting away all but duplicate toys—no sharing required! Babies and young toddlers still believe the world revolves around them, that they are the center of the universe. They want what they want, and they want it now! It takes time to develop the skills to share, but modeling sharing is a great foundation to start from.

At about three years old, children understand and try to work out on their own who will play with what and when. They are learning sharing skills, but they still need close supervision and occasional help. By age four, children should be able to cooperate and share toys with other children with ease.

You can encourage sharing skills by providing lots of practice opportunities for your children. Some people believe that too many kids on a play date can be overwhelming. In my experience with twins, the more the merrier! You have more opportunities to practice sharing and working on social skills. You are exposing children to others with different personalities, which allows them to learn to work things out with all types of people.

At the boys' house, we created a space called "the pit." This was an area with a padded floor, surrounded by the plastic play yard with toys attached. We had to connect two play yards together because we would have five kids over at a time! My charges are still friends with their first friends, another set of twins and a little girl. These kids got together in their first months of life, almost daily. They would play in the pit, lying on their backs looking at mobiles at first. Then they moved on to crawling on top of each other with glee, as we watched them carefully, making sure no one was getting hurt. Then they advanced to pulling themselves up on the sides of the play yard and learning to walk around. Next, they progressed to parallel playing, and finally to playing together. It was a joy to watch them grow and develop sharing skills, social skills, and compassion from a young age. Learning compassion for others goes hand in hand with learning to share.

Taking Turns

In the toddler world, it helps to refer to sharing as "taking turns." Young children often understand tangible concepts rather than abstract ones. When you use the phrase "taking turns," you are teaching your child that sharing is not permanent, often breaking the natural misconception that causes them to be upset. They are thinking, *This is mine! Why do I have to give it away?* They don't yet understand the concept of time . . . or the difference between temporary and permanent.

One way you can help children understand that taking turns is a time-sensitive process is to use a timer. "When the timer goes off, guess what? Your turn is over. When the timer goes off again, your friend's turn is over and you get the next turn! Isn't that a fun way to share and play?" Egg timers, microwave timers, and even cell phone alarms serve as great devices for keeping track of whose turn is whose.

Taking turns should be approached with a positive attitude. "Doesn't it feel nice when Sharon shares her toys with you? Wouldn't it be great to make her feel good by sharing with her?" Emphasize the win-win in sharing. Everybody is happy (at least, eventually!).

What's Mine Is Mine

Although it's important to teach kids to share, all kids should have some special treasures that they should not be expected to share. Maybe it's a favorite doll, a cherished truck, or a beloved stuffed animal. For older toddlers, these can also be the toys that they have the most trouble sharing with others. These toys should be set apart as "off-limits for sharing." Providing children with a few things that are "only theirs" teaches them that they do have choices over what they want to share, but that sharing is still an important part of life.

These special treasures should not be allowed to "attend" play dates or be around other children. You can also ask an older child, "Honey, which toys would you like to share with your friends when they come over today?" Then put out only what she wishes to share, and put the other toys away for the duration of the play date. Not only does this eliminate potential conflict, but it allows your child to have something reassuring and fun to return to after a day of sharing, something that is uniquely hers.

Think of some things that you love that are yours alone to use: a favorite journal, a pretty pen, a sentimental mug. You are happy to share most of the items in your life, but it is comforting to have a few things of your own that you can return to for personal satisfaction and comfort. The same is true for children of all ages. Wise parents understand this, even as they encourage their children to be generous with most of their worldly possessions.

When Other Kids Won't Share

It can be quite frustrating when you are working hard at teaching your child solid life principles ("Let's share our toys!") only to have your child experience the short end of the stick. What should you do if your child is sharing with another, but the other child won't share back?

Acknowledge and validate the feelings of both children. "Kate is sad because she doesn't want to part with her toy. You remember how that felt when you were learn-

Nanny Tips

Here are some wonderful ways to teach your child to have a generous and compassionate spirit:

1. Make cookies and take them to a new neighbor or a sick friend together.
2. Encourage them to color pictures for friends and family, and make sure to give them (or mail them) to the intended party.
3. Teach empathy by speaking kindly and gently to people and animals, especially the young, helpless, or injured. Ask your child things like, "What could we do for Aunt Eliza to cheer her up? Can you think of something we could give her or share with her?" Maybe your child will offer to lend or give a favorite stuffed animal to an ailing relative. Give it to Aunt Eliza with a big bow and explanation. She'll be touched by this beautiful gesture from a child, and it will do all hearts good!

ing to share?" Addressing the behavior, rather than the child, is always good practice. "I know you are sad that Kate won't share. It doesn't feel nice to not have a turn." Again, you are addressing the feelings, not the child. You are allowing your child to be sad and to learn to deal with these feelings. Not always getting what you want is a part of life.

It is more blessed to give than to receive.
—Acts 20:35

This is a good opportunity to teach your child how to handle momentary personal defeats. You can remind her that just because another child doesn't want to share, your child should still share. Why? You are teaching her, in essence, that it is as much a joy to give as it is to receive. Cultivating a giving spirit in the right way can empower your child. When you are alone later, say things like, "Isn't it happier to share and give? Aren't we sad for people who won't share and don't know how fun it is to make another person happy?"

Sharing after Age Three

Once a child is mature enough to understand the concept of taking turns and you have established which toys are "sharing toys" and which ones are "special treasures" (not for sharing), you can continue to enforce the principle of sharing by imposing consequences for not sharing. If two children are fighting over the same toy, put the toy in time-out. (It's interesting to watch their faces as you march the toy to the time-out chair.) If your child has a sharing toy out for others to play with and refuses to share it, and you've given him two warnings, the child can be put in time-out.

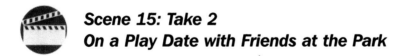

Scene 15: Take 2
On a Play Date with Friends at the Park

(Two-year-old Katie is playing with two-year-old Max in the sand pit.)
KATIE. That's mine! Give it back!
KATIE'S MOM. Honey, if you bring toys to the playground, you have to share
      with everyone. Can you share one with Max? *(She goes over and helps*
      Katie give a bucket to Max.)

MAX'S MOM. Hard lessons to learn, but worth it, huh?

KATIE'S MOM. Yep. It's easier to teach them now than later. She knows that she has special toys she doesn't have to share, but they stay home. If she brings toys on outings, they are for sharing with everyone.

MAX'S MOM. Max, can you say thank you to Katie for sharing her bucket? Remember we don't grab toys; we need to ask nicely first.

MAX. Thank you, Katie.

(Max gives Katie a hug. The moms express how proud they are of the kids' good manners.)

 ## *Nanny to the Rescue! Recap*

What Nanny Tips did these moms use to turn the sandbox struggle into the sandbox snuggle?

1. *Teach children to share from a young age.* Model the behavior that you want your child to mimic. The power of observation is one of life's primary teachers!

2. *Only allow children to bring toys if they are prepared to share them.* Set this clear limit from the beginning. If you bring it, you share it.

3. *Allow them special, nonsharing toys.* Call them "special treasures." Allow them to have special treasures that are only theirs.

4. *Teach them how to ask and receive graciously.* Teach them to ask nicely and to appreciate sharing by using good manners. When they do so, say, "Wow! What nice manners you are using!"

5. *Help them complete the task.* Give them the words and actions to use so that they can learn to share. Help them verbalize their thoughts and express their actions.

6. *Praise good sharing.* Remember: positive, purposeful praise. Praise the specific behavior. "I love how you shared your baby doll with Karen so nicely!"

CHAPTER SIXTEEN

CHORES AND MORE!

 **Scene 16: Take 1
The Playroom**

MOM. Jamie, don't throw that!

(Jamie picks up his toy truck and again throws it across the floor, adding to the heap of toys on the floor.)

MOM. Jamie! Put that away. No more toys!

JAMIE, *crying.* I want to play!

MOM. Help me pick up now!

(Jamie keeps on playing.)

MOM. Come on, help me. You made this mess, not me!

(Jamie continues to ignore Mom and keeps playing.)

MOM. All right, then, don't help me, but all your toys are going in the trash.

(Jamie cries hysterically.)

s that how your playroom cleanup time goes? If so, read on! Have you ever seen a toddler pick up his toys? It's a beautiful thing. If you want your child to be responsible and organized, it can be done! How? By teaching him from the get-go. When you teach a child something from the beginning, it becomes habit.

I remember growing up in a house that was always clean. Our house was definitely lived in, but it was clutter free. Growing up, a clean house was all I knew; because of that, I also maintained a clean and clutter-free home once I was on my own. My mom never told me, "Clean your room, Michelle!" It was just something that came naturally to me because it was the environment I was used to. It was the environment in which I felt things were safe, cheerful, and comforting.

Maybe some of you grew up in a messy and cluttered home environment. Perhaps now you are the type who knows exactly where everything is in a pile the size of Mount Everest. Cluttered chaos works for some, but I believe (and most studies show) that people, in general, tend to feel more productive and relaxed when their environment is structured and organized. Think of it as self-nurturing: you deserve a neat and organized environment, and that is a way of caring for yourself. Lots of the "messies" I know and love are really, at some level, rebelling against overly organized and critical parents. There's a middle ground, and you want to make sure you aren't punishing yourself in your rebellion against organization. Try thinking of organization as a treat you give yourself instead of an order to be fulfilled!

Organize Your Environment

Even before your baby is mobile, you can set the stage for an organized lifestyle. You can make his surroundings peaceful and his play area clutter free with room for exploration. We all know that environment affects mood. A peaceful, calm environment yields a peaceful, calm attitude. Are you stressed out when relaxing on the massage table at the spa? No! Why? The environment is tranquil, and it tends to produce a peaceful, relaxing attitude. A cluttered, chaotic environment yields an unfocused, frantic attitude. Remember the streets of Fenway Park when the Red Sox won the 2004 World Series? Sure, there's a time for a bit of controlled chaos, but you don't want to live that way for a very long time.

What can you do to make your baby's environment serene? You can use soft or neutral colors in his or her room to enhance relaxation. Use gentle lighting, such as a dim lamp that turns on with a touch. Use a CD player to set a relaxed mood by playing soothing music. There are even aromas that promote restful feelings. Potpourri isn't just for the rest of the home; use some calming fragrances in the nursery too. Keep the baby's area welcoming by limiting extra clutter. Decorate the walls with peaceful scenes and a soft carpet or area rug. These touches make it a place where your baby wants to be.

As your kids get older, you can also set up play areas in your home so that their toys have a specific place and purpose. A reading nook can be created with beanbag chairs and milk crates for their books. Open boxes and bins on the floor or on shelves are the easiest way to store things so that little ones can help with a quick cleanup.

You Play; You Put Away

Once your toddler has toys to play with, it is a good idea to establish how you want your child to care for his possessions. If you don't care if toys are thrown on the floor in the corner, then don't sweat it. But if you are a "cleanie" (rather than a "messie"), you need to have a place for everything and everything in its place. As soon as the boys

Nanny Tips

• You can create and organize almost anything by using tiered rolling units or plastic see-through storage containers.

• Use an old wooden hat hanger on the wall to hang costumes or jackets.

• Cleaned coffee canisters are great for storing crayons (even the oversized toddler ones fit well), and empty egg cartons work well for storing large beads and lacing.

• Even the most organized homes have a junk drawer. I have always had one bin labeled "Miscellaneous." This is where all the junk toys (the toys from McDonald's, cereal boxes, or the dentist treasure chest) go. That bin gets emptied pretty regularly and freshly stocked with other items that are waiting to be recycled.

were old enough to have their first baby toys, we set up a toy box where all the toys would go. Safety First and One Step Ahead make great plastic toy boxes that have lids that will not slam down or completely close.

As soon as the babies began having belly time on the floor with their toys, I would sing the "Clean Up" song as they watched me pick up their toys and put them in their box. You can pick any easy nursery tune and make up words to go with it for activities during the day. As I mentioned before, early childhood teachers use "transitional songs" all day long in preschool to help kids move from one activity to the next. You can make up a "Sweeping the Floor" song, a "Time to Get Dressed" song—a whole repertoire of ditties to do the chores by. As the boys became more mobile, they would mimic me. All I had to do was start singing, "Clean up, clean up, it's time for us to clean up," and the boys would automatically start picking up and putting away toys, thinking this, too, was a fun game!

As they got older, around age two, we had a bin system in place. Each bin had a label and a picture of what it stored. We had a truck bin, a ball bin, an animal bin, and so forth. Again, they would watch me match up their toys with their bins while singing the "Clean Up" song, and they would follow suit and have fun doing it.

I can honestly say that it is only on the rarest of occasions that I have picked up toys in the playroom after the kids turned three years old. They grew up around my philosophy "You play; you put away." So cleaning up their toys after playtime came as second nature to them. They grew up in a clutter-free, structured environment, and thus far, they both seem to have caught the "cleanie" bug. I am sure their future wives will thank me!

Assign Responsibility

The "You play; you put away" philosophy leaves no questions for who is responsible. When Austin plays with something, he puts it away—or at least contributes to the cleanup time when there is more than one child playing. Setting clear expectations for how toys, clothes, shoes, and so on will be cared for eliminates the "I didn't know I had to" mentality. Having a structured system also eliminates the "I didn't know where it went" whining as well.

Make sure your organizational requirements are age appropriate. For example, you cannot expect a two-year-old to neatly line his cars up in a box or on a shelf, but you can expect him to put his cars in a pile in a plastic, see-through tub designated as the car box (with a picture of a car on the box). As the children get older, you can expect more from them in this department. Remember, they will live up to the expectations that you set.

With older preschoolers, you can also assign responsibility to areas of the home or to specific tasks or chores. They need to feel they are a part of helping to make the family home run smoothly. Putting clothes in the hamper (or even in a pile in a designated corner of the room) is a great starting place. Having them make their bed each morning is also a great way to instill a responsible routine in young kids. I've found that a lightweight comforter is easiest for little ones to handle when making beds, and of course, it's not going to look perfect. Reward their effort with praise.

These early years are great for letting kids help, because children have a natural desire to contribute like big people to daily activities. By letting a young child help, you make her feel needed and let her know she belongs. Assigning age-appropriate tasks and responsibilities gives her a sense of satisfaction and reassurance in a job well done.

Taking care of your things and picking up after yourself is just part of life. It is the reality of our world. Just as you are responsible for your own actions, you are responsible for your own messes and possessions.

How can you turn something generally perceived as a negative into a positive? You approach chores as you would anything else: by being upbeat and matter-of-fact. You teach your children, "We take care of our things because that's what we do." And then, when they take care of daily tasks, follow up by asking your children, "Now doesn't that make you feel good about yourself?" This is a great way to affirm your children.

If you wonder where your child left his roller skates, try walking around the house in the dark.
—Leopold Fechtner

The older we get, the more things we have to take care of. The older we get, the more we can contribute to the family. These are not negative things. These are positive principles that will prepare your child for real life, where being a responsible person is valued.

Purposeful Praise

Most people would rather receive one specific phrase of praise than three general ones. Which would you rather hear: "You look nice today" or "Wow, that color looks great on you. It really lights up your face!"?

The same school of thought applies to children. Praise often, but praise purposefully. This is a great encourager to a child. But there also comes a point when you can lighten up on praise for certain tasks. For example, after a few months of a child successfully putting his cars in the bin, you don't have to go over the top with praise. Why? Because putting the toys in the bin is now becoming what is expected of the child, and you want this to become a routine, not a performance deserving special adulation. Sure, you can affirm your child on occasion for completing a daily task, just to let him know that you continue to notice and appreciate his efforts. But as a general rule, there's no more need for applause for putting away toys. It should become part of his routine of life, like eating, brushing his teeth, and bathing.

In real life, adults don't always get rewarded for doing daily chores, nor do we expect to be. However, it is a lovely thing to occasionally have a family member say, "Thank you for washing the clothes. They always smell so fresh, and I really appreciate it." So continue to praise your children randomly but in moderation. This way the thanks will continue to be meaningful but not something to which your children feel entitled.

You Break It; It's Gone

This is another law of natural consequences. Too often I have witnessed a child throw his favorite toy across the room and break it, then the parent runs off to buy a replacement. What does that teach a child? It teaches him that things have no value. It also teaches him that things are readily replaceable, regardless of how they are treated. It sends the message that possessions can be destroyed and automatically replaced.

We can find a new book to replace the one that has been torn apart or a new teddy bear to replace the one that lost his arm because a child swung it around in the wrong way. But just because we *can* readily replace these items doesn't mean that we always *ought* to. If you teach the value of the little things, you are preparing kids to learn to value the big things: people, pets, and—when they are older—your car!

Young children have no concept of money or how material things are acquired. To them, it's magic: new toys just appear. Don't we wish that were reality! When a toddler begins to throw his toys, we can teach him, "Toys aren't for throwing." We can remove the toy from the area. We can also redirect his attention to something else. To immediately give back a misused toy would teach your child that treating things inappropriately has no consequences. That's not a message you want to send.

When a preschooler begins to mistreat his possessions, consequences can be imposed. It is important to teach value and respect of possessions. If a child does not learn to value and care for family possessions, what attitude will he develop about the value of other things? How will he treat a borrowed library book? How will he learn to respect other people's property? Or books and equipment belonging to the school he attends? "You break it; it's gone" is a powerful lesson for older kids too.

You can teach a child there is only one way to replace a toy that has been broken or lost because of neglect or misuse—that is, to earn a replacement. This result mimics real life; we can replace something we've broken or lost only by earning money to replace it. Depending on the age of your child, you may want to let him do small chores to earn quarters in a jar, and when he has enough quarters, he can buy a new book, teddy bear, or whatever he wants to replace.

Far better, and kinder, is to teach your child to learn this lesson in a loving, secure environment at a young age rather than in the real world where people often don't value their own things, much less value the hurt feelings of others.

A friend of mine told me her hairdresser had a teenage son who was caught destroying some property belonging to a neighbor in an act of irresponsible mischief. The hairdresser's son also had a friend, an accomplice. The hairdresser insisted her son apologize for his thoughtless behavior and then get up early and work for the neighbor for two weeks to replace the property and atone for what he had done. The hairdresser continued, "Sadly, the other boy's parents required nothing of that kid to pay back what he'd destroyed. My son learned a hard lesson and never got in serious trouble again; the other boy is now in jail, having moved on to other crimes."

This story reinforces the importance of teaching our children to respect the possessions we have and share in a family. It begins here, at home. If this lesson is caught, our children will be respectful and responsible with possessions belonging to others.

In addition, when children learn to contribute to the family by doing small chores and daily routine tasks, they develop habits that will lead to responsible, thoughtful, and productive lives.

Scene 16: Take 2
In the Playroom

MOM. Jamie, trucks are not for throwing. Two minutes till cleanup.

(Jamie picks up his toy truck and again throws it across the floor, adding to the heaping pile of toys.)

MOM, *getting down on Jamie's level to make eye contact.* Jamie, it is time to clean up now. Put the truck in the truck bin, please. Trucks are for driving, not for throwing.

JAMIE, *crying.* I want to play!

MOM. I know that you want to play, but playtime is done. When you play, you put away. Can you help me sing the "Clean Up" song?

(Jamie looks at his mom with a pout on his face.)

MOM. Here we go: "Clean up, clean up . . ." *(She begins picking up the toys to the tune of the song.)*

(Jamie follows along, joins in the song, and starts picking up toys with his mom.)

MOM. Great work helping to clean up. I like when you take care of your toys.

(Jamie smiles, the room gets cleaned, and he and Mom go on to the next activity with a minimum of fuss.)

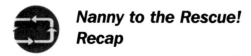

Nanny to the Rescue!
Recap

How did this mom make cleanup time go from crazy to cool?

1. *Set clear expectations.* You play; you put away.

2. *Give a warning before playtime is over.* "Two minutes left."

3. *Have an organized storage system.* "Trucks go in the truck bin."

4. *Stay positive.* "Cleaning up is what we do, so let's do it happily." A fun song is one way to enforce this.

5. *Model the behavior you want.* When you lead, your child is sure to follow.

6. *Don't assign blame; assign responsibility.* "You play; you put away" teaches responsibility but doesn't shame the child. "You made this mess; now clean it up" can discourage creative play and may send the message that her play was unacceptable and there's something wrong with messes. Messes are a part of creative play, but we do have to clean them up!

CHAPTER SEVENTEEN

SIBLING RIVALRY OR REVELRY?

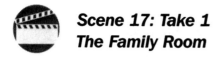 **Scene 17: Take 1**
The Family Room

CARA. Stop it! I had it first!

MILLIE, *pushing Cara.* No! It's mine! Give me!

CARA, *pushing Millie to the floor and grabbing the doll.* My doll!

(Mom enters the family room from the bathroom.)

MILLIE, *crying to Mom.* Cara pushed me.

CARA, *crying to Mom.* She pushed me first!

MOM. Who started it? Tell me this minute. You girls are being bad!

MILLIE AND CARA. She did!

MOM. You always seem to be picking a fight, Cara. Go to your room!

CARA. You always take her side!

U ntil you're on child number two, you may not understand that *siblings* and *rivalry* are practically synonyms. If they are not synonyms, they definitely have a cause-and-effect relationship.

How do you survive sibling rivalry? You have to switch roles. Remember the parenting team? Well, your team has secured a promotion and has been fast-tracked to "referees." Fortunately, you're still a team. Dad may be the home plate ump, and Mom may act as the field ump, the two of them working together to referee the family game, but new dynamics definitely come into play as new children are born. Welcome to the world of having more than one kid!

"Mom Always Liked You Best!"

Sibling rivalry is an inevitable part of family life with more than one child. There was a TV show in the 1960s called *The Smothers Brothers*, where the shtick centered around Tom and Dick Smothers' brotherly jealousy. "Mom always liked you best" became a famous phrase of the era.

The Smothers brothers' onstage rivalry was exaggerated for comedic effect, but you may be weary of the all-too-real sibling whines that are not always funny. It seems there is always somebody who feels left out, another who feels loved more, and someone else who thinks he is getting the short end of the attention stick and that life just isn't fair. The verbal intensity and complications of sibling competition take on different (and sometimes more intense) dimensions as the kids get older, but the race to rivalry often begins the moment a new baby arrives at the door of the (theretofore) only child's domain.

Each One Is Special

What ground rules can you set to help you minimize rivalry within the ranks? Most important, you really need to communicate from the start that your family unit is one team. Sure, everyone has different roles, but you are all on the same team.

Sibling rivalry is a package deal, starting from birth. It literally comes home with the new baby. One way to start the new sibling relationship out right is to prepare your child for being a big brother or sister before you come home with your new bundle of joy. Explain that being "the oldest" is a special and unique role that only he or she can fill. Encourage those who come to visit the new baby to bring a little something for the "new" big kid in the house. When friends and family come to visit, it's a great time for Mom and Dad to have extra cuddle time with the older child, while everyone else is doting on the newborn.

What role do siblings play on the family team? They are cheerleaders for each other. Their duty is to love and encourage each other, to stick up for one another, to respect and be loyal to each other, and to share and take turns with each other so that everyone gets a fair shake. In fact, you could give the older child a set of pompoms and teach her a little cheer to use when baby brother does something praiseworthy. Teach baby to clap when big sister turns a somersault or puts her cup in the dishwasher. Establish the spirit of being each other's number one fans as often and as creatively as you can.

As parents, you can do even more to foster this team mentality. You can spend quality time with each child individually so that he is secure in his personal value and thus more secure in the family unit. Whether it's going to the store, reading a book aloud, or taking a child out alone for a stroll, Mom and Dad must do things with each child so that he feels he is getting some individualized attention. Love, to a small child, is usually spelled T-I-M-E. Focused attention, when you are giving each child some eye contact and entering fully into his world, can do enormous amounts of good for his self-esteem and his ability to be less jealous when his sibling is getting attention. It reminds him that he is special and that he contributes something unique to the family team . . . and that you love him for that.

Just because two kids are siblings does not mean that they have to be joined at the hip. They should be taught to respect their sibling's privacy and not be expected to always play with each other. They should be allowed to have separate friends and not have to always incorporate their sibling into their play dates—although at times they will. It is important to encourage, acknowledge, and praise individuality. Convey to the child that it is great that he is different from his sister. It makes him special, and no one could ever take his place.

Just as a child needs to learn that the family doesn't revolve around his sibling, he must also learn the family doesn't revolve around him. He needs to understand that being part of a team also means sacrifice. Teammates will sacrifice for him, and he is expected at times to sacrifice for his teammates. If your child watches sports, you can use this idea of "teammates" as a way to help him grasp sibling roles, with a minimum of rivalry.

Although violence should never be permitted, sibling roughhousing is to be expected. Each family has its own limits on where the roughhousing line ends and fighting begins. Walk your line carefully. Younger children who don't yet have the verbal skills to communicate often physically lash out as a means of expression. This type of interaction is natural, and it will decrease as their verbal skills increase. But you still need to intervene and encourage your children to use words instead of hitting. Boys, especially, tend to love wrestling, and to some extent this is OK. But you need to establish a family rule: when one sibling stops having fun or says, "Stop!" the roughhousing is over, no matter how playfully it may have begun.

> *If you don't understand how a woman could both love her sister dearly and want to wring her neck at the same time, then you were probably an only child.*
> —Linda Sunshine

Age Has Its Privileges

Discipline must be age appropriate for your children. Each child must abide by the same rules, but the expectations have to be individualized based on each child's age. Your four-year-old knows, by now, that hitting is not OK. So if she hits, she will be sent directly to time-out. Your eighteen-month-old is just learning. She may get a warning first. When your children break the rules, consequences follow. But your two-year-old will get a two-minute time-out, and your five-year-old will get a five-minute time-out. The five-year-old may squeal, "Unfair!"—so be prepared to say, "You are older, and that means that you have bigger privileges sometimes. But it also means that your time-outs are longer because you understand better than your little sister when you are doing something wrong."

Make sure your older child also gets to stay up a few minutes later than the younger child, if he wants. Or find some other small privilege for the eldest to help even things out when it seems the little ones get all the breaks!

Dealing with children in different age groups is exhausting. You need lots of love and lots of patience. It takes effort to continuously explain to younger siblings why life just isn't fair. As a child's big brother gets more and more freedom, goes to school, or gets invited to fun outings, you'll have to reassure the youngest that her time is coming. When she gets older, she, too, will get more responsibility, more freedom, later bedtimes, larger cuts of food, or whatever else is causing her angst. I remember reading about a little girl, about age two, who watched as her dad walked out the front door with her big brother to go on a fishing trip. She said, "I want to go too!" The daddy got down on one knee and said, "Honey, you can go fishing with us when you get bigger," and then they walked toward the car. The little girl waited a couple of minutes, then put on her brother's cowboy boots and ran awkwardly out the door after the pair, announcing with gleeful assurance, "I'm bigger now!"

Bless her heart, there's not a younger sibling who doesn't remember the feeling of being left behind. But there's not an older sibling who hasn't felt the sting of being upstaged by a cuter, younger baby brother or sister. Life is not always fair, and you cannot create a totally pain-free world for your children. The greater gift is teaching them how to self-soothe and to overcome sorrow and find happiness again in the face of life's natural unevenness.

When a new baby arrives, the older child is usually curious about her new role as big sister. Perhaps you can go over some of the fun things that big sisters get to do (stay up ten minutes later, gently hold the new baby, make the new baby laugh and giggle, be Mommy's big helper, and so on). Usually she is going to attempt to model your parenting behavior. She will try to be a little mommy. Acknowledge the ideas she offers, and praise her for her attempts to help.

"He Started It!"

I've learned to rarely ask, "Who started it?" when I hear squabbling. As siblings get older, they should be encouraged to work things out on their own. Unless you hear bloodcurdling screams, try to let the kids work it out. Why? Because Mom and Dad can't see who started everything. When you hear, "She started it!" you have two choices: have the kids work it out on their own, or impose a penalty on both. A smart parent will always try to avoid what would appear to be taking sides. You can do this by encouraging siblings to try to work things out on their own and not assigning blame unless you know for a fact who did what.

Another important point when you are running interference between kids is this: *don't assume anything.* If you don't know, you don't know. It's better to play it safe than to make a blind call.

As soon as siblings can talk, they inherit another trait—the art of tattling. Whenever the kids are playing and I hear, "Shell, I have to tell you something!" my response is always, "OK, but first let me ask you, is this tattling?" If they say, as they usually do, that they don't know, I go on to ask, "Well, is someone going to get hurt? Does someone need my help? Have you used your words to try to work it out on your own? Is it something I need to know?" He can usually answer one of these questions with a no. When this happens, I tell him, "Thank you for your concern, but let me know when it is something that I really need to know and that I can help with." At school, when dealing with tattling, the teachers first determine whether the situation is *dangerous or destructive.* If it doesn't fall into one of those categories, they don't want to hear it, and neither should you!

I always encourage the boys to tell me anything, and I thank them for sharing with me. I let them know that I am there to listen, but I don't need or want to know every little thing. Also, I transfer confidence to them by saying, "I trust you two are capable and reasonable little human beings who can figure out how to solve most minor problems on your own. I'm here to help with the big stuff, but you guys can handle most disagreements yourselves."

If you happen to be in a more severe situation, and sibling rivalry has really taken over and is running out of control, check out the classic book *Siblings Without Rivalry* by Adele Faber and Elaine Mazlish.

If sisters were free to express how they really feel, parents would hear this: "Give me all the attention and all the toys, and send Rebecca to live with Grandma."

—Linda Sunshine

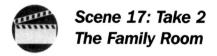

Scene 17: Take 2
The Family Room

CARA. Stop it! I had it first!

MILLIE, *pushing Cara.* No! It is mine! Give me!

CARA, *pushing Millie to the floor and grabbing the doll.* My doll!

(Mom enters the family room from the bathroom.)

MILLIE, *crying to Mom.* Cara pushed me.

CARA, *crying to Mom.* She pushed me first!

MOM. Girls, I don't know who started it, and I don't care. I'll give you two
minutes to work this out, and if you can't decide whose turn it is to
play with the doll, the doll can go to time-out.

CARA AND MILLIE. OK.

MILLIE. I'm sorry I pushed you. Can I have a turn when you are finished?

CARA. Yes.

MOM. Nice job solving this on your own. I am glad that you can share the doll.

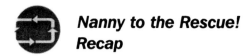

Nanny to the Rescue!
Recap

What Nanny Tips did this mom use to survive sibling rivalry?

1. *Address the behavior, not the child.* Kids are all good—their behavior sometimes
   stinks.

2. *Don't ask; don't care.* It doesn't matter who started the argument. What matters
   is that it is going on.

3. *Don't assume you know something that you don't.* Don't take sides!

4. *Encourage siblings to work things out on their own.* Tell them what you expect to happen: "You need to work this out and decide whose turn it is between the two of you."

5. *Offer a fair solution if they can't work things out.* If they can't work it out, the toy gets removed from the situation.

6. *Praise positive teamwork.* Tell your children, "Great job working together!"

CHAPTER EIGHTEEN

TAMING THE "ME MONSTER"

 **Scene 18: Take 1
Getting Ready for Swim Class at the YMCA**

JOHN. Hurry up and help me, Mommy! The door's going to open.

MOM. No need to rush; we still have a few minutes.

JOHN. Faster, Mommy! I want to be first!

MOM. Stop wiggling and get the suit on. Then we can go, and you can be first in line.

(Mom and John exit the changing area with the pool door in full view.)

JOHN. See? Now they are already there! I want to be first! *(He pushes his way through the kids and moms to be first in line.)*

MOM. Sorry, everyone. Johnny just has this "thing" about being first in line. Boys will be boys!

T he world doesn't revolve around you." I still occasionally hear that phrase directed my way by a close friend or (gulp!) even my mother. Why? Because our ego is part of our inner being, imbedded deep inside of us, and although we try to push it aside, it never completely goes away. It makes me think of those T-shirts that say, *Born with an Attitude*. Perhaps nannies and parents should band together to create one that says, *Born with an Attitude, but Raised to Be Compassionate*.

The goal is to teach your children balance. You don't want to squelch your little go-getter or your budding actress who sees the living room as her stage. We want to encourage our kids' self-esteem and sense of being special, while simultaneously teaching them to be aware of others' gifts and uniqueness—to be able to take the stage of life with confidence but be willing to graciously take a seat and applaud when it is others' time to shine. In other words, we want to give our kids self-esteem without creating the "me monster." We may chuckle at the caricature of a spoiled diva crowing, "It *is* all about me," but it isn't very funny when you've got a real-life, self-centered miniature drama queen on your hands.

As we learned in chapter 4, children are born with a natural sense of egocentricity, a sense of feeling that, like the sun, all planets (and parents) should revolve around them. Their first expressions of vocabulary revolve around "me, myself, and I." At first, of course, this is perfectly normal and natural. As children begin to grow and develop, however, their view should begin to expand. A slow realization should begin to set in that there is more to this world than "marvelous me." I have to believe that one of the reasons God gives us families is to teach us the basics of what it means to look to the needs of others as well as ourselves. From dealing with siblings to aging grandparents, crazy aunts, and colorful uncles, families are a perfect laboratory for adjusting to the variety of folks who populate this planet and learning the basics of respect.

Let's explore some practical ways that we can gently nudge kids out of complete egocentricity into a compassionate, honoring, balanced view of themselves and others.

> *An egocentric person walks into a room and says, "Here I am!" An empathetic person walks into a room and says, "There you are!"*
> —Becky Freeman Johnson

Teaching Respect

One of the paradoxes of life is that you must give respect to get it. Truly more is caught than taught when it comes to passing along the quality of respecting others. Children learn by example, so teaching them to respect you and other authorities begins with talking to your own kids kindly and calmly. You can also model thoughtful listening skills as they speak. The mom of a friend of mine used to say, "The world would be a better place if we treated our company a bit more like family, and our family a bit more like company." In other words, we should make company feel at home, and we should treat our family members with a little more practical courtesy and kindness.

Another great way to teach kids respect is to train them in using good manners with others. This is truly one of the most useful gifts you can impart to children. It will open doors for them and endear them to teachers and other adults and kids. Teach them to say please and thank you as part of their earliest vocabulary. Make use of natural teaching moments that come up in family life to reinforce politeness.

Handle Conflict Respectfully

If your preschooler blurts out, "You are stupid!" in a fit of frustration, fight the urge to yell back, "Don't you dare talk to Mommy that way!" Instead, try, "Amy, we do not use the word *stupid* in this house. It is a hurting word. If you ask me nicely to help you with your shoes, I'd be glad to help."

You also need to model for your children how to graciously handle arguments and disagreements. Conflict is a natural part of life, so equip your kids with the tools they need to handle upsets and differences of opinion and preferences. First, be sure to model how to disagree respectfully in your dealings with your mate and other adults. Next, be a living example of how to disagree with respect in dealing with your children. For example, your three-year-old might say, "I hate peas! They taste like green dirt balls." And you can say, "Hmm . . . that's an interesting way to put it. You know, you don't happen to like peas, and that is fine, but I love them, especially with mashed potatoes. I guess one person's 'yuck' is another person's 'yum'! Tell me your favorite veggies."

Think of Others First

It is vital to teach kids to express themselves respectfully by using kind words and, as soon as they are emotionally mature enough, to encourage them to put themselves in another person's shoes. This is another building block toward empathy, one of the most significant attributes of emotional intelligence. Before your child goes into a new experience—such as a nursery or preschool class—you can say, "Be sure to look for anyone who seems shy or lonely and ask them to play with you. That will make them feel so happy, because you are such a good friend to have." Do you see how this helps your child's self-esteem by teaching him or her to think of others' needs?

A great paradox of life is that our self-esteem often grows best as we actively think

---

 Nanny Tips

Here are eight great ideas to teach your kids good manners:

- *Model good manners to your children.* Say please and thank you to others in front of your kids. Learning by imitation is one of the greatest teaching instruments.
- *Make good manners part of your daily routine.* Encourage your children to practice politeness by holding the door for others, using their indoor voice when inside and outdoor voice when outside, and greeting other adults (act out "practice sessions") by looking them in the eye, shaking their hand, and smiling.
- *Point out when you see another child using good manners.* "Wow, wasn't that kind and courteous that he waited in line rather than shoving through?"
- *Teach your children telephone manners.* Use a toy phone to teach telephone manners, along with acceptable and unacceptable information to provide to callers.
- *Prompt children when they don't have the words or skills to perform.* "Oh, Aunt Sandy gave you a gift. What can we say?"

about the needs of others and dive in, shirt sleeves rolled up, to help them. In part, I think this must have been what Jesus meant when He said that in losing our life, we would find it (Matthew 10:39). In reaching out, we find our best selves. Anyone who watched the heroism and compassion of the rescue workers following the devastation of September 11, 2001, understands Christ's words. In helping others, these heroic men and women became the best versions of themselves. What a powerful lesson to begin to teach and model for our children at the earliest stages and ages of life!

Setting limits is another way to help your child learn respect for others. By being firm but kind in your discipline, you are clearly communicating that throwing fits just doesn't work. When Sam has a fit in the toy store, firmly but calmly ask him to

- *Write thank-you notes.* Since my charges began receiving holiday and birthday gifts, they have been required to write personalized thank-you notes. In their earliest years it was a handprint on a card, with a note written from me. Then it progressed to them drawing a picture and telling me what to write. Now they write their own personalized thank-you notes for each occasion, with little or no help (or nagging!).

- *Practice table manners at home.* Have special theme night dinners. Have BBQ night, where children can learn what foods are acceptable to eat by hand. Have a tea party to teach place setting and a formal dining experience. Teaching your children restaurant manners is a great way to teach lots of lessons at once: having patience while waiting, ordering from the menu, thanking the server, and staying seated until everyone has finished their meals. By age three, most children can grasp and understand what is and isn't acceptable at the dinner table.

- *Bring back the golden rule!* Help your children memorize some simple version of this wonderful admonition from the New Testament: "Do to others what you would have them do to you" (Matthew 7:12).

stop. If he doesn't, remove him from the situation until he does. When he has pulled himself together, give it another try and praise him for calming down.

Here's a method that has worked for me in teaching my charges how to get a grip on their emotions so they can proceed to act with more respect. When they hear me say, "Pull yourself together," they know to stop what they are doing, fold their hands, close their eyes, and count to ten. A lot can change in a little time.

Another method I use when going into an unfamiliar environment, especially when they are excited, is to say, "Let's talk about what kind of acceptable behavior we are going to use today at Mrs. Miller's house." Let them chime in. This way, they are mentally prepared to be on their best behavior.

Reinforcing the use of respectful words and actions by positive, purposeful praise will help ensure that good manners continue. Catch your child doing things right! "That was so courteous when you held the door open for Mom. Thank you."

Break the Sense of Entitlement

When evaluating children's (and adults') behaviors and personalities, there are some traits I can deal with and some things that, in all honesty, I simply can't abide. The sense of entitlement fits into my "Can't stand it!" category. Entitlement is when people expect to get something—in fact, think they are *owed* special benefits and privileges.

How does a sense of entitlement develop? Some children have to fight this tendency more than others, so I think, in part, there are some inborn personality traits that lead to this general sense that "the world owes me." More often, however, I think it comes from a culture that promotes immediate gratification. For example, we go to the ATM machine, we stick in a plastic card, and the machine spits out a wad of cash. We live in a fast-cash, fast-food, fast-forward society. Instant gratification has become the norm.

The problem with this is that we don't appreciate material things as much, nor do we realize the process that goes into an end product. In times past, a child helped water and weed a garden, picked the carrots, helped wash them, and watched their mother can them. When a child ate a carrot, he appreciated the work involved in getting the food from the garden to his plate. It isn't any wonder that many kids today think carrots magically appear in tiny plastic bags with no appreciation for how they arrived in the grocery store.

In a similar way, children might not comprehend that someone went to the store and bought a gift, especially with the child in mind, with the money that he or she earned from working. A child just knows it is his birthday, and presents show up! This is where you come in. You can explain to your child, "Grandpa worked hard at his job, then he thought of how much he loved you, and with some of the money he made from working very hard, he went to the store and picked out a red fire truck just for you. Wasn't that thoughtful? Let's color Grandpa a picture of you playing with the truck and send it to him in the mail to tell him thank you for doing such a kind thing for you." Or perhaps you can plant a little vegetable patch together and allow your child to tend to it alongside you and experience the work and joy of watching food grow from a seed in the ground. Such appreciation for process is a precursor to respect!

A good way to teach the rewards of delayed gratification and to help your child tie together effort with produce is to assign your child tasks and reward him for completing them. For example, if a child wants a special toy, you can develop a plan for him to earn it. Let's say that Jared gets a great report from his preschool teacher. He can put a sticker on a "Good job, Jared!" chart. After Jared acquires perhaps twenty-five stickers, he has earned the toy. Or maybe he can earn a quarter to put in his special bank each night that he remembers to pick up his room and brush his teeth and take a bath without fussing. As Jared gets older, perhaps you give him an allowance that goes with his completing his weekly chores. Whatever way you choose to handle it, what is important is that the child feels that he earned some of his special privileges and toys rather than just expecting to be given toys on a silver platter.

> *The love of our neighbor in all its fullness simply means being able to say to him, "What are you going through?"*
> —Simone Weil

Teaching Generosity and Compassion

Generosity and compassion are gifts that keep on giving. How wonderful I feel when my charge sees a man in a wheelchair and says, "Shell, I am sad for that man because his legs do not work. I am going to hold the door for him." Wouldn't it be great if adults were as sensitive and nonjudgmental as children? Young kids (unless they've been tainted by the world) see differences, but they don't judge. They see a problem, and they try to help. If encouraged to do so, they can truly feel empathy for another's pain at an early age and begin thinking of ways they might help or comfort.

Working with twins, I have been able to observe a unique early development of empathy and compassion. Because twins relate to each other, they learn sooner than most siblings that someone else has needs that have to be met too. Thus, twins often tend to relate better to others at an earlier age. Whenever Fraser saw a child who was crying, he would run over and give the child a hug, because that is what he and his brother did to soothe one another.

How can you teach your children the values of being generous and compassionate? Be generous with what you have been given, whether it is a little or a lot. Maybe each time your child finds a penny on the floor, you could have a special jar for him to put it in and send it to a chosen charity. Compassion International has a wonderful program for sponsoring a less-fortunate child in another country.[1] Perhaps you can have your child give clothes and toys to a shelter. At Christmastime, make sure your child is a part of creating a bit of Christmas joy for other children. Samaritan's Purse has a wonderful way for families to pack shoeboxes with gifts and donate them to needy kids.[2] The Angel Tree project is another way your child can help another child during the holiday season.[3]

The habit of giving to others can begin at an early age and continue to thrive into adulthood. Not only do you want to pray that your child will grow up and be blessed, but you should remember to pray that he or she will be a *blessing to others* as well.

Good Sportsmanship

Sports is a great training ground for life, so use your child's involvement in team sports to teach them greater truths about working with others, accepting defeat with grace, and doing their best. Instead of asking, "Did you win?" when your kid walks in the door after a game you missed seeing, try some of the following questions:

- How did you play?
- Did you try your hardest?
- Did you play fair?
- Did you shake hands with the other team at the end of the game?
- Did you cheer on your team while you were benched?
- Did you pass the ball?
- Did you listen to your coach?
- Did you have fun?
- Did you respect the referee?
- Did you try not to gloat when you did win?

If you can get your child to a point where he can answer these questions affirmatively, you've taught him how to be a good sport. And that goes a long way in taming the "me monster"!

Fraser used to sing, "I'm winning, I'm winning, I'm winning, winning, winning!" when he was ahead in a board game. I had him stop singing this gloating little ditty because I felt it showed a lack of respect for others' feelings and efforts. I told him, "Fraser, we will have to stop playing this game if you can't stop bragging, because that is unkind. Take a few minutes to pull yourself together, and then we'll continue playing more nicely."

Also, I firmly believe that we shouldn't let children always win when we play a game with them. First of all, they figure out pretty quickly that you are letting them win, and their victory is less satisfying. Second, how do they learn to lose? Third, how do they learn to win graciously? Your kitchen table or living room floor and a board game can be a wonderful teaching lab for handling life well. In fact, the tone of general respect for others that you set in the home will go a long way toward nipping the sense of entitlement in the bud.

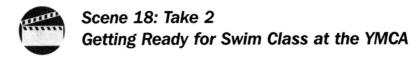

Scene 18: Take 2
Getting Ready for Swim Class at the YMCA

JOHN. Hurry up and help me, Mommy! The door's going to open.

MOM. That is no way to ask for help, Johnny. We don't need to rush; we still have a few minutes until class starts.

JOHN. But, Mommy, I want to be first!

MOM. Stop wiggling and get the suit on. Then you can join in line with the others.

(Mom and John exit the changing area with the pool door in full view.)

JOHN. See? Now they are already there! I want to be first! *(He pushes his way through the kids and moms to be first in line.)*

MOM. Excuse me, John. *(She gently guides him back to the end of the line.)* Other children have been waiting patiently for the door to open. It's not fair or polite for you to cut in line when others have been waiting. How would that make you feel?

JOHN. Sad. But I want to be first, Mommy!

MOM. I understand that you get excited about class and want to be the first one in the pool, but everyone is going to have their turn to get in. Someone needs to be first, someone needs to be in the middle, and someone needs to be last. Today it is your turn to be last. Now can you apologize to the others for pushing your way through?

JOHN, *to the kids.* I'm sorry.

MOM. For . . .

JOHN. For cutting in line.

MOM. That's much more polite! Good job, John.

Nanny to the Rescue! Recap

What Nanny Tips did this mom use to teach her child not to be the fool in line at the pool?

1. *Insist on respect.* Respect for others is critical.

2. *Don't stress the winning.* Stress the effort and the fun factor instead.

3. *Everyone needs a turn at being the "loser."* Someone has to win, and someone has to lose. If today is your turn to lose, do it graciously. Then you win at being a good sport!

4. *Validate your children's feelings.* Be ready to offer words to use to help your children express themselves when they can't do it on their own.

5. *It is not all about them.* Life doesn't always revolve around them. It's tough to accept but true in the real world. The younger your child learns this lesson, the better.

6. *Teach them defeat is only momentary.* There is always next time.

7. *You always have another chance to win.* Don't give up!

SECTION THREE

EMBRACING THE JOYS OF PARENTING

CHAPTER Nineteen

BIG QUESTIONS FROM LITTLE MOUTHS

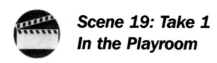 ### Scene 19: Take 1
In the Playroom

STACIE. Where do babies come from?

DAD. From mommies.

STACIE. How do mommies get them?

DAD. They get them when they get married.

STACIE. Does someone give them to mommies?

DAD. No, honey, babies grow in a mommy's belly.

STACIE. How do they get in bellies? Do mommies eat them?

DAD, *tired of the questioning.* Just ask your mom later, OK?

When kids ask questions, they want the answers . . . now. That puts you in a tough place. Your child expects you to have the answer in your pocket to virtually any question.

"How do clouds get made?"

"How many stars can you fit in the ocean?"

Or one of my personal favorite kid questions, shared by a friend of mine: "Does God have hair in His nose?"

One has to marvel at a child's capacity for curiosity and wonder at the world and beyond. I'm tickled at how parents are so eager to teach their babies to talk, but about the time that precious child is two or three—chatting about everything and firing questions with machine-gun speed while you are trying to cook dinner—parents (and nannies) sometimes wish there were a temporary Off switch to our child's voice box. Add to this the fact that many of the child's questions are indeed very good ones, questions that you need to think about before answering. These situations can be difficult, especially if you don't know what the answer is or if you don't know how to communicate it in a way that is appropriate to your child's ability to grasp.

There's a time when you have to explain to your children why they're born, and it's a marvelous thing if you know the reason by then.

—Hazel Scott

So what do you do? You can carry around a magic eightball in your pocket, ready to shake it up when the tough questions are asked. Or you can begin to strategize how you will respond to the questions every child will ask at one point or another. (Where do babies come from? Is there a God, and where does He live? Where do people go when they die?)

Prepare for the Questions

Now don't get me wrong: not even the best parent can plan out in advance the answer to every question a child can dream up or a response to every idea they conjure up, because at times, the questions or ideas that your children present will simply amaze (or embarrass) you. For example, your five-year-old daughter may approach an elderly woman who is clearly past her fertile years and excitedly say, "I know why your belly is so big! You have a baby in there!"

Though curiosity may have killed the cat, it is the fuel of a toddler's imagination. It gives children the desire and energy to explore their new world. To empathize, just imagine that you were plopped down on Earth from outer space, and everything around you was new and interesting. You'd be walking curiosity! Accompanying a young child through his first experiences in this world is one of the greatest joys of being a parent. To experience Christmas, a first snow, or a zoo through the eyes of your child is too marvelous for words. However, if your child's curiosity isn't guided by you, his loving parents, you may not be happy with the conclusions your child draws about the world. So you will want to make sure, as much as possible, that your little ones are getting loving, honest, and age-appropriate answers from trustworthy people when they are in their curious years.

> *If any of you lacks wisdom, he should ask God, who gives generously to all without finding fault, and it will be given to him.*
> —James 1:5

When Your Child Asks a Tough Question

Jessica Dunn and Judith A. Myers-Walls from Purdue University's Provider-Parent Partnership Project developed a process to follow when kids ask tough questions about sexuality. I've expanded this process a bit to cover a broader spectrum. Here's what they say to do when your child asks a tough question.

Find out what your child already knows. Ask a child how he would answer his own question. When your child asks, "Why do girls sit down and boys stand up when they pee?" Counter with, "Why do you think, honey?" Find out what your child already knows, and provide some additional, age-appropriate information. Your child may respond with, "I think that it's because they are different." Follow up with, "You are right; boys and girls do have different bodies."

Clarify the question. Find out what led the child to ask the question. Make sure you understand the question before beginning an answer. Children might ask,

"Where did I come from?" Some children might want to know how babies are born. Others may just want to know the hospital or city in which they were born.

Answer the question in a simple way. Try to keep answers short and simple. Children usually ask exactly what they want to know. Often, they want a simple answer and not a long explanation. They will ask more questions if they are not satisfied. Expect more questions, and keep answering with short explanations.

Be honest. Tell children what you know about the questions they ask. When it comes to questions about sex, avoid talking about storks or cabbage patches. It is not helpful just to say that babies are "gifts," however nice that sounds. To a child, that image is only confusing. (In their concrete reasoning, they imagine their baby brother arriving in a gift-wrapped package with a bow on top.) Instead, you can honestly say that it takes a mommy and a daddy to make a baby, and the baby grows in a special place in the mommy's body until it is ready to be born. If you do not know the answer to a question a child has asked, admit it, but promise to get back to him after you look it up.

Nanny Tips

• Keep lines of communication open. The earlier you start having conversations about the tough topics, the easier they are to discuss later on.

• Use teachable moments. For example, while your preschooler is in the bath, you can talk to him about his body parts. You can use the moment to explain that his body belongs to him and isn't for other people to touch.

Use the correct terms. Use the correct words for body parts so the child does not become confused. Children should know the correct names for basic anatomy. Call a penis, a penis—not a "dingo," cute as that sounds to you.

Let tough topics be a normal part of life. Don't whisper or change your facial expression when you talk about touchy topics. Keep communication open, and encourage your children to talk to you. You want your children to feel like they can talk to you about anything! If you are embarrassed, fess up, and communicate that no matter how embarrassed you may seem, you always want to hear what they have to say.

Be prepared. Think about questions that might come up. Imagine how you might answer them. For "Why is my skin brown?" you might have a simple answer in mind to explain pigmentation. But there are bigger questions like "Is there a God?" that require you to communicate your values and beliefs, and you want to do this naturally and clearly. Then there are the sexual questions. These are probably the ones that make most parents blush and stammer for answers.

Here's an example of how this conversation may play out in the real world. Three-year-old Joseph might ask, "Where do babies come from?" You respond, "What do you think?" He answers, "From Mommy's tummy." That is an age-appropriate answer for a three-year-old.

Another three-year-old may believe that children are burped up by their mothers (like my charge said!) or are delivered from a stork in the sky. In those cases, you could say, "There is a special place inside a mother where a baby grows." That gives an honest answer without giving too much information.[1]

Appropriate Answers to Common Questions

At one point or another, in one form or another, your child will ask you the following questions. As we all know, kids are different, and how much information they press for is individual, based on their level of maturity. You know your child. Give your child enough to swallow, but not so much that he chokes! Below I've given you some age-appropriate answers that should cover the bases fairly well until age six.

Where Do Babies Come From?

This question gets asked quite early, especially if you are expecting another child. Although preschoolers may be wondering how they got into the world, they are not ready to hear all the details yet. After you determine that your child indeed wants to know where babies come from inside you, rather than asking where you go to get one, an age-appropriate response to this question would be something similar to this: "Mommies are given a special place in

> *You know children are growing up when they start asking questions that have answers.*
> —John Plomp

their bodies for babies to grow called a uterus." If your child asks you what a uterus is, you can simply say that it is a special place in a woman's body, near her tummy, that is sort of like a warm sack or cocoon that protects the baby as it grows. This is a simple, honest answer that relates the invisible to something your child can imagine.

Why Is His Skin a Different Color?

Phyllis Katz, director of the Institute for Research on Social Problems in Denver, tracked the development of racial attitudes in children and found that almost half of the two hundred children had racial biases by age six.

Kids aren't color-blind. By age five, most children have discovered that people come in shades of a variety of colors. When they ask questions about skin color, it is because they see the difference and want to know what, if anything, that difference means. Your response and attitude will shape their future understanding of the value they place on the color of someone's skin.

Some preschool age-appropriate responses to why people have different-colored skin include that skin color is passed on from parent to child or that skin color is determined by the part of the world where the family originally came from. Acknowledge and affirm your child's observations. "Yes, you are right; John does have brown skin, just like his mommy."

Teach your children to embrace diversity from a young age. Expose them to different cultures and ethnicities that will give you opportunities to have open and honest communication. Read books that show pictures of children from all races. Many cities have great ethnic restaurants that can give your child a small experience in another culture's style of eating; often you can meet the owners, who can share even more about their culture and country and customs. What a colorful world this is, with so many delicious foods to taste, interesting people to meet, and fascinating cultures to explore! This is the attitude that you want to convey. This attitude doesn't ignore our differences in cultures; it embraces them!

Why Is She Fat?

I'm really proud of my new, improved eating habits and slowly shrinking figure. I had grown accustomed to my extra large frame—then it happened. At the age of twenty-six, I was at my biggest: five foot eight and 336 pounds. At this time, my charges were about three years old. We were walking out of the YMCA from swimming class one day when a boy, about the age of six, pointed at me and said, "Look, it's Ursula the sea witch!" I almost died. Kids are brutally honest. But I have to admit, this was a turning point for me. I used this child's honest observation as a personal wake-up call to lose 130 pounds. However, an innocent child's comment like this could plunge another overweight person further into despondency. So how do we teach our kids to be sensitive to others who are battling weight issues?

Very young kids communicate their observations, most of the time without making judgments. They don't associate a person's self-worth with physical size; that is something they are taught from media, from their peers, and even sometimes (unfortunately) at home.

When your child asks why a person is fat, acknowledge his observation and encourage him to use a term that you are comfortable with. I would always tell my charges that calling people "fat" can hurt their feelings because that word has turned into a hurting word. I then would give them alternatives. I once suggested that we use the term *overweight*.

So my charges would ask me, "Shell, why are you overweighted?" I told them that people come in all shapes and sizes. I also gave them some of the reasons: sometimes people eat too much of the "sometimes" foods, sometimes people do not exercise, sometimes people have medical health issues, sometimes people are born in families with bigger bodies, and sometimes we just don't know why.

Remember, your attitude and response will shape your children's future association between size and self-worth. Be honest and acknowledge their observations, but be careful not to associate their size with their value as a person.

Why Doesn't She Have a Mommy (or Daddy)?

There are certainly a lot of answers to this question, and some of the answers are becoming all too common. Today, half of the marriages in the United States end in divorce. That leaves a lot of kids in single-parent homes, many without an active second parent in the picture. Some children are born to unwed mothers; other kids have suffered the loss of a parent through death or divorce or abandonment. Regardless of the reason, at some point or another, your child is going to encounter a child who doesn't have a father (or mother). Or perhaps you are a single parent reading this book, and that child is *your* child. How do you respond when a child comments on another child having only one parent and asks you why this is so?

Begin by asking questions to figure out what prompted him to believe that the child is without a daddy. Ask why they are asking. Maybe it is because they simply have never *seen* the other parent because Dad works in the daytime while Mom takes care of the child. Maybe the child lives only with his mom, while his dad lives somewhere else. So before answering, figure out where your child's question is coming from.

The other day, I picked up Austin from school and he said, "Shell, guess what? I am not the only one without a mother!" I didn't understand what he meant, since I know Austin knows he has a mother. So I asked some follow-up questions and found out what he meant was that he wasn't the only child with a "working mother." He had just realized that other kids had nannies who picked them up from school too. He just thought the other kids' nannies were their moms.

So when you get hit with the question about why some kids don't have two parents and some kids do, you can explain that it takes a mommy and a daddy to have a baby, but sometimes only one parent to take care of the baby. Also say that lots of times other friends or family members help too. Grandmas and grandpas, aunts and uncles, or friends or foster parents or nannies might help raise a child. The important thing isn't how many or how few people raise a child; it is that the child grows up with lots of love.

If your child asks why a particular child lives with only one parent, you can be honest and say, "Sweetie, I just don't know." If you do know, you can give a simple, short explanation such as, "His parents are divorced" or, "He lives only with his mommy." If the questions continue ("What is divorce?"), give simple, straight, non-judgmental answers. ("Divorce is what parents do when they decide not to be married anymore.") If the questions continue, it may be because your child is worried that the same thing will happen to him. Reassure him of your love and say whatever you can (that is true) to assure your child that his family will stay intact. If that is not the case (perhaps you anticipate a divorce may happen, or there is other instability in the family), say, "You will always be loved and cared for! First of all, I *can* take care of you, but let's think of all the people in our lives who love us and would help us if we needed them to." Then make a list of grandparents, family friends, and grownups in the child's life who create a safe village of community and comfort.

Why Does She Have Two Mommies (or Daddies)?

However tempting it is to skate over this question, take a deep breath and prepare to answer. Evaluate your beliefs, and be prepared to share them. If you believe it is OK to be gay, communicate that. If you believe that it isn't OK, communicate that, but do so with sensitivity. Your child is looking for you to answer the question. If you choose not to share your beliefs, your child will find *someone* to answer this question, and you may not agree with the answer he finds.

Remember, you can hold true to your beliefs without judging the beliefs of others. One way to communicate your outlook on homosexuality in a noncondescending way is to answer, when asked, "I believe (or don't believe) that it is appropriate for girls to marry girls. But some people believe differently, and we treat everyone kindly, even if we believe differently." You are sharing your beliefs without making a judgment call on a person's worth.

As you undoubtedly know, your child expects you to have great wisdom. You are his resource. Be ready and be available! For any question that arises that I've not covered specifically (for example, questions about handicapped people, or death, or how butterflies come out of cocoons), you can use the basic format for answering. Let's review quickly:

- Clarify the question.
- Answer only what is asked.
- Answer simply.
- Answer honestly.
- Acknowledge when you don't know the answer.

There's nothing that can help you understand your beliefs more than trying to explain them to an inquisitive child.
—Frank A. Clark

Communicate Your Values

Too often today, parents don't want to address their child's "value" questions because they are afraid of offending someone or creating a bias in their child rather than letting the child discover religion and philosophy on his own. They rationalize that when the child is old enough, he can make his own decisions on tough issues.

Friends, I have news for you: if you don't answer your child's tough, eternal questions, someone else will. Think of your child as a lump of clay. If you don't help to shape and form them, someone else or something else will. Maybe the media, maybe the school system, maybe their peers, maybe a coach—I don't know. But I can guarantee you this: one way or the other, every child will be shaped and hold a set of core values and beliefs.

This is why it is important for you to know what you believe about God and the meaning of life. The Quakers use the term "centering down," which means to quiet oneself at the core and settle in one's faith in God. Parenthood seems to be, by nature, a call to "center down"—to explore and define what we believe so that we have a solid faith to pass on to our children. It is one of the greatest blessings and one of the greatest responsibilities we have to the next generation.

Is There a God?

Before you can answer this question for your child, you must answer the question for yourself. Do you believe in God? Is God real to you? If you seek for God, I believe you will find Him, for He longs to reveal Himself to us in the same way we long to love and encourage our children.

You may have guessed that I have a pretty strong faith in God. You might assume that this came from having been raised by perfect parents in a perfect home with a nice, regular, religious way of life.

Wrong.

Statistically, I should be a failure. Let's go down the list: From a broken home, check. Born to an alcoholic father, check. Child of divorce, check. Raised by a single mother struggling to make ends meet, check. Been obese, check. Been in a seriously abusive relationship, check. Been divorced, check. Been bankrupt, check. Look at the facts, and any one of those eight categories alone could be enough to classify me as a failure in this world.

The qualifications listed above would hardly qualify me for the title "Super Nanny," by which I am affectionately known. How did I end up where I am today? How did I beat the statistics? It was God's loving presence and guidance in my life, a presence that is bigger than all the baggage.

I'm a scientist by training; I hold a degree in chemistry. So you may be thinking, *How can you believe in something you can't see?* I often respond, "I can't see the wind either, but I can feel its effects." Yet that response hardly does justice to God's goodness.

I can't tell you what to believe; I can only tell you how my choice has affected my life. Believing in a good God who has a redemptive, restorative, amazing plan for our lives has given me an inner peace that I had never known before. It has given me Someone to turn to when things are bad and Someone to praise when things are good. It has given me victory when I should have been defeated. It has given me the ability to recognize my God-given gifts and use them to benefit others.

When you come to know God, the importance of earthly things seems to fade away, and what has true meaning (love for others, love of self, respect for people, respect for yourself) shines through. I have lived around people who seem to have it all—money, prestige, and success. But I have discovered that happiness doesn't come with a price tag; it is attached to a purpose beyond ourselves—a belief that our life matters not only to God but to others here on earth.

I think this is probably the reason for the phenomenal success of Rick Warren's book *The Purpose Driven Life*. We long to know we matter, that our life matters, and that there's a way out of the messes we came from or the messes of our own making. Though I realize that many people have centering faiths that come from other religions, I've found particular comfort in the Christian message.

If you saw Mel Gibson's powerful movie *The Passion of the Christ*, you may have been touched by the love in the eyes of Christ, shining through to humanity even as He suffered beyond description by human hands. It is a passionate look of divine love that really defies human words. It is this sacrificial love in the eyes of Christ that drew me to the heart of God. That lets me know my full worth to God, allows me fresh starts, and compels me to love others a little more each day, to become a bit more like He was in this world.

Why Do People Die?

Your child will eventually ask about death, and your response must be sensitive. Oftentimes the question comes up because someone (or a pet) dies. Kids naturally want to know what happened and why. You can approach the topic by being honest and empathetic. Everyone eventually dies. For a young child, you want to explain that in most cases, people die when they are really, really old and have lived a long time. By that time, their bodies have usually worn out and they need new bodies that are ready to live in another place, with God, called heaven. Heaven is a place where their bodies won't hurt anymore, where they can run and play again, like when they were young, only better! However, you don't want to tell your child that people *only* die when they are old. Why? Because how will you answer when your child asks, "Mommy, you said only old people die, so why did that baby die?"

There is a fine line between being honest with a child and scaring a child. Answer the questions as they come. If you don't know the answer, admit it. For example, when your child asks, "When and how will I die?" Respond, "None of us knows when and how we will die. What we do know is that we can focus on living. That is the job God gave us to do while we are here. Isn't that a fun job? When it is time for any of us to die, God will help us and send us angels, and it will be more like waking up in a new and more beautiful world. To us, death looks like someone has gone to sleep forever. But what we can't see is the best part. It is the part where someone comes to life in heaven with a brand-new body."

It is also important to communicate to a child that while death is an entry to heaven, it does mean that the person will not be back again on earth. (Otherwise, a child may keep looking and hoping for Grandpa to show up again.) Encourage the child to cherish the memories of the times that he shared with the person who has passed. Depending on the child's level of understanding, you might talk about keeping a person's memory alive in his heart or about windows in heaven (if you believe this to be true) where Grandpa can look down and see him.

Death and what is beyond—even for those with the strongest faith—are still somewhat of a mystery. But these types of images are comforting to those of us who have lost loved ones and long to see them again. Also, communicate that people are sad because they miss the person who has died. When your child asks, "Why is Grandma crying?" you could respond, "Because Grandpa died, and Grammy misses him very much because he won't be back. But the happy times they spent together will never leave her, and she knows they'll be together again someday in heaven."

Although they may not ask directly, children may wonder if it is their fault that the person or pet died. Two-year-olds have not yet grown out of the egocentricity stage and believe that their thoughts and actions affect everything around them. When the topic of death comes up, reassure your child, even if he doesn't ask, that when people die, it is not his fault.

Follow the process for answering tough questions. What is she asking? Why is she asking? Answer with short, simple answers. Be truthful. Be prepared. Little children deserve the best answers we can give their big questions.

> One Sunday, Pastor Joe told this story: "We used to take the kids camping. When they were about six, we were hiking up a trail. I pointed to the side of the trail and told them, 'Don't touch that; it's poison ivy.' My son asked, 'Dad, why did God make poison ivy?' I thought, Great, I have about three seconds to come up with an answer. God, give me wisdom. 'Son,' I replied, 'See those shiny leaves, the red ones and the green ones? They look so beautiful. God made poison ivy to teach us something. All that glitters isn't gold.'"

Scene 19: Take 2
In the Playroom

STACIE. Where do babies come from?

DAD. That is a really good question, sweetie. Babies come from their mommy's body.

STACIE. Does someone give them to mommies?

DAD. No, honey, they grow in a safe place inside a mommy's body, near her belly.

STACIE. How do they get in bellies? Do mommies eat them?

DAD. What good questions. Babies grow in a mommy's uterus where they are kept safe before they are born.

STACIE. Oh, OK.

Nanny to the Rescue!
Recap

What Nanny Tips did this dad use to answer his daughter's tough questions truthfully without terrifying her?

1. *He only answered the questions asked.*

2. *He gave simple answers.*

3. *He gave honest answers.*

4. *He encouraged her to talk and ask questions.*

5. *He used age-appropriate language.*

6. *He used correct terminology.*

CHAPTER TWENTY

A LIFELONG LOVE OF LEARNING

 Scene 20: Take 1
Walking to the Corner Store

HENRY. Dad, what's that?

DAD. Looks like a bug.

HENRY, *walking over to get a closer glimpse.* Ew! It's moving! What is it?

DAD. Come on; it's a bug. Let's leave it alone.

HENRY. What kind of bug? How did it get there?

DAD. Come on, I said. I don't have time for these questions. A bug is a
bug. Let's go.

D addy, what's this?" "Mommy, why is that?" You may feel like screaming as your pint-size scientist interrogates you day in and day out with unending questions. All parents and nannies of preschoolers have been there, standing at what seems to be the end of the parenting cliff. One more question and you think you might dive off, headfirst, because it truly seems less painful than answering the obvious, over and over again. Although it may appear that your child's purpose is to drive you certifiably insane, she really just wants to gain an understanding of the world around her. The school of life begins in your home, and a love of learning can be fostered or squelched at a young age.

Sometimes, if you stand on the bottom rail of a bridge and lean over to watch the river slipping slowly away beneath you, you will suddenly know everything there is to be known.

—Winnie the Pooh

Learning Is Fun!

As tempting as it is to resign from answering ten thousand questions a day, it is important to help your children develop the attitude that learning is fun in a variety of ways. Asking questions is the way we find out about life and how the world works. Here are some ideas to help foster the concept that learning is fun, which can easily be included in your daily or weekly routine.

Read to your child daily. From infancy, read regularly to your child. Read the newspaper aloud; read kids' stories; read anything! Your baby will enjoy hearing your voice and listening to new words. If you make reading part of their day from their earliest memories, it will be an easy habit to maintain.

Build a library. Start with a few classic books for preschoolers, and expand your library as your child grows. Building a library doesn't have to be expensive. Be creative—you can usually find great books at garage sales or secondhand stores. And be sure to read the classified ads in your local paper to find out when public libraries and church libraries are having their annual book sales.

Call things by name. Get in the habit of pointing things out by name to your child. This is a great vocabulary builder. When they are babies, say, "Tree" as you point to the oak trees lining the streets where you go for your morning walk. Shout,

"Airplane!" as you point up to the sky; then watch your child gaze up to see it fly by.

As your little one grows, you can also label things in your home with laminated index cards or clear contact paper. "Door," "window," and "chair" all make great first sight words. Labeling toy bins (with pictures and words) provides a vocabulary-building opportunity while also teaching children how to organize. (I love these "two-for-one" teaching opportunities!)

Talk to your baby. Carry on conversations with your child, even if she's too young to talk. "Do you like the peaches? Do they taste nice?" Judge her expression and reaction. When she smiles, say, "Looks like you are enjoying them!" When she pouts, say, "Looks like they might not be your favorite. We'll try them again another time." You can model expressing emotions and feelings for your child, even at an early age. She doesn't have the words yet, but she certainly has the feelings! Help her build her vocabulary and conversation skills.

For older toddlers and preschoolers, make mealtime a happy social event full of discoveries.

 Here are a few of my favorite books for preschoolers:

Classic Board Books

Pat the Bunny by Edith Kunhardt Davies

Brown Bear, Brown Bear, What Do You See? by Bill Martin Jr.

Mr. Brown Can Moo, Can You? by Dr. Seuss

Preschool until Age 4

The Very Hungry Caterpillar by Eric Carle

Goodnight Moon by Margaret Wise Brown

Corduroy by Don Freeman

Guess How Much I Love You by Sam McBratney

Ages 4 to 8

The Cat in the Hat by Dr. Seuss

The Velveteen Rabbit by Margery Williams

The Tale of Peter Rabbit by Beatrix Potter

Curious George by Hans Augusto Rey

Chicka Chicka Boom Boom by Bill Martin Jr. and John Archambault

Nanny Tips

Here are some great ways to help your children develop a lifelong love of learning:

- *Make a "Question of the Day" jar or box.* Stuff it with slips of paper with questions on them. A fun book called *201 Questions to Ask Your Kids: 201 Questions to Ask Your Parents* by Pepper Schwartz has some great conversation starters. You can even fit this in your purse or glove box.

- *Join a walking group.* If your child is still in a stroller, get together with some moms and take walks in a variety of places—neighborhoods, indoor and outdoor malls, botanical gardens, zoos. Give your children the gift of a rich and varied environment to explore.

- *Have unstructured playtime.* Playtime is an amazing learning tool. Kids get to learn how to occupy themselves, find ways to entertain themselves, and discover their world at their own pace. Have a kid-safe cabinet in the kitchen with some pans, bowls, and spoons for your babies and toddlers to bang on. They can entertain themselves when you are cooking!

- *Use your library.* Libraries are great resources for free kids' events and activities. Most libraries offer free weekly sing-along programs, holiday programs, and special events for kids under five. They also often provide discount passes to local kid-friendly attractions, such as museums, aquariums, and other educational venues.

- *Participate in story times.* Story times by age group are a great way to meet others with kids in the same age range. Most libraries and large bookstores have story times for all ages. From lap time to pajama story time, we have visited them all. This is a networking opportunity to build a play-group. Pack a lunch after story time, and see where it goes!

Have everyone share the two best things that happened that day or the one most interesting thing they saw.

Take one adventure a week. Visit the zoo, take a trip to the children's museum, or even go for a nature walk. Check out your world! Most major cities have some type of tourist book for families vacationing in the area. Make your city's tourist book part of your home library. You'd be surprised at the hidden gems in your backyard. Maybe there is a farm that allows kids to come and milk cows, a garden co-op that allows children volunteers to pick fruits and vegetables, maybe even a great picnic spot or playground that you didn't even know existed before. Be up for adventure yourself, and your kids will catch that spirit of exploration.

Each week before the kids entered preschool, we would have "Fabulous Fridays" with other nannies and their charges. This was our adventure day. Each week, we would pick an outing and do a day trip, the cars lined up ready to head out in the nanny motorcade. This is something any parenting group, formal or informal, could get together and do. Some of our adventures included going to the farm, going to the beach, and going to the Boston Public Garden to ride the famous swan boats.

We even turned some of these outings into annual traditions. For example, the last week of each September since 2000, we have gone apple picking. Each July we visit Edaville Railroad in Carver, Massachusetts, where families can ride on real steam-driven locomotives, take a spin on an original carousel, ride on the lake in a foot-pedaled swan boat, and get dizzy on traditional amusement rides.

When the kids were younger, the nanny brigade would also do really simple and inexpensive adventures that provided quite a thrill. We would take the train two

 Some of the best places and activities for kids of all ages include these:

- Children's museums
- Science museums
- Nature walks
- Apple or berry picking
- Farms
- Aquariums
- Historical sites
- Parks
- Lakes or ponds
- Zoos
- Eateries that cater to kids

stops, get off, have a picnic lunch, and head back. We would visit the mall to watch people, stroll, and chat. It was great to introduce them to as many environments as possible. They got to experience the diversity of life. Get a book of family-friendly local outings—and get going!

Find a friend with a child the same age. Commit to get out of the house once a week. It will help you keep your sanity. It is also comforting to have an extra set of hands to hold a stroller when you need to run to the bathroom.

Do your errands with the kids. Wait in line at the bank, go to the post office, grocery shop, and continue with life as usual—with your kids! What are daily errands to you can be learning opportunities for your child. Imagine you are a preschool teacher on a field trip, and point out the fascinating facts in the everyday world.

Create a Learning Lifestyle

Here are some more ideas to make learning a part of your child's everyday life.

Enroll in a class. Gymboree, Music Together, and other national chains offer great programs for children under five. Local facilities also offer gymnastics classes, art classes, creative movement classes, and the list goes on! Attending a local class gets you out of the house and provides a structured time and place for your child to get some energy out. This is especially important during the cooler times of the year when you can't spend as much time outdoors.

Eat out. In all my positions, we made a practice to dine out at least once per week. This is such a practical learning opportunity for families. The children learn manners and patience while they experience different environments and people. You can introduce your child to different cultures and cuisines. It is also nice to have a planned night when you don't have to cook.

Alternate having dinner with another family. Have a theme cuisine. One week try Mexican, then next week try Chinese. Every other week, one gets to cook and the other gets a break. You can even incorporate the kids by having them set the table, make place settings, draw up a menu, and send thank-you notes. Older kids can even help serve. If you don't want to go that far, you can arrange to take turns making "double dinner" and just picking it up, like takeout. This still provides a break for

Mom and Dad from cooking and allows the kids to experience something different than what they are used to.

Participate in your local church. Churches are a great source of fun activities for kids and parents. MOPS (Mothers of Preschoolers) is a popular church-sponsored organization that provides encouragement for moms and an organized time for the little ones as well.

Turn Your Home into a Learning Zone

Turn your home into Adventure Island! Have a fresh stock of age-appropriate art supplies that include materials of various textures, colors, and mediums. Even a ten-month-old can finger-paint with baby yogurt, a toddler with pudding, and an older

Nanny Tip

Here is my favorite play dough recipe:

What You Need

- 1 cup flour
- 1/4 cup salt
- 2 T. cream of tartar

- 1 cup water
- 2 tsp. food coloring
- 1 T. vegetable oil

What to Do

1. Mix the flour, salt, and cream of tartar in a medium pot.
2. Add water, food coloring, and oil.
3. Stir over medium heat for three to five minutes. Don't worry if the mixture looks like a lumpy mess; it will turn into dough.
4. When the mixture forms a ball in the center of the pot, turn off the stove and let it cool. Then take it out of the pot and put it onto a floured surface. Knead it several times.
5. Store in an airtight container in the fridge.

toddler with shaving cream or nontoxic paints. Have an art supply closet. Some of my favorite multipurpose art supplies include these:

Crayons—all shapes and sizes	Cotton balls
Paper—all textures and colors	Coffee filters
Tissue paper	Clothespins
Glue sticks and Elmer's glue	Foam letters, numbers, and shapes
Paints	Stamps and washable ink
Paper plates	Child-safe scissors

Help Your Budding Scientist to Bloom

Encourage a child to answer his own questions. Be the lab supervisor for your young scientist. "Mommy, what is this?" your child asks as he points to a beetle on the ground. "Let's see," you respond. Take a closer look at the bug and then begin investigating. "Isn't this interesting? How many legs does it have? Can you point to its antennae? What color is it? Let's see if we can find out more about the bug in a book or on the computer, OK?"

Your kids are never too young to learn about how and where to find answers to their questions. Libraries are wonderful places to find answers to all the information you could want. (Not to mention the information highway in your computer.) Teach kids the joy of following a research trail at an early age.

Check out some books at the library on how to do kid-friendly experiments, and keep a magnifying glass in your purse or glove compartment to let them better examine their nature finds. Teach them how to do rubbings by placing a paper over a leaf and rubbing a crayon over it lightly.

An experiment can be as simple as dropping a raisin and a peanut in a glass of Sprite and seeing what happens to each. The raisin eventually attracts bubbles to itself and rises to the top of the glass. The bubbles burst and down the raisin goes again . . . then up again, then down again. This is a fun thing for kids to watch and an interesting science lesson at the kitchen table. (There are many books on easy experiments for kids, and these can be tons of fun to do together.) Keep a "scientific journal" to chart your child's observations and a "science box" where kids can keep their nature treasures.

Let a child grow a seed in a paper cup full of dirt. You can also grow a vine from an avocado pit by suspending it with toothpicks in a shallow bowl of water. For the more adventurous, there are preplanned garden packets of seeds for planting small child-friendly gardens in nearly every plant store. You can grow giant sunflowers, green beans, carrots, and more.

Get outside as much as possible, especially if you have a fenced, childproofed backyard. Have an age-appropriate play structure professionally installed if possible. (Make sure you have the recommended depth of soft material underneath, and ensure that the structure is built solidly.) If that's out of the question, you can purchase inexpensive play items from the paper or garage sales. Have a sandbox (with a proper mesh cover to keep visitors from "dropping" in) and lots of outside toys. Let your kids experience all types of weather, including rain, sleet, and snow! Even if for a few moments, they will learn about temperature, precipitation, and the effects of weather on the grass, shrubs, and trees. Never underestimate the value of the little red wagon either. Kids love these and use them in imaginary play in a variety of fun ways.

Learning Opportunities Are Endless

Here are some ways to keep your children's curiosity fresh and flowing.

Subscribe to your local town or parenting paper. Also, many bookstores and grocery chains will have stacks of free family newspapers and magazines at the entrance and exit. Or use the Internet and do a search for family or parenting or kid activities and events in your hometown. Many Web sites list special events for children and provide invaluable resources and links to your community. Even the major newspapers often have a monthly calendar insert that includes a special section geared toward families.

Learn about your community resources. Most towns have community education programs that offer parenting classes and workshops. Some towns even hold special family-centered events, including block parties, town fairs, holiday tree lightings, and special presentations, such as puppet shows, for families. My work town has an "Arts in the Park" program that offers two free weekly events throughout the summer. The boys and I have seen jugglers, clowns, puppeteers, music men, and so on—all free!

These events are also great places to meet locals with kids the same age, kids your children may end up sharing a classroom with.

Subscribe to at least one parenting magazine. If you have multiples, *Twins* magazine is a must! *Parenting, Parents,* or any of the others offers great monthly parenting tips and craft ideas for kids of all ages. When people ask you what you want for a gift, this is a great suggestion! It's relatively inexpensive, an easy purchase, and truly a gift that keeps on giving.

Join a playgroup. Playgroups are great for kids' social interaction, but they are just as great for moms! Chatting with an adult is sometimes the lift that can get you through the day. A playgroup is also a great place to meet other moms with kids the same age. You can share outing ideas, swap clothes, share your special parenting tips, and enjoy knowing that you are not alone in your daily joys and struggles of parenting. Many playgroups are now formed on-line. Check a parenting Web site for bulletin boards to connect with moms in your area.

Visit local coffee shops. Some coffee shops, bagel places, and kid-friendly restaurants offer free weekly sing-alongs and story times. It's a great first place to take your children to see if they are interested in participating in these types of events.

Network with other moms. Print up a business card with your first name, child's age, and an e-mail address that you can use to network with other moms. Hand out these cards at social events.

Read the bulletin boards. I can't tell you the number of new places, new playgroups, and kid-friendly community events I have learned about just by stopping to read the bulletin boards at the library, coffee shops, and grocery stores. These are definitely worth the look! Be proactive. You can also post events. If you want to start a playgroup, an exercise group, or any other kind of kid-friendly group, ask if you can post a flyer.

Have fun incorporating some of these practical ideas into your daily routine. Remember, you are your child's tour guide to the world! Show your kids what is out there, and teach them how to use the resources around them. What may be routine to you is a new adventure to your child. If you start early, a child can develop a curious nature that grows into a lifelong, self-sustaining love of learning. This is one of the most precious gifts we can give our kids and model for them.

Scene 20: Take 2
Walking to the Corner Store

HENRY. Dad, what's that?

DAD, *walking over to get a better look.* Hmm . . . Come closer and see; what do you think?

HENRY, *walking over to get a closer glimpse.* Ew! It's moving! What is it?

DAD. Come on and take a closer look.

HENRY. Is it a bug, Daddy?

DAD. Looks to be that way. What kind of bug could it be?

HENRY. I don't know.

DAD. Well, what can you tell me about it?

HENRY. Well, it's black, it's small, and it's moving.

DAD. Great observations. What is it?

HENRY, *excitedly.* An ant, Daddy! It's an ant!

DAD. You got it, kiddo. Come on and let's see what else we find on our way to the store. Maybe when we get home, we can get our magnifying glass and our bug book and see what other critters we can find in our backyard.

HENRY. That will be fun!

DAD. You bet it will be. Learning is always fun!

Nanny to the Rescue!
Recap

How did this dad use the Nanny Tips to survive his child's interrogation without going insane?

1. *He listened.* It's important to listen to your child. Take his questions seriously, and don't just ignore them.

2. *He appreciated the value of the questions.* He knew his child was experiencing something new, and he wanted to encourage and be part of the learning process.

3. *He let the child problem solve.* Let your child attempt to solve some problems on his own. Be there to lend a helping hand when he needs it, but encourage him to think for himself.

4. *He praised specifically.* Praise your child by saying things like, "Great job observing." "Great thinking." "Nice problem-solving skills." "Way to go!"

5. *He encouraged further opportunities for learning, using what was happening as a springboard.* Give your children opportunities to grow and learn!

CHAPTER TWENTY-ONE

YOU ARE AWESOME!

 ### Scene 21: Take 1
In the Hallway Heading Out for Preschool

DAD. Come on, Julia! We're late! Move it!

JULIA. I'm putting my shoes on.

DAD. Come here; I'll do it. We don't have time for this.

JULIA. I almost have it. Golly, I can't do anything right.

DAD. Give me your foot. Stop messing around. Let's go. In the car, now!

JULIA. What about my snack?

DAD. Julia Marie, forget about the snack. It's too late now. You need to be
   ready on time! You are so frustrating!

JULIA, *sniffling*. OK, Daddy. I'm sorry.

DAD. Good. Now let's go.

We all have times when we don't feel great about ourselves or our life circumstances. How do we get through those trying times? For me, it is remembering who I really am at the core, beyond the current circumstances—a beloved child of God. I know my value. I also know that my life situations are temporary and that my feelings do not define me. I have found it's the people who are not confident of their worth and value who have a hard time getting through the ruts of life.

> *It is easier to build strong children than to repair broken men.*
> —Frederick Douglass

In my home, I was taught that God loved me no matter what and that I could talk to Him anytime about anything, and He'd listen and help me. My mother modeled unconditional love to me daily. She taught me that I was valuable and precious in her eyes and in the eyes of God. I was taught that even though I came from a broken home, with an unreliable father, my circumstances didn't define me. My sense of self-worth mattered much more than any temporary situation.

Building Your Child's Self-Esteem

Building a child's self-esteem is like constructing a tower. It's a slow process that requires attention to detail. It is important to build a solid foundation, or as the tower grows, it will topple. Building a solid foundation is showing your children, in words and in deed, that they are valuable. That regardless of circumstances or other opinions, they have inherent worth.

On my fridge at work we have a magnet titled "100 Ways to Praise a Child." It comes in handy! Even when my charge is having a bad moment or acting out, I can always find one thing on that magnet to say to him. "Austin, you are special to me." How does that translate to a child who is on the floor throwing a fit? He thinks, *Wow, she loves me even when I'm acting out.* Enough of those experiences, and a child is going to grasp the truth: *No matter what I do, no matter what I say, no matter how many time-outs I sit through, I am loved.* The power of unconditional love is amazing.

When I talk about discipline, keeping your child's self-esteem intact is one of the reasons that I am adamant (and I urge you to be) about always addressing the behavior, not the child. Calling a child bad, saying he is a brat, or labeling him a loser breaks his spirit; it doesn't help shape his will. You could be building the fourth floor of your child's self-worth tower and yet demolish it with a single word. Then it takes twice as long to build it back up.

I have known nannies who have spent hours undoing one unkind word a parent said to a child. One conversation has gone like this:

"Michelle, I am so annoyed. James told little Bobby today that he throws like a girl."

"Oh no. How did that comment come about?"

"They were throwing the ball around, and Bobby's just learning to throw. His dad, not thinking, got frustrated and thought he'd tease Bobby into better performance—but that was the end of their fun. Bobby was all done. He dropped his glove and came running to get me. He was so hurt that tears were streaming down his cheeks."

"What did you say?"

"I told him that I would be sad, too, if someone said that to me. But I assured Bobby that his dad loved him and must have been trying to be funny—it is just that the joke wasn't very funny. Still, this thoughtless comment hurt and cut deeply at Bobby's desire to have his dad's approval, to feel like a big boy. So much damage had been done in a matter of seconds. Bobby said he'd never play ball again."

"I'll never understand why some people think insulting a kid is going to make him want to play or improve his game."

"I know. I don't get it either. I decided it would be a good idea for Bobby to get back on the horse, so to speak, so I said, 'Come on, champ, let's go outside and throw the ball around.' I had to start all over, standing two feet from him, tossing the ball right into his glove and having him throw it back to me, cheering and praising him with each effort. Then we would back up more and then a little farther. It took me over an hour to get him to realize that he could really play ball again."

One careless word, one thoughtless phrase can make your child's self-esteem tower crash to the ground. Your words are something you can never take back, so it is always better to think first before speaking. And if you do blow it, apologize quickly and sincerely. "Bobby, I am so sorry I hurt your feelings. I was trying to be funny and said something my old coach used to tell us when he wanted to get us to throw better. But really, I was just acting dumb. You are my big guy, and I love you and I'm proud of how you are working at this sport. Can you forgive me, slugger?"

Your Children Never Outgrow Affection

Never assume your kids will outgrow their need to be hugged, patted, and told, "I love you." I remember dating a guy who thought it was bizarre that I always told my mom I loved her when our phone conversations ended. This guy was thirty-three and could not remember the last time he had told his parents that he loved them, or vice versa. I was so saddened by that; it was beyond my comprehension. I grew up in a house where we got a kiss good night, a hug on the way to school, and a pat on the back after a sports game. People say, "Yeah, but kids grow out of that." Well, I am twenty-nine, and I still love my mom's hugs. Each day when I get into work, I greet my charges lovingly. When I drop them off at school, they give me a kiss. When I leave at night, it's always "Love you." You cannot reinforce love enough.

I remember being interviewed for a newspaper when I received the 2004 Nanny of the Year Award. Austin was five. In a sidebar in the article, he said, "Shell, I love you this much!" as he extended his arms as far as he could reach. I was so touched as I realized my love had come full circle.

Studies show that children with high self-esteem tend to take pride in their accomplishments, are able to act independently, can handle their emotions, are helpful to others, and are willing to try new things. Children who suffer from low self-esteem tend to put themselves and their accomplishments down, are withdrawn, are easily influenced, avoid trying new things, and have a general feeling of being unloved and rejected. Granted, your child may have come into this world with a less sanguine disposition than his sibling by nature, but your nurture can help even a naturally melancholy child achieve the highest setpoint of good feelings and joy possible for his personality type.

Parents need to fill a child's bucket of self-esteem so high that the rest of the world can't poke enough holes to drain it dry.
—Alvin Price

Dealing with Disappointments

An unkind word is just one of the many life disappointments your child will experience. Think about some of your disappointments over the years, both small and large. Maybe you were passed up for a promotion, maybe your dating relationship ended, or maybe someone close to you died suddenly. For those who do not have the tools to deal with disappointment, recovery is almost impossible—or at least takes a lot longer.

If you want to equip your children with the tools to handle disappointment, you must first teach them that disappointment is a part of life; it is not a personal issue or a reflection on them. Then you have to let your children experience disappointment.

Maybe your child's first friend moves away, and he is disappointed. His friend is gone, and he is sad. Too often, we try to gloss over it to make our child feel better

Nanny Tips

Here are five creative ways to help your child express anger in a healthy way.

1. *Give them the words to use.* "When you are mad, say, 'I'm mad!' and stamp your feet." (Just stay away from other people's toes!)
2. *Show them healthy ways to express their anger.* Have them "shake" the anger out with a special "I'm angry" dance.
3. *Play a sport to get out some energy.* Kick a ball around the backyard.
4. *Have an "emotion poster" covered with all different types of faces with labels.* Draw a face with a frown and write "sad" underneath. Draw a face with a smile and write "happy." Posters like these are often available in teacher supply stores.
5. *Encourage them to draw their feelings.* Sometimes they can draw what they are feeling when they don't have the words to verbalize it.

with unrealistic promises. We say, "Don't be sad; he will be back to visit," even though we know he moved across the country and most likely this just isn't going to happen. Maybe your pet has passed away, but instead of telling your child the truth, you tell them that Fido "went off to the old dog farm." Why are we afraid of allowing our children to feel disappointment, pain, or hurt? We are not doing a service to them by covering up the situation so that they can avoid working *through* the feelings.

When your child's best buddy moves away, acknowledge that your child is sad. Help him work through the emotions he is feeling. Give him the words to use if he doesn't have them. "Trevor, I know that you are so sad that Chad has moved far away. It is OK to be sad. After all, you guys were great friends." What can you encourage him to do to help him work through the emotion? Try to find something for him to do that can help him express his feelings. "Hey, Trev, why don't we make Chad a picture for his new home? You can tell me anything you want to tell Chad, and I'll write it down for you, word for word. Then we can mail it to him." This helps give your child a sense of control over a situation that he has no control over.

Another way to equip your child with handling disappointment is to teach that feelings are temporary. You can tell your daughter, who is feeling blue today, "I know that you might think you are going to feel this sad forever. But you will be happy again, I promise. It just takes some time. When we are really sad, it helps to cry or be sad, and the happy feelings will slowly come back again."

You can teach a child that her feelings do not have to govern her actions. When you are mad, you don't have to punch something. When you are sad, you don't have to go off and be alone. Although punching a pillow or being alone for a bit may be one of many ways to handle anger and sadness, teach a child that there are a variety of healthy and unhealthy ways to handle emotions. Give her ideas for how to handle anger and sadness in ways that are self-soothing and nondestructive.

You can teach your children that difficult emotions will pass and that you are there to support and help them through whatever they're feeling. You might tell them it is kind of like getting a shot. A shot hurts no matter what, but it is less scary when you can hold someone's hand, and the hurt does go away eventually! By making yourself available as friend and comforter, you are showing your children their value to you. A child needs a soft place to land when the world outside seems hard and cold. A parent can provide this.

Children who learn how to handle disappointments, work through them, and then get up and go again are ready to meet the bigger challenges that life has in store. Children who are not allowed to experience disappointment as a part of life from a young age will be in for a shock. Prepare your child for life by allowing him to experience disappointments.

Self-Reliance

Even though children have learned that you will not abandon them, it is equally important to teach them that they are OK on their own. "While self-confidence relates to specific skills and aptitudes that an individual may have, self-reliance refers to the confidence that a person has in his inner resources to cope with any situation on his own."[1]

Self-reliance is knowing that even in the worst-case scenario, a child can rely on himself to make it on his own. "A self-reliant person has better control of his life and can handle any curveball that life may throw his way."[2]

It is hard for parents (or nannies) to let their kids grow up. Letting go isn't easy! When I talk about never doing for a child what they can do for themselves, it is not because I am mean; it is because I know this is the most loving way to train a child. I know that part of their self-esteem means they need to learn to be resourceful and self-reliant. It is like the old truth, "Give a child a fish, and he has a meal. Teach him to catch his own fish, and he can nourish himself for a lifetime."

When you encourage your child to step out and try things on her own, when you give her challenges, you are letting her practice life. When she succeeds, you are teaching her self-reliance. Rather than sit and stew, she learns how to solve real problems.

If you are a family of faith, teaching your children to rely on God and His strength to help and guide them is an amazing gift. You cannot always go with them everywhere, but if you teach them that God does go with them everywhere and that He is available to talk anytime, it helps a child not feel so alone in this world.

Setting Their Own Boundaries

Once a child knows who he is and is confident that he is loved and worthy, you will be amazed at how well he handles life's ups and downs. You will see your child show empathy and love to others, handle disappointments with grace, and rely on his own ingenuity to figure out problems.

My charges often put themselves in time-out. At times, I don't even ask why. I know that whatever they did, they knew it wasn't acceptable and took action to correct it on their own. I often hear the "perpetrator" apologizing to the other, only to overhear the "victim" saying, "Thank you. I accept your apology." I don't need to know exactly what happened. The boys resolved it on their own. They have begun to set their own boundaries for what is acceptable and unacceptable based on their life experiences.

Treasure the Journey

I have kept a comprehensive scrapbook for the family I serve. It is currently three volumes, which cover the time their mom was pregnant to the present day. There are pictures of every little milestone. The first time Daddy held the boys, their first tooth, their first haircut, their first kiss, their first day of school, their outings with nanny, and so on. This scrapbook encompasses our annual traditions, such as picking apples and visiting the Enchanted Village. It captures them skiing with family. It shows them playing with friends and exploring their world.

To me, it is so important for the boys to have a photo journal of their life. It shows them that the things that have happened in their lives are worthy enough for others to see. They love looking at the scrapbooks and reminiscing over each photo. They recall the feelings of how special they felt when Santa brought them exactly what they wanted. The time the Easter Bunny shook their hands. Even the little things like hugging each other are moments that are cherished.

Capturing such moments on film, looking at the pictures over and over, and commenting on them show the boys they are special enough for me (and their mom and dad) to treasure their journeys—big and small. It reminds them of who they are and of all the love that surrounds them—and that everything that happens to them matters.

Scene 21: Take 2
In the Hallway Heading Out for Preschool

DAD. Come on! We're late! Move it!

JULIA. I'm putting my shoes on.

DAD. Oh, OK. Keep trying. Holler if you want some help. I'll get the car started.

JULIA. I almost have it!

DAD. All right, honey. Keep working on it. I'll be right back in to get you.

JULIA. What about my snack?

DAD. Good remembering. Grab it on the way out. Your snack, your responsibility.   We are running late, so let's get into high gear now!

JULIA. OK, Daddy. I gotta grab my snack, then I'm ready.

Nanny to the Rescue!
Recap

How did this dad use Nanny Tips to tackle the tying while keeping Julia from crying?

1. *He allowed her to try solving her own problem.* He was there to encourage and help if she couldn't do it on her own, but he allowed her to try, knowing she may or may not be able to complete the task.

2. *He praised her purposefully.* "Keep trying" praises persistence. "Good remembering" praises responsibility.

3. *He held her accountable for her own things.* "You want to eat, you'd better get your food!" shows your child you believe in her! She can do it! (Of course, this assumes that your child knows where the acceptable snacks are and how to safely get them.)

4. *He realized that sometimes it's worth being late to teach a more important lesson.* Some lessons take time to learn and are worth the extra few minutes that they take.

CHAPTER TWENTY-TWO

A PEP TALK FOR PARENTS

 Scene 22: Take 1
In the Car

MOM. I am going crazy. I swear, Luke, I am on the edge of a nervous breakdown. The kids are out of control, and you and I aren't on the same parenting page with anything. Can things get any worse?

DAD. And we thought those parents on the nanny shows seemed dysfunctional! Where can we get *our* family a Mary Poppins to control this chaos?

MOM. I'm just at my wit's end. Whatever happened, I feel helpless and hopeless and flat-out exhausted. I never dreamed having kids would be this hard.

DAD. I know, I know. Parenthood feels more like a life sentence right now than a privilege. We have got to find a way to do this differently, or our marriage and family are gonna blow up.

Congratulations on making it to the end of this book! Reading it may have felt like a labor of sorts, complete with mental contractions *(Ouch! This hurts!)* and perhaps a transition stage *(How much longer before the good part?).* But in the end, my prayer is that the process will be worth the result: a healthy, functioning, contented, smiling family!

All families have their own unique set of issues and personalities. I am sure you could see yourself in at least one of the scenes that were sprinkled throughout this book. Childrearing struggles don't happen because parents aren't good people, don't try hard enough, or don't love their kids. The issues continue to exist because most parents aren't given or taught practical skills. We don't learn parenting skills in school.

So unless you came from terrific parents who modeled a peaceful, loving, smoothly running home, you likely haven't seen a great example.

> *It's not that [parents] are not trying; it's that they lack training.*
> —Dr. Tod Bolsinger

The nannies I know well (including the nannies on the top two most popular TV shows) not only have the knack for working with kids, but through education and experience (and the advantage of objectivity), they've discovered the secrets to creating less stressful homes. In some ways, the parents agree to apprentice with a nanny for a period of time. The results, as you've probably seen, are not only fascinating but heartwarming.

Since not every family can afford to hire a nanny for a week, my goal in writing this book is to have been a kind of literary nanny-in-residence. You can keep "me" on your shelf to pull out whenever you need a dose of encouragement or an idea to try when you feel stuck. (You're also invited to drop by for a visit at my Web site, www.nannytotherescue.net, for tips of the day and other parenting resources.)

It's unrealistic to think that you can read through this book and magically apply all of the principles, tips, and tricks at once and—voilà!—life is perfect and the chaos disappears. Chaos doesn't happen overnight; it can take months and even years to build. It also takes time to restore lost order.

My challenge to you is this: Go back through this book and pick out your favorite top twelve Nanny Tips. Write them down and tuck them inside this book. Choose one tip to focus on each month. By the end of a year, you will see a drastic change in your family life. If you are zipping along and find you want to do more, try implementing a tip a week or every two weeks!

One of the most important strategies in this book, you will find, is getting Mom and Dad on the same page. Successful families are like strong trees. You, the parents, are the roots, and your kids are the branches. The stronger and healthier the roots are, the more fruitful the branches will be. Now look ahead at that tree twenty years from now. Is it big, with lots of branches? The strength of each branch is a reflection of those same roots. You are not just parenting a houseful of little ones; you are someday going to be the matriarch and patriarch of an entire family tree. What will your legacy be?

If you are a single parent, I applaud you. Build your support system strong. Draw on the resources available to help you: family, friends, church members, single-parent groups, neighbors, and even parenting chat rooms (that is, if you have any time to surf the Web). Asking for help isn't being weak; in fact, it is a sign of great strength. There are enough times when you must face the lonely task of parenting all by yourself, so make use of every available resource to create a village of adults who will not only support you but also love and encourage your kids. My mom did a great job of raising me alone, so I'm living proof that it can be done!

If there is just one thing I could hope for as a result of your reading this book, it would be that you feel empowered. I want you to believe in yourself and your God-given parenting abilities. You are an awesome creation, you are a loving parent, and you are trying your best. You now have the training, the best Nanny Tips. Put them to use, and I know you'll see amazing results.

In closing this book, I have to share a very poignant experience. Being a nanny is the only position that you sign up for where the end result, the highest promotion, is working yourself out of a job. As I finished this book, I came to the realization that my promotion is shortly awaiting. Like Mary Poppins says, the wind is blowing and is about to change directions.

I am experiencing right now one of the hardest of all nanny moments: letting go. My charges are transitioning into full-day school, with after-school activities keeping them busy most days until the time when I'd be heading out the door. Soon they will no longer have the need for a full-time nanny.

However bittersweet the transition will be, I take great comfort in knowing that what I have put into the lives and hearts of these precious boys will help them thrive, grow, and learn in the next phase of their lives. The love and lessons that they have given me in return will also help me as I open new chapters in my own life. Since being named the International Nanny Association's 2004 Nanny of the Year and writing books, I sense that I'll become a mentor to other nannies and to parents who need guidance and encouragement. Wherever the wind takes me, I'm excited to see what lies around the corner.

I'm amazed to think that God has taken the most unlikely girl, with so many strikes against her, and given her the privilege of nurturing two precious lives on a daily basis for the last six years. Now I have the joy of passing on what I've learned to the world. If He can do this for me, He can certainly equip you to be the most amazing mom or dad to your children that you can possibly be.

Take advantage of this short, intense period of time with your children. Be firm. Be kind. And don't forget to take them out to fly kites, up where the air is clear! If you can follow these simple guidelines, you'll be practically perfect in every way.

Or at least as close to perfect as any parent (or nanny) ever gets.

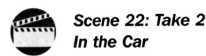 ### Scene 22: Take 2
In the Car

MOM. Can you believe just this time last year I felt like I was on the edge of a nervous breakdown?

DAD. That seems like forever ago, doesn't it?

MOM. You know, I really believed that things would never get better. I thought we were stuck in that chaotic way of life, and there was no way out.

DAD. We sure tried hard and loved our kids—but something was missing.

MOM. You're right. It certainly wasn't a lack of trying that got us where we were, but a severe lack of training.

DAD. Yep—a little training, a little practice, a good plan, and lots of prayers! Honey, I think we might not blow up the kids after all!

MOM, *giggling.* Yes, they are keepers. And so are you. Thanks for partnering with me to get us back on track. The time will come when the kids leave home and when it is just you and me again, you know. And we'll spend the rest of our lives enjoying the fruits of our labor.

DAD, *dreamily*. Yeah . . . We'll travel, see the world, kick up our heels. But in the meantime, maybe we could celebrate a good year in a small way.

MOM. Do you have anything particular in mind?

DAD. Why don't we get a great nanny to watch the kids for the weekend, and you and I take off for a midlife honeymoon to a hotel by the beach? We'll promise the kids a trip to a theme park next month.

MOM. You find a great nanny, baby. I'll put on a Beach Boys CD and a bathing suit, and start packing! We deserve to celebrate.

(To find a credentialed nanny in your area or to find out more about nannies in general, check out my Web site at www.nannytotherescue.net, and I'll point you in the right direction!)

If children live with hostility,
they learn to fight.
If children live with ridicule, they learn to be shy.
If children live with tolerance, they learn to be patient.
If children live with encouragement, they learn confidence.
If children live with praise, they learn to appreciate.
If children live with fairness, they learn justice.
If children live with security, they learn faith.
If children live with approval, they learn
to like themselves.
If children live with acceptance and friendship,
they learn to find love in the world.
—Author unknown

Nanny to the Rescue!
Michelle's Top Thirteen Nanny Tips

1. *Love each other.* With love, you may lose battles but never a war.

2. *Be a parent, not a friend.* Follow this tip, and twenty years from now your child will be your best friend.

3. *All kids are good.* Remember, it's their behavior that sometimes stinks.

4. *Have a positive attitude.* It's hard to be negative when everyone else has a positive attitude.

5. Discipline *and* training *are synonyms.* The Bible says to "train a child in the way he should go, and when he is old he will not turn from it" (Proverbs 22:6).

6. *Discipline is out of love; punishment is out of anger.* Discipline is an act of love.

7. *Be a parenting team.* A unified team is a winning team. Be on the same page of the same book.

8. *Communicate.* Communication is the key to the success of any relationship.

9. *Be a proactive parent.* Proactive parents are prepared; reactive parents respond.

10. *Be consistent.* Rules are only effective when they are consistently enforced.

11. *Listen to your children.* You are given two ears and one mouth for a reason. Listen more than you speak and listen actively: use good eye contact, nod your head, and ask pertinent questions.

12. *Positive, negative, positive.* For every one negative word, give two purposeful praises.

13. *Pray!* The family that prays together stays together.

NOTES

Chapter 1—Who's the Boss?
1. Diana Baumrind, "Child Care Practices Anteceding Three Patterns of Preschool Behavior," *Genetic Psychology Monograph* 75 (1967): 43–88.

Chapter 6—Getting Your Infant to Sleep
1. Dr. Richard Ferber, interview on *The Early Show*, March 18, 2005; accessed at www.cbsnews.com/stories/2005/03/18/earlyshow/saturday/main681634.shtml.
2. Hope Keller, "Pillow Balk," *Baltimore Magazine*, April 2005; accessed at http://www.sleeplady.com/am_pillowbalk.htm.
3. Dr. Richard Ferber, interview on *The Early Show*.

Chapter 8—Popsicles for Breakfast and Other Nanny No-Nos
1. Charnicia E. Huggins, "Sweet Drinks Help Some Preschoolers Pack on Pounds," Reuters Health article, accessed at http://www.somersetmedicalcenter.com/114306.cfm.
2. American Dental Association, "Diet and Oral Health," accessed at http://www.ada.org/public/topics/softdrink_faq.asp.

Chapter 12—The Great Pacifier Debate
1. www.drgreene.com/21_608.html.

Chapter 18—Taming the "Me Monster"
1. Find out more about Compassion International at www.compassioninternational.org.
2. Find out more about Samaritan's Purse and Operation Christmas Child at www.samaritanspurse.org.

3. Find out more about the Angel Tree Christmas Project, a ministry of Prison Fellowship International, at www.angeltree.org.

Chapter 19—Big Questions from Little Mouths

1. http://www.ces.purdue.edu/providerparent/Health-Safety/AnsweringTough.htm.

Chapter 21—You Are Awesome!

1. http://www.indiaparenting.com/confidentchild/index.shtml.

2. http://indiaparenting.com/raisingchild/data/raisingchild050.shtml.

RECOMMENDED READING

Amen, Daniel G. *Change Your Brain, Change Your Life: The Breakthrough Program for Conquering Anxiety, Depression, Obsessiveness, Anger, and Impulsiveness.* New York: Three Rivers Press, 1999.

Baker, Dan, and Cameron Stauth. *What Happy People Know: How the New Science of Happiness Can Change Your Life for the Better.* New York: St. Martin's Griffin, 2004.

Baumrind, Diana. "Child Care Practices Anteceding Three Patterns of Preschool Behavior." *Genetic Psychology Monograph* 75 (1967): 43–88.

Deci, Edward L., and Richard Flaste. *Why We Do What We Do: Understanding Self-Motivation.* New York: Penguin, 1996.

Faber, Adele, and Elaine Mazlish. *Siblings Without Rivalry: How to Help Your Children Live Together So You Can Live Too.* New York: HarperResource, 1998.

Ferber, Richard. *Solve Your Child's Sleep Problems.* New York: Fireside, 1986.

Gordon, Jay, and Maria Goodavage. *Good Nights: The Happy Parents' Guide to the Family Bed (and a Peaceful Night's Sleep!).* New York: St. Martin's Press, 2002.

It's Potty Time. DVD. Video Distributors, 2004.

Ladd, Karol. *The Power of a Positive Mom.* West Monroe, La.: Howard, 2001; *A Positive Plan for Creating More Calm, Less Stress.* Nashville: W Publishing Group, 2005.

Maas, James B. *Power Sleep: The Revolutionary Program That Prepares Your Mind for Peak Performance.* New York: Perennial Currents, 1999.

Once upon a Potty for Him and *Once upon a Potty for Her.* DVD. Barron, 2004.

Omartian, Stormie. *The Power of a Praying Husband.* Eugene, Ore.: Harvest House, 2001.

———. *The Power of a Praying Parent.* Eugene, Ore.: Harvest House, 1995.

———. *The Power of a Praying Wife.* Eugene, Ore.: Harvest House, 1997.

Peale, Norman Vincent. *The Power of Positive Thinking,* reissue edition. New York: Ballantine, 1996.

Phelan, Thomas. *1-2-3 Magic: Effective Discipline for Children 2–12,* 3rd ed. Glen Ellyn, Ill.: ParentMagic, 2003.

Schwartz, Pepper. *201 Questions to Ask Your Kids: 201 Questions to Ask Your Parents.* New York: HarperResource, 2000.

Seligman, Martin. *Learned Optimism: How to Change Your Mind and Your Life.* New York: Free Press, 1998.

Table Graces for the Family. Nashville: W Publishing Group, 2005.

Warren, Rick. *The Purpose Driven Life: What on Earth Am I Here For?* Grand Rapids: Zondervan, 2002.

West, Kim. *Good Night, Sleep Tight: The Sleep Lady's Gentle Guide to Helping Your Child Go to Sleep, Stay Asleep, and Wake Up Happy.* New York: CDS Books, 2005.

ABOUT THE AUTHOR

Michelle LaRowe, the 2004 International Nanny Association "Nanny of the Year," has been a career nanny for eleven years. Among other jobs as a professional nanny, she was nanny for a former first family and is currently nanny to a set of twins whom she has cared for since weeks after their birth. Michelle, a credentialed nanny, is the founder and president of Boston Area Nannies, Inc., and a proud member of Christian Nannies.

CPSIA information can be obtained at www.ICGtesting.com
Printed in the USA
239099LV00002B/3/P